Transecting Securityscapes

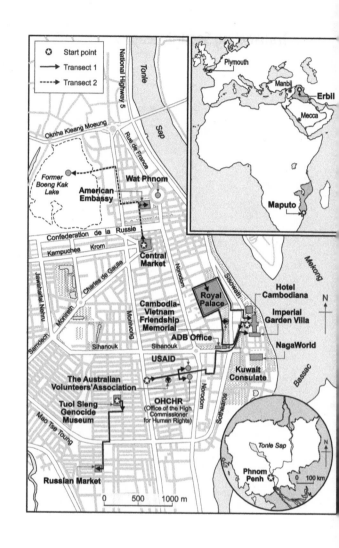

Start point
→ Transect 1
⇢ Transect 2

National Highway 5

Tonle Sap

Plymouth
Manbij
Erbil
Mecca

Maputo

Oknha Kleang Moeung

Rue de France

Former
Boeng Kak
Lake

Wat Phnom

American
Embassy

Confederation de la Russie

Kampuchea Krom

Charles de Gaulle

Jawaharlal Nehru

Monireth

Samdech

Central
Market

Norodom

Mekong

Cambodia-
Vietnam
Friendship
Memorial

Monivong

Royal
Palace

Sisowath

Hotel
Cambodiana

N

Imperial
Garden Villa

ADB Office

Sihanouk

Sihanouk

USAID

NagaWorld

The Australian
Volunteers'Association

Kuwait
Consulate

Tuol Sleng
Genocide
Museum

Mao Tse Toung

OHCHR
(Office of the High
Commissioner
for Human Rights)

Norodom

Sothearos

Bassac

Russian Market

0   500   1000 m

Tonle Sap

N

Phnom
Penh

0   100 km

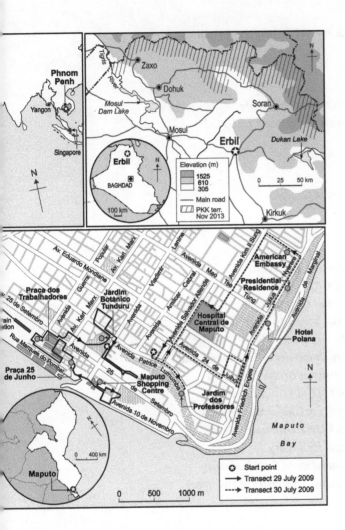

Phnom Penh

Yangon

Singapore

N

Zaxo

Dohuk

Mosul
Dam Lake

Mosul

Soran

Erbil

Dukan Lake

Tigris
River

N

Erbil

BAGHDAD

100 km

Elevation (m)
1525
610
305

— Main road
PKK terr.
Nov 2013

0   25   50 km

Kirkuk

Av. Eduardo Mondlane

Av. Karl Marx

Popular

Guerra

Vladimir

Lenine

Avenida   Mao   Tse

Avenida Kim Il Sung

American Embassy

Presidential Residence

Julius   Nyerere

Tung

Avenida   da   Marginal

Praça dos Trabalhadores

Jardim Botânico Tunduru

Av. 25 de Setembro

Avenida

Av. Karl Marx

Amílcar   Cabral

Avenida Salvador Allende

Hospital Central de Maputo

Avenida

Hotel Polana

Main station

Rua Marquês do Pombal

Avenida

25

Avenida

Avenida Patrice Lumumba

Avenida   24   de   Julho

N

Praça 25 de Junho

Maputo Shopping Centre

de   Setembro

Jardim dos Professores

Avenida Friedrich Engels

Avenida 10 de Novembro

Maputo

Bay

N

0   400 km

Maputo

Start point
Transect 29 July 2009
Transect 30 July 2009

0   500   1000 m

Transecting Securityscapes

DISPATCHES FROM CAMBODIA, IRAQ,
AND MOZAMBIQUE

TILL F. PAASCHE
JAMES D. SIDAWAY

THE UNIVERSITY OF GEORGIA PRESS
Athens

© 2021 by the University of Georgia Press
Athens, Georgia 30602
www.ugapress.org
All rights reserved
Set in 10.25/13.5 Minion 3 Regular
by Kaelin Chappell Broaddus

Most University of Georgia Press titles are
available from popular e-book vendors.

Printed digitally

Library of Congress Cataloging-in-Publication Data

Names: Paasche, Till F., author. | Sidaway, James D., author.
Title: Transecting securityscapes : dispatches from Cambodia, Iraq, and Mozambique /
    Till F. Paasche, James D. Sidaway.
Description: Athens : The University of Georgia Press, [2021] | Series: Geographies of justice and
    social transformation; 52 | Includes bibliographical references and index.
Identifiers: LCCN 2021021243 (print) | LCCN 2021021244 (ebook) | ISBN 9780820360607 (hardback)
    | ISBN 9780820360614 (paperback) | ISBN 9780820360591 (ebook)
Subjects: LCSH: Security sector—Mozambique. | Internal security—Mozambique. | Security
    sector—Iraq. | Internal security—Iraq. | Security sector—Cambodia. | Internal security—
    Cambodia.
Classification: LCC HV8271.A2 P33 2021 (print) | LCC HV8271.A2 (ebook) | DDC 363.209567—dc23
LC record available at https://lccn.loc.gov/2021021243
LC ebook record available at https://lccn.loc.gov/2021021244

For Jasmin Leila Sidaway and our parents

CONTENTS

LIST OF FIGURES AND TABLES

ABBREVIATIONS

ASEAN	Association of Southeast Asian Nations
CPP	Cambodian People's Party / Kanakpak Pracheachon Kâmpuchéa
Frelimo	Mozambique Liberation Front / Frente para a Libertação de Moçambique
G4S	Multinational security company headquartered in London
KDP	Kurdistan Democratic Party / Partiya Demokrat a Kurdistanê
KRG	Kurdistan Regional Government / Hikûmetî Herêmî Kurdistan
PJAK	Kurdish Free Life Party / Partiya Jiyana Azad a Kurdistanê
PKK	Kurdistan Workers' Party / Partîya Karkerên Kurdistanê
PUK	Patriotic Union of Kurdistan / Yekêtiy Niştîmaniy Kurdistanê
PYD	Kurdish Democratic Union Party / Partiya Yekitîya Demokrat
RCAF	Royal Cambodian Armed Forces
Renamo	Mozambican National Resistance / Resistência Nacional Moçambicana
SDF	Syrian Democratic Forces / Hêzên Sûriya Demokratîk (HSD)
UNTAC	UN Transitional Authority in Cambodia (February 1992– September 1993)
YPG	People's Protection Units / Yekîneyên Parastina Gel
YPJ	Women's Protection Units / Yekîneyên Parastina Jin

ACKNOWLEDGMENTS

Transecting Securityscapes has been long in the making. James initially wrote about power and space in Maputo and wider Mozambique in the early 1990s, following doctoral fieldwork there (1989–90). However, the journey to *Transecting Securityscapes* started with a visit the two of us made to Maputo in 2009. This was funded by a grant from the pump-priming research fund of the School of Geography and Environmental Sciences at the University of Plymouth, England, where James was a faculty member and Till a graduate student. When James moved to the National University of Singapore (NUS) in 2012 while Till held a postdoctoral fellowship at the Université de Neuchâtel, Switzerland, we had the opportunity to work in Phnom Penh. We also decided then to work together in Iraqi Kurdistan, subsequently enabled by Till taking up a position as a faculty member at a Kurdish university in 2013.

Hence this book is the result of recurring research, reflection, and writing. Portions of chapters 2, 3, and 4 draw on articles that appeared in *Environment and Planning A* (Paasche and Sidaway 2010, 2015; Sidaway et al. 2014). In that earlier incarnation, what here has become our dispatch from Phnom Penh also had two other authors. We thank Piseth Keo and Chih Yuan Woon for working with us in Cambodia and allowing us to adapt the results here. In Maputo, Manuel Francisco Ngovene was an efficient research assistant and Aurelio Mavone was a superb host and source of facts and opinions. Robina Mohammad also joined us in Maputo, and for tolerating our stories from Iraq and for continually reminding him that an embodied feminist perspective on security should never be lost sight of and greatly complicates assumptions about security and insecurity, James is especially grateful.

The research in Cambodia and Iraq was funded by a grant from the National University of Singapore (Crucibles of Globalization: Landscapes of Power, Security and Everyday Lives in Post-Colonial Asian Cities, R-109-000-

133-133). The grant also enabled James to join NUS-based graduate student Jasnea Sarma in Myanmar in 2015. Returning there with Jasnea since and applying the transect method described here in chapter 1, "Yangon thereby becomes a site for critical reflections about complex and multiple imbrications of frontiers, security and the urban with implications for how these may be conceptualized elsewhere" (Sarma and Sidaway 2020, 447). A Humanities and Social Sciences grant from the Office of the Senior Deputy President at NUS (then headed by Ho Teck Hua) allowed James a semester free of teaching and service and hence a return to Iraqi Kurdistan during the fall of 2014, when he was generously hosted by Soran University. The Politics, Economies and Space and the Social and Cultural Geographies research groups within the Department of Geography and the Inter-Asia Engagements Cluster of the Asia Research Institute at NUS have offered sounding boards to discuss some of the arguments that unfold in *Transecting Securityscapes*. James also thanks Neil Coe, Robbie Goh, Brenda Yeoh, and Henry Yeung who enabled sabbaticals from January through May in 2015 and 2019. These offered time to advance the manuscript.

Earlier versions of some of the material in the introduction was presented in the session on "Peripheral Visions: Security By, and For, Whom?" at the April 2015 Annual Meeting of the American Association of Geographers in Chicago and at a Research Roundtable on Geopolitical Economies of Development and Democratization in East Asia held at the Peter Wall Institute at the University of British Columbia, Vancouver in May 2015. A later version of the introduction was presented at the 4th Workshop on the Geopolitical Economy of East Asian Developmentalism co-organized by the Department of Geography, Osaka City University and the East Asian Regional Conference in Alternative Geography (EARCAG) in November 2019. We thank the organizers, hosts, and audiences in Canada and Japan. In addition, conversations about security and insecurity with Shaun Lin have been helpful, especially in September 2019 when he accompanied James through Beijing's Forbidden City and Tiananmen Square on the eve of the commemorations for the seventieth anniversary of the founding of the People's Republic of China. For comments on a range of drafts and sections of the manuscript as it evolved, we thank Francisca Azevedo, Katherine Brickell, Andrew Brooks, Padraig Carmody, Sara Fregonese, Nathan Green, Chris Harker, Miles Kenney-Lazar, Felix Mallin, Virginie Mamadouh, Nick Megoran, Martin Müller, Patricia Noxolo, Adam Ramadan, Ananya Roy, Vani S., Ian Slesinger, the late Peter Sluglett, Matt Sparke, Simon Springer, Nigel Thrift, Richard Yarwood, Sallie Yea, and Sheyla Schuvartz Zandonai. Mat Coleman read the entire manuscript twice, first in an early draft and again following extensive revisions. We are immensely thankful for his guidance and backing as well as that of Mick Gusinde-Duffy at the University of Georgia Press, whose patience was consistently reassuring and whose encouragement was inspiring. Two anonymous readers for the press challenged us to sharpen the analysis and specify its limits. We appreciate their constructive feedback. Of course, none of those people or institutions named above bear responsibility for what follows.

* * *

Finishing the book was deferred after the completion of fieldwork in Iraqi Kurdistan in 2014, when Till became a participant observer with the Kurdish People's Protection Units (YPG) in northern Syria (known in Kurdish as Rojava) from 2015 to 2017. However, the deferral sharpened our reflections on bearing witness to (in)security—as becomes evident in the coda.

Transecting Securityscapes

INTRODUCTION

Situating Securityscapes

> "Security" grabs people in different places in myriad ways.
> —**Katherine Verdery, 2019**

What do we mean by securityscapes, and why are we adopting this term here? To answer these questions requires an appreciation of how the securityscape idea has been used by others. In staging this review, we focus on scales and intersections as a prelude to the three dispatches that follow.

Security and insecurity take many forms. Drawing on ethnography in East Timor, which she describes as "a country with a long and violent history of colonization and foreign occupation ... compounded by a legacy of mass human rights violations, unresolved grievances and trauma," Bronwyn Winch (2017, 198) reflects on how people met during her fieldwork had used the common phrase "la iha fiar, la iha seguransa" (without belief, there is no security). Feeling secure, in this sense as a lived experience, was invested not in sovereignty or any "state-based security provision," but in a spiritual landscape.[1] Similarly signified in many other contexts of unravelling violence and trauma, the Quranic term *iman*, often translated as "faith," also speaks to safety and security, "guarding all from danger, corruption, loss etc." (Yusuf Ali [1934] 2009, 1214n5402).[2] Recognizing "that factors of security and insecurity are 'embedded' in context and culture," Winch (2017, 207) concludes "that there is no 'universal ontology' of security, that it is a subjectively lived and formed experience and emotion."

In English alone, the meaning of *security*—partly a borrowing from Middle French *sécurité* and Latin *sēcūritās* according to the *Oxford English Dictionary* (*OED*), whose account of its etymology, meanings and derivatives runs to more than nine thousand words (*OED* Online 2020)—ranges from freedom from (care, doubt or want), confidence, protection (of people, states, sites, or-

1

ganizations and systems), fixity, property and assets pledged (and grounds for their guarantee), and measures to safeguard the interests of something or someone. Early uses, from the fifteenth century to the seventeenth, mostly refer to individuals being protected from dangers and fears as well as the (now rare) false sense of this yielding complacency and (now rare) figurative uses. References to state and public security were present early on but have greatly multiplied in the past century. The *OED* records the first use of the compound noun "security guard" in 1920 from an article in the *Times*.

The plurality of notions guiding how everyday security is understood, practiced, or experienced are frequently overwritten or erased by national security narratives that seek to set the scales and scope of what security is. More recently, however, the security-speak of these disembodied, militarized, and trenchantly patriarchal perspectives has been provincialized, liberated from national or state modifiers by feminist and other critical security studies scholarship and popular movements that engage security via a focus on conditions of its counterpart, "insecurity," and at a range of intertwined scales. Even without delving into spiritual realms, scholars, states, social movements, globalized commerce, and media may use security to signify disparate concerns connected with what Kezia Barker (2015, 357), writing about biosecurity narratives, portrays as living with and managing "the complex, contingent and emergent circulations of life." In these contexts, Lucia Zedner (2009, 9) describes security as "a promiscuous concept . . . wantonly deployed in fields as diverse as social security, health and safety, financial security, policing and community safety, national security, military security, human security, environmental security, international relations and peacekeeping." For Clive Barnett (2015, 257), security encompasses "a whole range of empirical objects, including terrorism, migration, food systems, logistics and supply chains, financial networks, environmental issues and precarity in labour markets." Mary Kaldor (2018, 13) suggests that even a commonly understood meaning "is very difficult to pin down," and ultimately relative: "When we use the term in everyday language it can refer to an objective, what we might call safety, or to stability and predictability (as in repressive societies). And at one and the same time, it tends to refer to a security apparatus or set of practices from locking doors, to airport scanners, to pensions, to surveillance, police, intelligence and military forces and even nuclear weapons. And both these different meanings can be interpreted in a myriad of ways. Whose safety are we talking about—the individual, the nation, the state, the world?"

So although, on the one hand, security becomes, in Krasmann and Hentschel's (2019, 181) words, "a 'live' mode of government," it also takes multiple forms and interpolates multiple subjectivities (while silencing others) entangled with countless modes of power. Each variant will have its own genealogy that intersects with, reflects, and refracts another. In the United States, for example, energy security emerged as a subset of national security discourses in the early 1950s that would be reanimated in the 1970s (Tidwell and Smith 2015).

The difficulty in mapping any variant of security is compounded when different discussions about security intersect. Marieke de Goede (2012, xx) traces the imbrication of finance, security, and surveillance, so that "the pursuit of terrorist monies" becomes a matter for police and financial intelligence monitoring, another domain of surveillance and "security intervention." Similarly, examining juxtapositions and overlaps of how "finance/security/life" become cojoined, Paul Langley (2017, 174) notes how "finance and security share an ontological conundrum—how to confront an uncertain future—and an epistemology of risk that is manifest in the deployment of a panoply of risk management techniques and tools in order to render the future actionable in the present." That investments in corporate shares are themselves termed "securities" and "securitization" refers to debts turned into tradeable financial products reveals this shared ontology. As Audrey Macklin (2004, 78) sums up, "The shared feature of security across different discursive domains is that it signifies both a valuable condition of well-being and a precondition to the attainment of other ends. Security is a utility that states, corporations and people seek to maximize."

Although there are frequently tensions between the logics of security and trade, the art and science of logistics (propelled by battlefields and preparation for war) seeks to square them (Cowen 2014). However, neither logistics nor the grand strategies of national security (dissected in accounts such as Gaddis 2005; Halliday 1986; and Morrissey 2017) form the primary focus in *Transecting Securityscapes*. Although such big-picture security narratives are part of the frame, we concentrate on forms and roles of private security, military, and police in strategic and symbolic power centers in three postcolonial polities. Sites of incarceration, though not encountered in our research, are also always in the background in the sense that Brett Story (2019, 49–50) unpacks: "Thinking about the city and the prison as dialectical spaces whose transformations are structurally bound by shared imperatives and relations of power not only reveals the prison as an expression of the property relation and its centrality to contemporary urban economies but also simultaneously invites us to consider the prison as an urban exostructure." Moreover, what Deborah Cowen and Amy Siciliano (2011, 1536) describe as "the overlapping space of prisons and militaries" reconnects such urban exostructure with city streets and military bases, and hence with national security narratives. Given the U.S. combined global imperial role and its scale of incarceration (which peaked early this century at over two million prisoners—more than one-fifth of the world's incarcerated, in a country that has one-twentieth of the world's population), these overlaps become particularly legible for the American case. And starkly racialized: African Americans are incarcerated at five times the rate of white Americans. More than a decade before the tagged movement #BlackLivesMatter, Loïc Wacquant (2002, 56) noted, "The conflation of black-ness and crime in collective representation and government policy (the other side of this equation being the conflation of blackness and welfare) thus re-activates 'race' by giving a legitimate outlet to the expression of anti-black ani-mus in the form of the public vituperation of criminals and prisoners."

While this American system—and associated policies like zero-tolerance policing and privatized prisons—became an export industry, more directly overseas the rendition and other apparatus finessed during the War on Ter-ror have yielded a kind of planetary imprisonment "exostructure" to Ameri-can national security narratives, with a node in Guantanamo. These networks of imprisonment, torture, and rendition came into focus, apparently concom-itant with post-9/11 security obsessions. However, a genealogy of what Andrew Preston (2014) calls "the monster" of national security in universalized Amer-ican narratives traces its roots to the imperial projection (to Cuba and espe-cially the Philippines) of American power after the 1898 war with Spain (Mc-Coy 2009), then growing into concerns about importing subversives (from Europe) through the First World War, into increasingly weaponized Ameri-can reactions to the rise of communism and fascism. Nonetheless, it was only in the 1940s that the term *security* as a watchword for *defense* displaced mean-ings bound to the New Deal and economy (Fergie 2019).[3] Soon after the Tru-man presidency (1945–53) institutionalized the structures—including estab-lishing the CIA, National Security Council, the posts of Joint Chiefs of Staff and Secretary of Defense—this national security system was buttressed by multiple government agencies and an industry of private subcontractors with global reach. Conservatives, liberals, and radicals then and since have voiced concerns about what this vast and electorally unaccountable security appa-ratus—a structure of "double government" according to Michael J. Glennon (2015)—means for the vaunted American tenets of "freedom and democracy."

Subsequently, as David Campbell (1998, 351) describes in the landmark *Writing Security*, "United States foreign policy has interpreted danger and se-cured the boundaries of the identity in whose name it operates." By the 1960s, national security led the United States into new counterinsurgencies and then full-scale war to shore up the campaigns of the anticommunist regimes installed in South Vietnam. Announcing the U.S. invasion of Cambodia's "parrot's beak" salient that abutted South Vietnam, in a 30 April 1970 televised address to the American people, President Richard Nixon described this as "necessary to defend the security of our American men" (Nixon 1970). Paradoxically, that American war yielded many insecurities, and not just for the populations of Indochina and the other prolonged counterinsurgencies, pacifications, and military regimes elsewhere in Southeast Asia. Writing about how anger over Vietnam as a failure fed into far-right white supremacist movements, leveraging military experience in the United States itself, Kathleen Belew (2018, 16) argues that "the story of white power as a social movement exposes something broader about the enduring impact of state violence in America. It reveals one catastrophic ricochet of the Vietnam War in the form of its paramilitary aftermath. It also reveals something important about war itself. War is not neatly contained in the space and time legitimated by the state. It reverberates in other terrains and lasts long past armistice. It comes home in ways bloody and unexpected."

Dispatches

America's Cold War interventions in the Global South have yielded vast scholarly literatures and reportage. Among the voluminous record, a short set of *Dispatches* from the front lines in Vietnam by the journalist Michael Herr (1977) caught many eyes and soon established itself as a classic account of American misadventures amid violent conflict that became normalized as national security. *Dispatches* helped establish what Mark Pedelty (1995, 23) calls "the lore of Vietnam" among foreign correspondents, describing how in El Salvador in the 1980s they would "quote lines from Herr's *Dispatches* . . . and the fictional forms he inspired, including *Apocalypse Now* . . . drawing constant comparisons between the two conflicts, only half of which truly apply." For Gearóid Ó Tuathail (1996, 171), noting that Herr ends his book with the words "Vietnam, Vietnam, Vietnam, we've all been there," *Dispatches* signaled how, "no longer a map or place, Vietnam became part of the structure of feeling of an era, a ubiquitous presence that bled into the consciousness of an emergent global movie time culture." For Hollywood, and wider American culture, Vietnam became an archetype, script, and syndrome. For many military strategists, Vietnam became the experience to learn lessons from, to overcome, and to reaffirm American exceptionalism. Thereby, the Vietnam War was increasingly retold and remembered, to "win itself" (Nguyen 2016). One telling consequence, according to Marguerite Nguyen (2018, 3), is that "'Vietnam' and 'Vietnam War' are stereotypically conflated, resulting in a willful neglect of pre-conflict contexts that must inform our comprehension of the war's enduring effects."

Yet, when introducing *Dispatches*, Herr describes a fading map of French Indochina on the wall of his Saigon apartment, left there by a long-ago tenant: "*Some nights, coming back late to the city, I'd lie out on my bed and look at it.... That map was a marvel, especially now that it wasn't real anymore.... The paper had buckled in its frame after years in the wet Saigon heat, laying a kind of veil over the countries it depicted. Vietnam was divided into its older territories of Tonkin, Annam and Cochin China, and to the west past Laos and Cambodge sat Siam, a kingdom*" (1977, 3, emphasis original). A third of a century on, a critical review of the literature about Herr's distillation of his in-country experiences of Vietnam as a war correspondent in 1967 and 1968 noted how the imperial French state's tripartite division of Vietnam into Tonkin, Annan, and Cochin China had evolved into North and South, supposedly divided by a demilitarized zone (DMZ) "that never achieved its signified, given that that DMZ never became fully demilitarized. As such, Herr believes the American 'map' of Vietnam to be as much an ill-fated Western conceit as was the French map" (Hawkins 2009, 133). As Ty Hawkins goes on to note, in Herr's reportage American military expedience subdivided South Vietnam and its cities into "war zones whose boundaries made little sense on a topographical level," such that by the time Herr arrived, "just months before the Tet Offensive of early 1968, '*even the most detailed maps didn't reveal much anymore*'" (citing Herr 1977, 3, emphasis original).

Although military strategists, police, and an array of private agencies may seek to freeze-frame and depict security and insecurity cartographically, something as multidimensional, embodied, and multiscaled as security cannot be readily mapped. Security is dynamic and can quickly shift depending on vantage point. As Barry Buzan (1983, 1) elucidates,

> In much of its prevailing usage, especially by those associated with state policymaking, this concept is so weakly developed as to be inadequate for the task. I seek to demonstrate that a simple-minded concept of security constitutes such a substantial barrier to progress that it might almost be counted as part of the problem. By simple-minded I mean an understanding of national security that is inadequately aware of the contradictions latent within the concept itself, and/or in-

adequately aware of the fact that the logic of security almost always involves high levels of interdependence among the actors trying to make themselves secure.

Hence, state/national security is sometimes projected as being at odds with civilians' security, whereby regime or state security is calculated as contriving the insecurity of its dissenting and competing others. Likewise, forms and meanings of private and public security do not always coincide, and publics are diversely constituted, by class, ethnicity, and gender. Private/public security maps unevenly onto sociospatial divides. Thus, Shona Loong (2018, 11) records in regard of the policing and surveillance of low-waged predominantly South Asian migrant workers in Singapore that security becomes "an unfinished project that is often exerted unevenly and paradoxically within state territory." Likewise, and drawing on feminist geopolitics demonstrating "how our understanding of security changes when we examine emotions about and with those who experience fear," in a case study from Honduras, Maaret Jokela-Pansini (2020, 848) studies how militarism intersects with patriarchal norms promoting "masculinist understanding of protection as to who should be protected and by whom—and from what." Security not only signifies a wide array of activities and objects, but it tends to overpower whatever else it is associated with. Building on Buzan's work, critical scholarship on the processes by which an activity, theme, or site becomes a reference point for security discourses legitimating exceptional or emergency measures—securitization theory—emerged as a research field.[4] Additionally, there are the huge literatures on international, bio, digital, environmental, systemic, psychological, social, and financial security. References to climate and planetary security proliferate. Others have used the term *vernacular security* to refer to discursive boundary making at different scales (Bubandt 2005; Vollmer 2019).[5] More recently (in a rich empirical study of security and power in the Central African Republic, Somaliland, and South Sudan) with an "actor-focussed, process-oriented viewpoint," Tim Glawion (2020, 8) develops the analysis of different forces shaping "security arenas."

Textbooks (Jarvis and Holland 2015) and readers in security studies (Collins 2012; Salter and Mutlu 2013) are challenged to encompass this multiplicity of approaches, dimensions, and definitions. Negotiating this vast scholarly arena and approaching the spatiality of security through three dispatches that follow, we develop the idea of securityscapes as a distinctive analytical pathway and method through the complexity. In our dispatches, we encounter, narrate, and analyze securityscapes in Maputo, Mozambique, Phnom Penh, Cambodia, and the Autonomous Kurdistan Region in Iraq. All three sites share fractious emergences from colonial pasts, revolutions, and the resurgence of dynamic and uneven modes of capitalist accumulation. Applying a grounded perspective that develops a walking transect method, we investigate how security is being enacted differently across these sites. We focus on the formal apparatuses of security that protect, or contest, spaces of political and financial power. While it has become easy to picture security becoming increasingly privatized everywhere in the context of incentives and mandates for neoliberal policies, the situation is more complex. Different historical trajectories and political economies yield variegated securityscapes. At the same time, securityscapes are a mirror to wide social, political, and economic conjunctures.

Moving through Securityscapes

The idea that the contemporary moment might productively be explored through intersecting "scapes" was codified at the start of the 1990s by the then Pennsylvania-based anthropologist Arjun Appadurai (1990, 296) arguing that "disjuncture and difference in the global cultural economy" could be explored through

> the relationship between five dimensions of global cultural flow which can be termed: (a) ethnoscapes; (b) mediascapes; (c) technoscapes; (d) financescapes; and (e) ideoscapes ... with the common suffix scape to indicate first of all that these are not objectively given relations that look the same from every angle of vision, but rather that they are deeply perspectival constructs, inflected very much by the historical, linguistic and political situatedness of different sorts of actors.

Of course, history and global space manifest many disjunctures and cultures (and the economies they are entangled with) and are always composed of fragments and reconstructions. Matthew Sparke (2005, 60) subsequently dissected the "profound" yet creative "ambivalence defining Appadurai's treatment of space," whereby scape is both deterritorializing and reterritorializing: "While most of the time he [Appadurai] describes each 'scape' as a flow, he does not shy away from activating the concept-metaphor's appeal to the more spatial connotations of landscape and the related notions of mapping and navigating one's way through space." Sparke reads Appadurai against the neoliberal landscapes of cross-border regionalization in the Pacific Northwest that rework earlier bioregional concepts of Cascadia—"stretching from Monterrey through western Canada to Alaska" and "defined by the ecology of the Cascade Mountains and their cascading waters, rainforests and salmon" (2005, 67)—into an entrepreneurial, networked, and globally connected region. Underpinning this reworking are the intersecting geopolitics and geoeconomics of state power (American, Canadian, and Mexican) and corporations (led by aerospace and computer technology) and a backdrop of American military and economic power projection into the Pacific.

Habitually with a nod to Appadurai's visions, the suffix "scape" has been attached to diverse aspects of social existence, from borderscapes (Rajaram and Grundy-Warr 2007) to consumerscapes (Cachinho 2014), deathscapes (Maddrell and Sidaway 2010), and hazardscapes (Khan 2012). Anindita Datta (2016) referred to "genderscapes of hate" when writing about violence against women in India. And narrating the conflict that enveloped Sri Lanka after 1983, through the long (and ultimately failed) struggle for Tamil statehood there, Jonathan Spencer et al. (2015, 98) describe "a warscape, marked by heightened military presence, military checkpoints, guerilla attacks by Tamil militants, counter-insurgency measures, killings, and 'white van' abductions." The notion of riskscapes has also been extensively discussed in terms of the anticipation of emergencies (Neisser and Runkel 2017). By 2020, the deep and promptly globalized emergency triggered by the COVID-19 pandemic impelled new surveillance and tracking measures. A fracturing and recomposing of all prior scapes rapidly unfolded, at a scale and speed that hitherto— for a century—had been associated only with wars. Their recrystallization, and the enforcement of biosecurity measures, will shift the kaleidoscope, with perspectives on security and configurations of biopolitics and risk accordingly realigned. While surveillance deepens, COVID-19's impacts were, to use Lois Beckett's (2020) term, being "warped" by intersecting racism and class divisions and caught up in culture wars that became especially visible in America and Brazil. In each of the research sites, fears of COVID-19 transmission became enmeshed with security responses. As the first cases were registered in Mozambique, videos of protests over the forcible relocation of downtown street vendors in Maputo, with the police using rubber bullets and tear gas, were circulating on social media. In Cambodia, a state of emergency law was formulated, ostensibly in responding to virus transmission, with arbitrary arrests in Phnom Penh (Human Rights Watch 2020a). And Iraqi Kurdistan, according to Reporters Without Borders (2020), saw a "wave of arrests of journalists since Covid-19's arrival."

Pertinently, an earlier (though far more limited) viral epidemic, that of the mosquito-borne Zika virus in 2016, when pregnant women contracting the virus faced the risk of having babies with microcephaly (a condition where the head circumference is smaller than the usual range), had led Claudia Rivera-Amarillo and Alejandro Camargo (2020, 414) to employ the idea of "assemblage" in approaching the imbrications of nature, society, and risk "as a way to understand the scalar connections of viruses, mosquitoes, and human bodies within broader spatial, political, and climatic processes. . . . The Zika assemblage operates through the constitution of zones of epidemiological surveillance, which involve spatialized forms of security and the control of human bodies, mosquitoes, and places."

Assemblage—defined in one anthropological study as "the product of multiple determinations that are not reducible to a single logic" (Inhorn 2015, 21)—has proven another fruitful way to conceptualize security (Haggerty and Ericson 2000; Lippert and O'Conner 2003; Topak 2019). In her study of "reprotravel" for assisted reproductive treatment (in vitro fertilization), Marcia Inhorn (2015, 23, emphasis original) proposes that "one scape of significant medical anthropological interest—namely the *bioscape* of moving biological substances (such as blood and semen) and body parts (for example, gametes and organs)—might be added to Appadurai's list. Using Appadurai's language of scapes, global travel for IVF might also be thought of as a more complex *reproscape*—a kind of metascape combining numerous dimensions of globalization and global flows." Inhorn finds analytical value in both concepts, but prefers scape to assemblage: "In short, a reproscape is both spatial and dynamic, involving geography and movement. Whereas the global reproductive assemblage entails a coming together of diverse IVF elements, the notion of a reproscape is more dynamic, entailing the movements of reprotravel in a way that a global reproductive assemblage cannot" (2015, 24).

While we want to keep in focus what, in an oft-cited paper, Kevin Haggerty and Richard Ericson (2000, 606) called "the surveillant assemblage" amid "desires for control, governance, security, profit and entertainment," like Inhorn we find more mileage in scapes, which bring space and perspective into the center of analysis. Yet though the analysis of intersecting scapes has been widely adapted and Appadurai's original typology productively extended, the idea of securityscapes was relatively slow to garner momentum. In *People of the Bomb: Portraits of America's Nuclear Complex*, anthropologist Hugh Gusterson (2004, xxi) seems to have made the first use, suggesting "in a friendly amendment to Appadurai's portrait of the world after bipolarity as a fluid panorama . . . we should also be on the lookout for 'securityscapes.'" Critiquing anthropological narratives of globalization that ignored "the national security state"—"as if nuclear weapons and the cold war did not exist"—

and thus surrendered all insights on "international security" to political scientists, Gusterson's work on state security offered inspiration to a collection on *The Anthropology of Security: Perspectives from the Frontline of Policing, Counter-terrorism and Border Control* (Maguire, Frois, and Zurawski 2014) and was in the meantime adopted by others (Eski 2016). In particular, Daniel Goldstein (2010, 512) argued, "We fail to engage—intellectually, politically, and with the problems of the world—if we refuse to go beyond the local cases or 'narratives' suggested by our research, in the present instance by neglecting the evident continuities that run between and across global 'securityscapes.'" A decade on from Gusterson, bringing a feminist and postcolonial stance to bear, Patricia Noxolo (2014, 291) proposed the "concept of an embodied securityscape, arguing that asylum seekers embody the point of articulation between two differently located security nexuses: security-migration and security-development." And in describing the range of "'scapes' that comprise the landscape of the world system," Jeff Halper (2015) briefly invoked "securityscape," though his account of Israel's pivotal role as an exporter of security systems and weaponry perfected in its governance of Palestinian populations offers little wider conceptualization of the concept.

Subsequently, the term *securityscapes* subtitled a set of essays on *Spaces of Security: Ethnographies of Securityscapes, Surveillance, and Control.* Providing a useful review of anthropological writing about security—described as "one of the most prominent topics in anthropology" (Maguire and Low 2019, 1)—the editors' introduction to the collection acknowledges Gusterson's early adoption of securityscapes, adding that "to date anthropologists have deployed the term 'securityscape' as a synonym for the U.S. national security apparatus. Despite the gravitational attraction of U.S. national security's planetary power, it is important that anthropologists attend to a more diverse universe" (2019, 11). The essays assembled in *Spaces of Security* pursue that, with studies ranging from Argentina, via India, Israel, Guam, Kenya, and New York, to South Africa. Although the studies are not in direct dialogue with each other, they do signal how (when attendant to seeing, projecting, enacting, and embodying security) the idea of a securityscape has clear potential. It critically engages with security as a way of seeing (practiced, but not solely defined by security companies and states) and its conduct. According to Mark Maguire and Setha Low (2019, 11–12), "If one thinks of security in terms of securityscapes, questions of temporality (including speed), vector and scale spring to mind. . . . We are suggesting that securityscapes can be individually contained (an airport, a gated community, a bomb shelter) as well as ethnographically studied, but that they are part of a network of spaces and securityscapes that ultimately provide a cultural code for living as well as a material map of their social and political production."

Security thereby produces a landscape that foregrounds and evaluates risk and enacts securitization. This process is a key moment in the wider social production of space that articulates populations, nature, capital, and states. Drawing on a mapping of transit corridors in the Gulf of Aden (between Yemen and Somalia), Zoltán Glück (2015, 655) argued, "The production of security space is . . . a kind of production of circulation infrastructure." And yet it is most often sovereign actors or para-sovereigns that garner most attention. Taking stock of the writing that adopts the term *securityscapes*, Marc von Boemcken (2019, 96) notes that "Appadurai did not refer to such a thing as a securityscape himself. And while some publications have occasionally done so, they curiously always reinserted the term into highly state-centric frameworks. . . . If conceptualized in Appadurai's original intention, however, a securityscape would encompass a lot more than this. In fact, the suffix 'scape' has mainly been used to foreground individual agency and the potential heterogeneity of social practice. To analyze scapes is to assume the perspectives of the individuals traversing them, to follow them in their daily practices, movements, habits, routines."

Working with others, von Boemcken has traced how collective securityscapes increase personal insecurity for LGBTQ people in Bishkek, Kyrgyzstan, where blending in, avoidance, hiding, mimicry, deception, and sometimes confrontation are required to evade normalized homophobic violence. Similarly, for Kyrgyzstan's Uzbek and Lyuli minorities, experiences of "*existential* danger" embody the "disjunctures" that Appadurai signaled in his account of intersecting scapes: "The securityscapes of socially marginalized groups, in particular, are likely to differ from the 'national security' rhetoric of elites. . . . A feeling of 'existential danger,' especially with regard to physical violence and collective belonging, is not some abstract fear instilled by policy-makers or newspaper headlines. It is a very concrete and conscious experience of everyday life" (von Boemcken, Boboyorov, and Bagdasarova 2018, 71, emphasis original). A subsequent edited book by Marc von Boemcken and his coworkers in Central Asia develops further alternative (alternative, that is, to definitions focused on state-security) notions of securityscape. According to a chapter on strategies developed by Kyrgyz women to avoid everyday sexual violence (which may take forms such as staring or verbal harassment as well as violent assault), "Thus securityscapes can be considered as recurrently applied acting strategies like ignoring, avoiding or making oneself unapproachable, subsuming a variety of relationally subsidiary and situationally adapted actions aimed at ensuring one's safety" (Oestmann and Korschinek 2020, 131). And, in similar terms, writing of their work in Pakistan, Mahvish Ahmad and Rabia Mehmood (2017, 511–12) ask, "How do we make sense of the overlapping forms of surveillance—not just from the state, but criminal groups, Islamists, militants, political groups, families—that bleed into one another?"

In fact, all relationships between seeing, sensing, and doing security have a complexity that is not readily unpacked. In a series of vignettes redefining policing as *Violence Work*, Micol Seigel (2018, 98) follows American visions of development, counterinsurgency, order, and extraction from Alaska to Arabia (via Indochina and Latin America, then back to American cities) through agents of the (discontinued) U.S. Office of Public Safety, whose "travels take us deeper into the coils of this transnational, imperial history of the security world, where state-market assemblages sprawled over national borders, entwining themselves into Leviathans of fearsome proportions." Seeing like a state involves security, and seeing like a security company is something that states enable and intersect with (O'Connor et al. 2008), though the actions and gaze of both state and corporations are highly territorialized and far from being homogenous grids (Ferguson 2005). Yet, in a broad sense of articulations, the idea of a securityscape becomes a useful path through the proliferating literatures on security linking to a vast range of issues. Scapes describe an interactional and intersubjective dimension to ways of seeing space, foregrounding certain technologies, social relations, and characteristics such as media, capital, and ethnicity.

The idea of securityscapes then helps to code our observations and analysis to decipher how security configures and cues architecture, urban zoning, clothing, semiconcealed (or conspicuously displayed) weaponry, behavior, friendly nods or stern warnings and glances, tacit (or unambiguous) displays, and exchanges. Moreover, those forms of insecurity (gendered and sexual violence and other subjectivities of security and insecurity) that are not always readily seen or visualized, or those that are not tabulated in official statistics, refocus attention onto the ways that securityscapes (following Appadurai's original scapes) are "deeply perspectival constructs."

Crucially, securityscapes also involve the *connections* of physical landscapes to microscales, cyberscapes, and other digital arenas. Drones exemplify such connections. In what they call the "liminal security-scapes" of "warzones in Afghanistan, Iraq and northern Pakistan and borderzones and urban areas in the USA," Tyler Wall and Torin Monahan (2011, 240) write, "While drones appear to affirm the primacy of visual modes of surveillance, their underlying rationalities are more nuanced and problematic. As complex technological systems, drones are both predicated upon and productive of an actuarial form of surveillance. They are employed to amass data about risk probabilities and then manage populations or eliminate network nodes considered to exceed acceptable risk thresholds." In other words, drones connect places, scopic regimes, and databases into a complex securityscape of physical and digital space that, as Ian Shaw (2016, 5) argues, "complicates the apparent division between the technical, the political, and the existential."

Scales and Intersections

Notwithstanding that the Kurdistan Workers' Party (PKK) base areas in Iraqi Kurdistan are surveilled by Turkish military drones and that wider air power enters our narrative in the closing pages, our focus in the three transects is ground-level securityscapes. The site choices in the three dispatches that follow arose through serendipity, connections, prior familiarity, and linguistic capacity. Moving between these sites required working in three vernaculars and negotiating diverse area studies literatures. Cambodia, Iraqi Kurdistan, and Mozambique all experienced decolonization, revolution, and the Cold War, mediated through powerful neighbors. Studying security in these sites means negotiating what Heonik Kwon (2006, 161), writing of Vietnam, calls the "disjunctive parallax effects between decolonization and [Cold War] bipolarization." Taking seriously the injunction by Goldstein (2010) for going beyond local to map global securityscapes, in advance of our three dispatches we develop two analytical points within our core argument for "securityscape" as a valuable epistemological device. The first concerns the variety of securityscapes. Our second point is about rethinking their intersections with other scapes, specifically the junctures between securityscapes and political economies.

DIVERSE SECURITYSCAPES

Beyond the Cold War and in its aftermaths, there is a tendency to generalize security as ever more privatized and/or fragmented. Many case studies have explored this fragmentation, as in the valuable review and striking Bolivian case study by Daniel Goldstein (2012) following an earlier influential study by Teresa Caldeira (2001) on São Paulo and Stephen Graham's (2010) wide-ranging account of the new military urbanism and the urbanization of security. But we need to be circumspect about generalizing. Pow Choon-Piew (2014, 1) has criticized a trend in urban scholarship that he sees as "often overwhelmed by recurring case studies documenting the proliferation of urban fortressing and segregation that often warn of an impending urban dystopia with cities being besieged by neoliberal forces of privatism." In security studies, this is seen in literatures on failed states that similarly aggregate postcolonial sovereigntyscapes (Sidaway 2003) and so misrepresents diversity. For beyond a security-development nexus mantra articulated by the World Bank and in a growing policy literature, as Søren Friis (2014, 6) emphasizes, "it is still unclear how the widespread acceptance of this nexus have (a) influenced the component concepts of security and development and (b) been adapted into a variety of national/institutional policy settings."

In what has become a widely cited text on the relations between private security and public police, Trevor Jones and Tim Newburn (1998) distinguish different domains of security. The first, the domain of informal security functions, is associated with the roles of caretakers, conductors, concierges, and municipal staff in parks; the second is the formalized security function of private security companies; and the third domain of security refers to the police. Jones and Newburn's (1998, 169) study finds that the domain of informal security has been shrinking, while the domain of privatized security is expanding by adding those informal customary functions to their core tasks in security provision: "Surveillance and other forms of 'low level' social control had previously been part of the everyday job of staff such as receptionists, caretakers, and gardeners. They would, for example, take note of suspicious strangers, ask people if they need help, and open and lock gates and doors. These functions had been taken on by a more formalized 'policing' presence in the form of uniformed security guards."

Jones and Newburn's findings are drawn principally from the case of London. Elsewhere, the second domain of privatized security might also feature armed response companies or business improvement districts and surveillance patrols in shopping malls, whose operations increasingly structure urban spaces and lives (Bènit-Gbaffou, Didier, and Peyroux 2012; Németh 2010; Paasche 2012; Shearing and Wood 2003). This growth of private security has led scholars to explore themes of plural policing, describing a network of police and private security, and voluntary policing (such as neighborhood watches) (Button and John 2002; Crawford et al. 2005; Jones and Newburn 2006; Loader 2000; Stenning 2009; Yarwood 2007). According to Rita Abrahamsen and Michael Williams (2011, 3), who also study global security assemblages as emanating transformations in global structures of governance, these diverse security actors "interact in a field of tension structured by the opposition between the public and the private and their different forms of material and symbolic power." Rather than eroding the authority of the state, the proliferation of private security companies become an integral part of policing networks enfolded within the final authority of the state/law. A further theme linked to the transformations in policing networks is the outsourcing of some police and military functions to private security companies. This includes basic guarding activities, training, logistics, cash in transit, security in courts and prisons, and security around sports and other significant public staging. Notably, duties that demand less training, or tasks that demand very specialized knowledge and therefore require substantial funding, are being outsourced to private security companies (Ayling and Grabosky 2006; Leander 2005; Minnaar and Mistry 2004; Minnaar and Ngoveni 2004; Singer 2005). This has opened lucrative prospects for the private security industry.

However, generalized trends of a growing privatization of security in selected cities and other putatively revanchist or neoliberal sites critically miss out on the variegated dynamics defining so-called neoliberal securityscapes brokered by different constitutional arrangements and conjunctures. For example, a legacy of the 1990s UN-brokered peace process in Cambodia forbids private security agencies from bearing arms, so to fill the requirement for armed protection and escort, the army has been privately hired by those with wealth and close connections to the ruling party. In comparison, in Mozambique's capital city of Maputo, private security firms have far less significance than informally hired guards, who have neither equipment nor job security. And in Iraqi Kurdistan, the scope for private security firms is now strictly limited (deployed mostly around oil facilities and hardly elsewhere), overwritten by the past and present of conflict, first with Baghdad and later with Dāʻish.[6]

JUNCTURES

In addition to recording and analyzing variations and diversity in securityscapes, *Transecting Securityscapes* explores their intersections with the technoscapes and financescapes that Appadurai originally flagged. Matt Sparke's work on the ideoscape of Cascadia offers some pointers on how such intersections operate there. Chris Philo (2014, 756) has noted that the contemporary moment might be conceived as one where "geopolitics and biopolitics invariably fold into one another . . . [so internal and external relations] become topologically entangled as a pervasive 'biogeopolitics' or 'geobiopolitics' of state (in)security." It is important to dissect these entanglements and conceptualize security, following some who critique its analytical centrality "not as some kind of universal or transcendental value but rather as a mode of governing or a political technology" (Neocleous 2011, 26) "that imbues itself on all social relations and attaches itself to almost all commodities" (Rigakos 2011, 63).

This is evident at different scales and contexts in different ways. All are however caught in a planetary web of surveillance and security led by the United States—the state that for all its travails, described already under Barack Obama's presidency by Oliver Stone and Peter Kuznick (2013, 549) as a "wounded empire," remains a hyperpower. Yet among the most important aspects of America's national security system, beyond its surveillance capacity or geopolitical role that garner most critique (Greenwald 2014), are its geoeconomic impacts in respect of strategic electronic innovation benefitting from federal largesse that has enabled the U.S. techno-capitalist edge in IT. This argument has been persuasively crafted by Linda Weiss (2014) in her *America Inc? Innovation and Enterprise in the National Security State*. Weiss indicates how the close connections between the U.S. national security system, surveillance, and techno-industrial innovation lends the system a creative dynamic, albeit one that rests on enormous destructive capacity. With well over one billion Global Positioning System (GPS) receivers in use worldwide, all taking their coordinates from a U.S. military satellite system, this continues to develop at fast pace. William Rankin's (2018, 5) acclaimed study of the prehistories of the GPS captures the key to such dynamics early on: "After all, what made the technologies of gridded space so ubiquitous and transformative is that they were widely adopted—and sometimes co-opted—for new and unforeseen uses in dozens of non-military fields all around the world."

These accounts, and allied critiques of online corporate *Surveillance Capitalism* (Zuboff 2019), largely miss the emerging synergy of security and economy in China, which conceivably has the potential to become a motor of innovation rivaling that charted in America by Weiss. In the past few years, Chinese firms and the state (often the same thing) have rapidly rolled out facial recognition and other surveillance technologies, first in Xinjiang Uighur Autonomous Region and then across the People's Republic. In tandem with the widespread internment of Uighur citizens based on association, movement, and suspicion, Darren Byler (2019) characterizes this development as "terror capitalism," resting on a massive data system using AI (artificial intelligence) predictive technologies, biometrics, cameras, and checkpoints. Associated techno-security startups have seen spectacular growth, and Byler notes how Xinjiang became the incubator for terror capitalism, now poised to corner export markets in other authoritarian states: "In just the last two years, the state has invested an estimated $7.2bn in techno-security in Xinjiang. As a spokesperson for one of these tech startups put it, 60% of the world's Muslim-majority nations are part of China's premier international development project, the Belt and Road Initiative, so there is 'unlimited market potential' for the type of population control technology they are developing in Xinjiang."

The further rollout of these surveillance and control technologies since the beginnings of the COVID-19 pandemic may be a portent of future trends in China and elsewhere (Chen, Marvin, and While 2020). Yet decades before "smart city" initiatives extended fine-grained surveillance, development, security, sovereignty, and geopolitics have been woven closely in East Asia. One way forward in examining these intersections is offered by Jim Glassman and Young-Jin Choi (2014, 1177), whose historical work on the start-up origins of Korean chaebol in South Vietnam during the American war argued that a geopolitical economic analysis of East Asian development "that makes the enrolment of Asian states in the U.S. MIC [military-industrial complex] a centerpiece of industrial transformation provides one important corrective to this absence of war from the story of East Asian industrialization." Cold War security operations became the glue that connected a range of economic, political, and social landscapes. We return to the range and choices regarding security's creative and destructive powers on recounting Till's active participation in Rojava's securityscape and events there since in our coda, which describes security's power to become something "we cannot not want" (to borrow from Spivak 1993, 267).

CHAPTER 1

Transecting Securityscapes

Writing about the relation between a sweeping vision of a city from above and "the turbulence of street life," David Harvey (1989, 1) acknowledges that "many a battle is fought over the 'proper' way to see." *The Urban Experience* charts the urbanization of capital and its consequences, how this produces (a struggle over) urban spaces.[1] Although some of Harvey's analysis necessarily proceeds at a relatively abstract level,[2] he offers a study of late nineteenth-century France, when, following the turmoil of Franco-Prussian War and eventual French defeat in 1871, the revolutionary Paris Commune emerged and was subsequently crushed by the regular French army. Twenty thousand communards were slaughtered. Harvey (1989, 214) describes how the army "swept quickly through the bourgeois sections of western Paris and cut slowly and ruthlessly down the grand boulevards that Haussmann [between 1853 and 1870] had constructed into the working-class quarters of the city." A reactionary clerical order was restored, exemplified by the construction of the Basilica of the Sacred Heart on the hill of Montmartre, on the rubble of the commune. A century on, leftist protests (in 1971) and a bomb (in 1976) led to police actions inside the Basilica. Harvey draws on the tragic destruction of the commune for a striking example of how (re)securing conditions for the urbanization of capital rests on and requires control over both strategic sites and the ordinary streets that surround and connect them. Landscapes of capitalist urbanization mandate certain forms of order and security. This holds for the microscales of individual firms and properties, wider neighborhoods, and metropolitan and national scales. As Harvey (1989, 58) puts it, "Capitalism has survived not only through the production of space as Lefebvre insists, but also through superior command over space—and that truth prevails as much within urban regions as over the global space of capitalist endeavor." Within this struggle to command, establishing security in service of capital becomes key. Security—conventionally, private and police—safeguards (or conversely neglects some) property and places and determines and regulates access to allow (or prevent some) business to proceed, rents to be enforced, and capital to circulate. At the same time, the wider corporate, public, and inter- and para-state orders are secured. We have argued in the introduction that these combined moments may be critically conceptualized as a multiscalar, multiperspectival securityscape articulating (or, as some would prefer, assembling) an array of social relations and spatial structures.

In studying securityscapes—as the next three chapters do—through the three conflicted postcolonial contexts, geopolitical considerations necessarily become central. Notably this means we must examine the interfaces between imperialism, national sovereignty, revolution, and the forms of capitalism that have been established in Cambodia, Iraq, and Mozambique. Framing our dispatches from these sites of post- (and ongoing) conflict, *Transecting Securityscapes* also draws on an analytical field of critical geopolitics. As indicated by Gerard Toal and Carl Dahlman (2011, 9–10), "'critical geopolitics' is an approach that produces 'categories of analysis' to grasp and explain the too-often unproblematized 'categories of practice' of banal and not-so-banal nor benign geopolitics. While well established within political geography to analyze foreign policy discourse and international relations, it has not been systematically used in the study of what political scientists classify as 'civil war' and 'ethnic conflict.'"

A related source of inspiration in shifting a key referent in critical geopolitics from the abstract global and state scales to quotidian spaces in cities has been the growth of work in the domains of "urban geopolitics" (Rokem et al. 2017) and "urban peacekeeping" (Björkdahl 2013). During the past century, warfare not only mechanized but also increasingly urbanized (Kaldor and Sassen 2020). In February 2017, a leading urban studies journal spotlighted a series of essays under the banner of "The City at War: Reflections on Paris, Beirut, Brussels, and Beyond" (Jaffe 2017), which occasioned reassembling articles and symposia it had published since 9/11 "on the geographical shift of conflict towards cities" (seen in Light 2002; Molotch 2003; Coaffee 2004; Graham 2006, 2012; Marcuse 2006; and Kinder 2014).

Analytically, to juxtapose "the urban" with "the geopolitical," as these investigations do, is to rub together two terms that each signify multiple things and have generated huge literatures (Sidaway 2017). Additionally, and especially in the tracks of Nick Megoran's (2006) call "for ethnography in political geography," other scholars' commitments to and advocacy of a wide range of methods in political geography and critical geopolitics encouraged us along the pathways to the transect methods that underpin our dispatches in *Transecting Securityscapes* (Dittmer and Gray 2010; Fregonese 2017; Kuus 2008; Lentz 2014; Müller 2008; Woon 2013).

Transects as Method

Transecting Securityscapes blends textual analysis and interviews with an ethnographic commitment to observation. We do however recognize that what is seen and interpreted via transects in our dispatches is partial, and that many (in)securities escape our focus. In other words, whereas "scapes" can encompass multiple meanings and practices of security, this book foregrounds aspects of them. As Sara Koopman (2011) argues, "other securities are happening" that involve grassroots practices, that are less visible, or that are at scales and sites requiring other modes and means of research.[3] While mindful of these limitations, we negotiate what Alexander Bridger (2013, 285) describes as "using bodies as research 'instruments' [which] means that innovative data may be gathered through the experience of walking and seeing." This brings to mind Raja Shehadeh's (2007, xviii) inspirational *Palestinian Walks*, kept up over a period of twenty-seven years of encroaching Israeli annexation and settlement, "to record how the land felt and looked before this calamity ... to preserve, at least in words, what has been lost forever."[4] In *Transecting Securityscapes*, we move far from the (mostly Western) metropolitan contexts suggested by ideas of "walking and seeing" associated with psychogeography and prefer to engage the "transect," invoking a term from geography that signifies a sectional sample of an environment or community.[5] Thus, "The notion of the section or the transect is not restricted to the study of natural phenomena. Introduced during the nineteenth century in reference to the altitudinal zonation of social forms (or ways of life, or of civilizations) from mountain to plain, it was used as a metaphor and figuratively by geographers and specialists in the social sciences during the late nineteenth and early twentieth centuries" (Robic 2004).

In a review of literature on (and an example of) transects, Peter Hemmersam and Andrew Morrison (2016, 23) describe them as a method for "critically reading and writing, of moving and locating, of seeing and picturing place." However, the transects informing *Transecting Securityscapes*, unlike those in ecological or urban design research that traces a line across a site, are not linear. Like Trevor Paglen's (2009) photography of secret/secured sites, we approach sites of security and sight geopolitics. This productively supplements a focus on speech acts and geopolitics as discourse. Our approach tackles the same questions that such discourse-centered critical geopolitics strives for, but less often can embody.[6] While therefore more than casual walks through cities (in chapters 2 and 3) or drives from cities into contested territories (in chapter 4), our transects are nonetheless complemented with qualitative interviews. Yet the transects remain at the heart of our dispatches as the mode of engaging with the experience of everyday security. Given the evolution of the approach through each of the sites, we argue that transects offer a critical perspective for others interested in ground-level research on security and space—not just for what Carolyn Nordstrom and Antonius Robben (1996) termed *Fieldwork under Fire*, or when *Surviving Field Research ... in Violent and Difficult Situations* (Sriram et al. 2009), *Researching Conflict and Violence* (Rivas and Browne 2019), *Doing Fieldwork in Areas of International Intervention* (de Guevara and Bøås 2020) or approaching *Fieldwork as Social Transformation: Place, Time, and Power in a Violent Moment* (Bridgen and Hallett 2021)—but anywhere.

James had previously used journeys, specifically walking, as a mode of encountering the geopolitics of the Portuguese-Spanish border (Sidaway 2002, 2005, 2007b). One of those papers sketched how "the methodology rests not only on the collection and critical scrutiny of published narratives about the Portuguese-Spanish border or about discussions with those who live along it, but a series of journeys and walks through its landscapes—in particular across the section of the border, between the Portuguese Alentejo and Spain's Andalucía, that also intersects the rolling hills of the Sierra Morena" (Sidaway 2007b, 162). Walking was the only practical way to reach those hilly sections of this long, mostly rural border, whose demarcation, history, and reconfiguration trace contexts of sovereignty and European integration. This series of writings drew on archives and grounded border encounters. James recovered the history and walked to and between dozens of spaced and numbered border stones (known as *hitos* in Spanish and *marcas* in Portuguese) on sections of the border. The archival research and the walks were then rendered into a narrative "collection of fragments of the border—thoughts and reflections on the boundary stones and rivers, the maps and marks that signify this frontier" (162).

Subsequently James elaborated the walking transect method in the British naval port of Plymouth, using a walk through that city as a means of critical geopolitics and critique of War on Terror narratives about security and insecurity (Sidaway 2009). This included walking with his daughter, Jasmin Leila, who soon afterward was suddenly killed in that city, aged ten years, on 19 January 2007. A subsequent publication, coauthored with Robina Mohammad (Jasmin's mother), explored the implications for thinking about insecurity and geopolitics (Mohammad and Sidaway 2011). Even as the method evolved through the three research sites in *Transecting Securityscapes*, we continue to work with the commitment to traverse space, slowly and attendant to ground details. Introducing his paper on the Plymouth walk, James described the aims "to illustrate how geopolitics *affects* us; to illustrate how the repercussions of military violence are folded into the texture of everyday urban life in a provincial English city and thereby how we are constantly touched by multiple overlapping tragedies operating at different scales and yet intensified in certain sites. This is done through the device of recounting an evening's walk along a section of the South West Coast Path in Plymouth (made on 6 December 2006), negotiating spaces of capital, sovereignty and militarism" (Sidaway 2009, 1094, emphasis original). In that case, the route was predetermined. James followed an urban section of a waymarked long-distance path that was established around the coast of southwest England in the 1970s. The history of the trails that were incorporated into the path themselves reflects strategic and state origins, having been used centuries before by customs patrols seeking to control smuggling. The Plymouth walk was then used as a mode of encounter and narrative strategy for an extended reportage of sites of security and insecurity.

Our joint research began three years later, early in 2009, at a meeting in James's office at the University of Plymouth. At the time James was a co-advisor for Till's doctoral research. While Till was planning his fieldwork on private security in Cape Town, James had successfully applied for funding for joint fieldwork in Mozambique that was to be combined with Till's already planned research in South Africa. Connecting at Johannesburg's O. R. Tambo Airport on 27 July 2009, we took the short flight to Maputo. Till had visited that city a couple of years before, and James was returning to a city he had spent months in during his own doctoral research two decades before and had occasionally returned to since. In Maputo we therefore walked in city streets that James had vivid memories of from the start of the 1990s, when the city was partly cut off from its immediate hinterland by the forces of the Mozambican National Resistance (Renamo). Neoliberal sociospatial transformations following a brief and profoundly contradictory period of state socialism in postcolonial Mozambique were already legible at that time (Sidaway 1992, 1993; Sidaway and Power 1995). By 2009 they had unfolded further.

Following the work in Maputo, we worked together in Phnom Penh, Cambodia, in 2012–13 and Iraqi Kurdistan in 2013–14. While the selection of these three sites reflects our interests, connections, and research opportunities, the simultaneity of the revolutionary process in Cambodia and Mozambique established a striking parallel, whose consequences still reverberate. For Cambodia, 1975 marked the end of American military intervention and the U.S.-backed order and the fall of Phnom Penh to the Khmer Rouge. Mozambique was one of the five Portuguese African colonies where leftist forces came to power in 1975, following the fall of the fascist-imperial regime in Lisbon the preceding year at the hands of a faction of its own armed forces. For Iraqi Kurdistan, 1975 heralded a turning point too, when Baghdad and Tehran signed an agreement (in Algiers) to put aside their territorial disputes and cease support for opposition and insurgent movements in each other's territory. However, the Algiers agreement was revoked by Baghdad soon after the Iranian Revolution, and during the subsequent Iran–Iraq War, Iraqi Kurdistan became a kind of second front. Describing the situation in the summer of 1984,[7] Marion Farouk-Sluglett, Peter Sluglett, and Joe Stork (1984, 24) wrote,

> Kurdish politics are complicated, and the various factions grievously divided. The [Iraqi] regime seems to have thought that the Algiers agreement of 1975 had solved the "Kurdish question" once and for all. Nevertheless, the repressive measures which it adopted in carrying out its policies led to renewed clashes between the army and the Kurdish guerrillas in 1977. In 1978 and 1979, over 600 Kurdish villages reportedly were burned down and some 200,000 Kurds "relocated" in other parts of the country, as part of a scorched earth policy aimed at creating a *cordon sanitaire* some 12 miles deep and 500 miles long along the borders with Iran and Turkey.

Hence, in the third of our dispatches, from Iraqi Kurdistan, we trace securityscapes from Erbil, the capital of the Autonomous Kurdistan Region, to the front lines with Dā'ish at Kirkuk, as well as to insurgent PKK base areas at Qandil, near to the Iran–Iraq–Turkey border. Till then spent an extended period in the majority Kurdish areas of northeastern Syria (known as Rojava) as a participant observer with the Kurdish People's Protection Units (YPG) in what became the Kurdish-led, American-backed armed struggle against Dā'ish, later moving back to Iraq as a participant observer in the liberation of Mosul from Dā'ish.

After finishing the joint fieldwork in Iraq that has become chapter 4 here, we did not meet again until more than three years later, when Till visited Singapore for two weeks in February 2018. Our reunion was at the entry barrier and gatehouse to the condominium where James then lived, staffed by employees of a private security firm. We took the draft manuscript of *Transecting Securityscapes* with us on the short ferry ride to Batam island, Indonesia, where (until travel was curtailed by COVID-19 in the spring of 2020) James periodically returned, seeking space and time to finish it.[8]

Indonesia offers a poignant site to reflect on security that starkly illustrates some of the contradictions and dilemmas running through *Transecting Securityscapes*. Put simply, these are what, who, and where is secured. How does one mode and scale of securitization (of the state, by a regime for example) yield insecurities (repression, death or detention) for some and secure safety or privileges for others? Around the midpoint of the Cold War (when that war was very hot indeed in most of Southeast Asia), the Indonesian archipelago became the scene of one of the most violent campaigns of internal repression in the postcolonial era. On the first day of October 1965, a putsch, whose dynamics were long disputed and remain in the domain of mythology in Indonesia, eventually brought to power a group of fiercely pro-Western anticommunist officers whose leader, General Suharto, would soon consolidate power. President Suharto's New Order endured until the late 1990s, establishing many of the economic, social, and political parameters of the Indonesian democracy that followed in the new century. On a regional and global strategic scale, what was secured in 1965 extinguished the anxieties about Indonesia's geopolitical stance that had preoccupied Cold War strategists in Washington, D.C. (and their fellow travelers in Europe and Canberra) since the 1950s. In their eyes, Indonesia was no longer part of what U.S. president Lyndon B. Johnson (1971, 606) had depicted in his recollections of the early part of his presidential years (1963–69) as "the Communist pincers—Djakarta-Hanoi-Peking-Pyongyang axis on the move: Hanoi in Laos, Cambodia, and South Vietnam; Djakarta into Malaysia and Borneo; Malaysian Communists and Hanoi-trained guerrillas into Thailand; Peking-trained guerrillas into Thailand and Burma; Pyongyang sends its guerrillas into South Korea."

In a section focused on 1964–65, Johnson's memoirs depicted the pincers cartographically (Figure 1), resorting to the arrows that have long featured in much classical geopolitics and its protégés (Boria 2008). According to Johnson (1971, 136), "What we saw taking shape rapidly was a Djakarta-Hanoi-Peking-Pyongyang axis, with Cambodia probably to be brought in as a junior partner and Laos to be merely absorbed by the North Vietnamese and the Chinese." Without American intervention, South Vietnam would collapse. Johnson thought that British support for Malaysia and Singapore was becoming financially unviable for London. China had detonated a nuclear weapon in October 1964 and was deepening its relationship with Indonesia, which in turn was staging a confrontation (involving frequent armed clashes) with

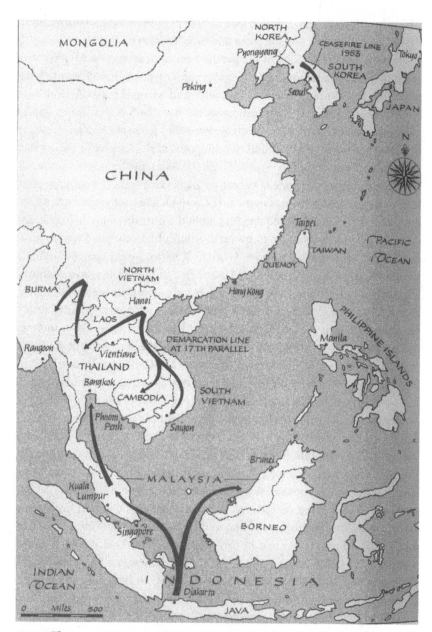

FIGURE 1. The communist pincers—Djakarta-Hanoi-Peking-Pyongyang axis—on the move. Reproduced with permission of the LBJ Foundation from Lyndon Baines Johnson, *The Vantage Point: Perspectives of the Presidency 1963–1969* (New York: Holt, Reinhart and Winston, 1971), 606.

Malaysia, whose legitimacy and broadly pro-Western stance it questioned. In these contexts, the October 1965 putsch in Indonesia and the coming to power of General Suharto there was momentous. In his broader tally of the Cold War, Fred Halliday (1986, 85) noted the importance of what transpired in Indonesia, where "the defeat of the [Indonesian] communist forces, in the early stages of the U.S. intervention in Vietnam, provided the USA with a protected flank that was of immense, if undeclared, importance."

President Johnson's (1971, 357) memoir devotes less than a page to what he calls "a major event in the history of modern Asia" in which "nationalist officers . . . routed or destroyed the Communist organizers and forces who had tried to capture the world's fifth largest nation." He disclaims any U.S. role (documents released in 2017 indicated the extent of U.S. knowledge of the slaughter, complicity in suppressing discussion of it, and assistance to the Indonesian military in identifying communists). Johnson (1971, 357) writes, "Of course, we welcomed the news that this rich nation of more than 100 million people had been saved from falling under Communist dictatorship, though we regretted the bloodshed involved." But the only "bloodshed" mentioned in Johnson's memoir is of high-ranking officers purportedly killed by "Communists" in the lead-up to the coup. Johnson claims the coup was a "nationalist" military response to intrigue and assassinations by communists. This story, long encased as an official chronicle of events in Indonesia, was questioned early on by a group of Cornell-based scholars of Indonesia, whose counterpoint continues to yield debate (Kammen 2017). Yet whatever the precipitating circumstances, as Geoffrey Robinson (2018, 4–5) describes, "In its sweep and speed, and its profound political and social implications, the violence of 1965–66 was comparable to some of the most notorious campaigns of mass killing and imprisonment of the postwar period, including those that occurred in Bosnia, Cambodia and Rwanda, and it far surpassed other campaigns that have become iconic symbols of authoritarian violence in Latin America, such as those in Argentina and Chile." Coming a year after another U.S.-backed coup installed right-wing generals in Brazil, Washington had obtained huge Cold War gains in both countries, without itself firing a shot. That same year—1965—President Johnson ordered forty thousand U.S. troops into the Dominican Republic—at a cost of forty-four American military casualties (twenty-seven killed in action)—establishing an "international security zone" in Santa Domingo. Although the invasion of the Dominican Republic was in a long tradition of American gunboat diplomacy, the immediate context was Cold War anticommunism (Chester 2001). The American strategic gains of 1965 were a decade after the military stalemate in Korea, a few years after losing control of Cuba, and just as America was mobilizing for deeper involvement and escalation in their Vietnam War. With anticommunist generals embedded in Brazil and Indonesia and the left eliminated as active forces in both, these hemisphere-spanning territories were locked into the Western strategic perimeter. They became subordinate and vigorous bases for strong-arm anticommunism and bywords for slaughter to secure globally linked capitalist and sovereign order. Vincent Bevins (2020) refers to this violent mode of securing order in the Global South as the *Jakarta Method*, framing 1965 in more insidious (multiperspectival) rolling out of CIA support (and U.S. military training) in regime change: *¡JAKARTA VIENE!*—the spray-painted graffiti in Santiago Chile in 1973, forewarning Pinochet's 9/11 *golpe*, with extreme suppression and silencing/forgetting in aftermath too.

In Indonesia itself, the events that accompanied state-orchestrated violence and repression were represented in a mythic morality tale of protecting and saving the nation, the "sexualized slander" of traitors being a central motif. Communism and the wider left were demonized. Reviewing some of the critical writing about that moment and its aftermaths, Rohana Kuddus (2017, 56–57) sums up the sweep of the violence:

> The PKI—before October 1965, the largest Communist party in the world outside Russia and China—was physically annihilated . . . the number of those murdered hovers between 500,000 and 1 million, perhaps more. . . . Another 1.5 million leftists or suspected sympathizers were held without any legal process in prisons and labour camps . . . many were subjected to torture, forced labour, sexual abuse or summary execution. . . . If they were released, they were put under close surveillance, required to report to the local Army command several times a week, ostracized by their communities, their identity cards marked with *Tapol*—political prisoner—status, excluded from work and deprived of political rights.

The relative domestic and international erasure of the significance and memory of 1965 and its aftermaths is testimony to the selective representation of (in)security linked to differentiated valuations of life and death (Olds, Sidaway, and Sparke 2005), and that might, in turn, be traced to everyday scorching that was the modus operandi of colonial rule in the Global South. The violence enacted later by the Indonesian state and local collaborators during its occupation of East Timor (1975–99) is better known. It ended, according to a stunning account by Joseph Nevins (2005, 7), with a "scorched-earth campaign [that] was unprecedented in terms of its destruction in the context of departing colonial powers in the twentieth century." His outrage is justified. Yet certainly all colonial counterinsurgencies also left plenty of earth and bodies scorched in Cambodia, Iraq, and Mozambique, for example—a backdrop to the dispatches that follow here.

The power of security narratives is caught up with powers of representation. For Ilana Feldman (2015, 13), introducing her study of security and surveillance in Gaza prior to Israeli occupation of the Strip in 1967, "Foucault's work can be helpful," noting how Foucault's investigation of security is of "a practice that he distinguishes from both sovereignty and discipline . . . involving a particular relationship of space, event and population." Anticipating events and managing degrees of uncertainty are central to this relationship. Feldman's work is part of an evolving literature on histories of and alternatives to policing (see Chazkel, Kim, and Paik 2020). An important strand of this work has excavated the colonial forms of police and their legacies, both for the postcolonial states constituted after the collapse of formal empires and back in the metropoles of the Global North.[9] Writing about the British Empire in India, Mark Condos argues that a collateral effect of the trend to excavate the ideological basis of imperialism and the variety of hidden or subaltern resistances to it has sometimes been to sidestep the violence of the imperial state, whose deep obsession with security had persisting legacies. For Condos (2017, 234), "we now seem mired in the same state of permanent war and anxious emergency that British officials so forcefully insisted existed in colonial India." Another variant of enduring legacy of imperial security derives from the policing of "Black lives" under transatlantic slavery, the focus of an important study by Simone Browne (2015). Post-emancipation America folds this into a racialized regime of surveillance, repression, and incarceration. Investigating this, Mat Coleman (2016, 78) advocates studying policing as a branch of state coercive powers, and in his work "approached state power as a site-specific undertaking rather than engaged in abstracted accounts of who the police are and what they do." Coleman uses a range of standard qualitative methods (interviews, participant observation, and focus groups), but notes how "the world of practice—gleaned through ride-alongs" was closed to him.

We, however, were able to ride with security forces in some of the driving transects in our dispatch from Kurdistan. What we do and the sites that we draw from in *Transecting Securityscapes* are varied. Our dispatch from Maputo, where James had first done fieldwork thirty years prior and where he had longtime contacts, has a longitudinal backdrop, insofar as James recalls the city at the end of the 1980s. Cambodia was readily accessible from Singapore, and contacts there were enabled by then NUS-based graduate student Piseth Keo. Although James had visited Kurdish-majority regions of Turkey in the mid-1980s (including areas proximate to the Iraqi border) together with

Kurdish intellectuals linked to the then nascent PKK, the Kurdistan region in northern Iraq opened to us when, in 2013, Till took up an academic position at a Kurdish university.

All three research sites have seen colonialism, revolution, and multiple insurgencies. Two have been invaded in the last half century. While the intersections of war, state building, and the aftermaths of revolution loom large in framing our dispatches, from the outset transects set the stage for a grounded perspective on security. We focus on the visible forms of security—though we are aware of and connect analysis with other, less legible, security and insecurities. While *Transacting Securityscapes* is more about experiencing the operation of security in charged public space, in each case, however, this also means considering the visions upheld by formal security actors as well as taking stock of extensive literatures on the trajectories of our research sites. Although we integrate interviews into the narratives, the research was embodied, drawing on a positioned experiencing of security and insecurity as much as talking and reading about it. In turn this sharpened our understanding of each site and some big-picture geopolitical themes, but resting on the little things that can easily escape attention. When we adopted this method and rendered it into transects that structure our dispatches, there were no fixed routes to follow. Instead, we selected key places (hotels, memorials, iconic buildings, and public spaces and sites of power and capital) and move between them. As we do so, in each of the dispatches, we record the locations and narrate our encounters with security forces and police. We also talk with both, supplementing our accounts with more formal interviews.

As the method evolved and we continued the work begun in Maputo, first in Phnom Penh and then Kurdistan, instead of trying to bring order into the almost certain uncertainty over where we could go and who we might encounter, we immersed ourselves in transects to embrace uncertainty preemptively by letting go of set plans and move through spaces of interest. Transects provide a methodological frame that translates uncertainty into opportunity and yields potential narrative structures. In Maputo, the method was born out of a need to improvise, given the relative lack of existing work on security in the city, and following in the footsteps of James's modes of encounter/narration in Plymouth. We adopted a similarly improvised attentive approach in Phnom Penh. In Kurdistan, especially after Till moved there to work, we had a rich set of interviews and observations. Still, the focus on transects structured a grounded perspective on security formations and setups: the smell of gun oil, pralines shared with the guerrillas, the bumpiness of rides in old Toyotas. Interviews were used to provide context, confirm observations, and point to scapes that we had bypassed and, sometimes, to enable access to spaces that were otherwise closed. While recognizing its limits, we find this method enabling. Planning transects required a mix of careful design and openness to opportunities and detours. Histories of and attentiveness to reconfigurations of power, class, and violence always loomed large. Besides a review of expansive area studies literatures, this requires local guidance.

Our first dispatch, from Maputo, is mostly based on our street-level observations. It took conviction, fortified by James's prior work on the city, to proceed in this way. There were a dozen interviews done in tandem with the walking transects, but these are not foregrounded. We were worried that feeding in interviews that confirmed the observations and narrative from transects could overwhelm the perspective these develop or reduce transects to impressions corroborated through interviews. We became more confident when planning the Phnom Penh research. Having satisfied ourselves that transects would yield worthwhile work, we began modifying our approach, opening it up, and integrating more formal interviews into the research and writing. In Phnom Penh, it was apparent that street-level security was overwritten by power struggles on a national political level, and interviews became important in understanding this. The three dispatches form an interleaved and evolving process: we needed the commitment to transects and their narration from Maputo to develop a sense for the method. Consequently, we created a template that we could subsequently experiment with. For the Kurdistan dispatch, the context was different. Till was working as a lecturer at Soran University, and connections from his position as a state employee made it possible to conduct in-depth interviews with key actors. But here too transects (through disputed territories and front lines) are the basis through which the research is narrated.

Our approach also has affinities with and derives inspiration from the feminist work on security. This field—as part of a wider critical security studies—has insisted on questioning the selective focus on the security of states that silence the linkages with embodied, personal, and familial security in "the sites where geopolitics is felt, negotiated, mediated and interpreted that are both within and beyond the body" (Botterill, Hopkins, and Sanghera 2020, 1157). As Shelly Feldman, Gayatri A. Menon, and Charles Geisler (2011, 2–3) note in their introduction to a collection of essays on *Accumulating Insecurity: Violence and Dispossession in the Making of Everyday Life*, this follows from "rejecting the equation of security with the stockpiling of armaments and embracing instead a notion of social reproduction as the crux of human security . . . [that] illuminates the banal ways in which the administration of violence—and a calculus of risk we typically associate with the battlefield—configures civilian space."

The feminist critique of security involves two other steps. The first has been a critique of masculinity embodied in the ways that state and international strategic security operate. Perhaps the most striking example of this work is Carol Cohn's (1987, 712) classic account of "sex and death in the rational world of defense intellectuals," enacting an ethnography that focuses on the hyper-hetero-masculine language of a group of "likeable and admirable men" charged with control of weapons of mass destruction. Her feminist critique of their world building is mindful of its seductiveness to draw one in. In similar terms, and speaking quite directly to some of our own work in *Transecting Securityscapes*, Cynthia Enloe (2010) engages with *Making Feminist Sense of the Iraq War*, developing eight vignettes that link its waging with domestic violence, racism, and sexual assault, as well as codes of beauty and valor. The second related step in feminist security studies is the advocacy of what Kathrin Hörschelmann and Elisabeth Reich (2017, 73) term "geosocial approaches," in which they argue for

> greater attention to four issues that are rarely thematised in security studies and which geosocial approaches bring more squarely into focus: 1) social relations as a key connective tissue through which different dimensions of (in)security are entangled and through which these entanglements are given shape; 2) social relations as sources of security and insecurity; 3) security practices as including the emotional and practical labour invested in sustaining, moulding or dealing with the breakdown of social relations; and 4) the topographic stretching and hybridisation of social relations that furnishes not just cultures of fear but can also generate greater senses of security.

We are unsure that all four of these issues are rarely thematized (although perhaps not simultaneously), at least in critical security studies, especially given the breadth of feminist studies that have emerged in the past two decades. However, we are mindful (in the light of the focus of some feminist work on the critical scrutiny of masculinity) that our dispatches here could invite the same charges that Michael Herr's attract. Reviewing the literature on Herr's *Dispatches*, Ty Hawkins (2009, 132) summarizes these as an author and book that succumb to "the hypermasculinity and sexually charged violence of the [Vietnam] war" or that shift attention away from the local toward a "quintessentially [Western] rock-and-roll adventure" caught up in a death drive. While those readings are plausible, Herr's *Dispatches* are internally complex and ambivalent. In regard of these ambivalences we find backup in Debbie

Lisle's (2016) account of *Holidays in the Danger Zone: Entanglements of War and Tourism*. She cites Herr among other dispatches from war zones, noting how "multiple entanglements" in the encounters of "political tourists" and soldiers emerge "in relation to the Others around them, the material objects they form attachments with, and the environments that sustain them. And it is precisely this condition of being *in relation*—of being constituted by multiple relations—that creates the possibility of revealing unexpected attachments and opening new spaces of encounter outside of the given coordinates of domination" (285, emphasis original).

Connecting the Transects: Maputo, Phnom Penh, and Kurdistan

As Appadurai highlights, scapes are intersubjective. Encountering security via transects is affective and tangible. Our intention is to enhance, in some measure, critical understandings of how security becomes an active element in the wider social production of space. The three dispatches that follow—one on each research site—are in the chronological order in which the research was conducted. Of course there are, as we have indicated, commonalities between the sites. The commonalities relate to some significant parallels in terms of exit from empire, revolution, and geopolitical contest. However, while Maputo and Phnom Penh became national capitals, Erbil, the capital of the Kurdistan region, does not enjoy that (international) status, despite, as chapter 4 details, the aspiration of Kurdish political forces and a majority of the population there. Moreover, the legacies of the Ottomans, British, and Americans in Iraq and the impacts of President Saddam Hussein's security regime, amid what Roger Owen (2014) charts as *The Rise and Fall of the Arab Presidents for Life*, differ from the trajectories of Portuguese and French empires. The Mozambique Liberation Front (Frente para a Libertação de Moçambique) or Frelimo, who established the People's Republic of Mozambique after the Portuguese imperial collapse, embarked on Marxist-Leninist-inspired revolution before embracing neoliberalism in the 1990s. In Cambodia after the French empire came the American war, violent revolution, and Vietnamese invasion, followed by UN-brokered peace settlement and the consolidation of a strongman neoliberalism. As we go on to detail, their contemporary securityscapes vary significantly.

Yet there are also intriguing connections. All three sites are shaped by an oceanic world of interconnectivity that predated Western colonial hegemony and had the Indian Ocean (extending into the Persian Gulf and across the Bay of Bengal into the South China Sea) at its heart. Fahad Ahmad Bishara (2020, 398) notes the "challenges that scholars face when trying to reconcile fixed, territorial notions of society—and of nation—with a history of circulation, entanglement and imbrication with contending imperial projects." The analytical challenge is compounded by the ways that colonial and postcolonial polities themselves interwove these and other connections. Oceanic circulations facilitated early Indic influences on Cambodia and subsequently a significant Islamic presence, especially in Mozambique. French and Portuguese colonial scholarship and governance rescripted and managed these "civilizational" influences. In turn, the discourses and policies developed by the French and the Portuguese imperial systems would, respectively, shape the anticolonial and postcolonial subjectivities of Cambodian intellectuals and political parties about Cambodia's past who celebrated the grandeur of the Khmer Empire as a template for modern Cambodia (Edwards 2007) and inform contemporary Mozambican narratives about Islam (Kaarsholm 2014; Machaqueiro 2012).

Connecting more directly with events in Iraq, since 2017, the littoral of the northernmost Mozambican province of Cabo Delgado has seen insurrection by a group whom Dāʿish claim as an affiliate. The uprising has seen spectacular violence directed mostly at civilians as well as the targeting of police and state forces, in turn triggering further repression. What locally has been variously called al Shabab and Swahili Sunna has links with insurgencies in Kenya, Somalia, and Tanzania as well as roots in unequal structures of political and economic power, seriously compounded by the development of extractive industries—gems and natural gas (Devermont and Columbo 2019; Morier-Genoud 2020) and illicit trade in narcotics, timber, and ivory (Haysom 2018). An American private security firm also operating in Iraq reportedly tendered contracts with the gas companies and the Mozambican state, losing out to Russia's state-linked Wagner Group of private military contractors (McGregor 2019). South African private security firms and special forces are also involved. However, as in Iraq, the humanitarian impacts are dreadful. In mid-November 2020, the UN Refugee Agency reported that over 355,000 people had been displaced, fleeing insecurity in northern Mozambique (UNHCR 2020).

In similarly entangled contexts, what Nile Green (2014, 559) has suggestively highlighted as "the exchanges of both long-term networks and short-term circuits" will crop up in the dispatches that follow.[10] However, distinct foci emerge. For Maputo, we spotlight micro enclaves. In Phnom Penh, we center on the landscape of complicit corruption and "development." Our dispatch from Kurdistan foregrounds autonomy and territory.

Chapter 2 describes how Mozambique's capital Maputo is secured. This includes policing. The ruling Frelimo party evolved from a 1960s national liberation movement, via a commitment to be a Marxist-Leninist vanguard in the 1970s (coming to power after the collapse of the Portuguese empire in the middle of that decade), to one espousing a neoliberal economic stance in the past thirty years. Although they have had to contest elections since the early 1990s, when Mozambique became a multiparty state following years of (almost entirely rural) civil war, Frelimo have won all six general elections since the first in 1994. The securityscape in central Maputo comprises private enclaves, where almost every building, condominium, and apartment complex is secured by some form of private security. Here the range of private security providers is remarkably wide, including professional, well-equipped personnel from national or international private security companies, minimally equipped guards in old uniforms, and many more in plain clothes sometimes armed just with a stick. While the state uses police to secure vital interests, they hardly patrol other public sites and spaces. To bridge this security gap, commercial and ad hoc security providers are contracted to protect private businesses and homes, and the complex patchwork of privately secured micro enclaves relay and rework enclaving on larger scales.

Chapter 3 charts Phnom Penh's transformative boom in urban redevelopment including the construction of malls, casinos, and skyscrapers and filling up inner-city lakes that served as seasonal flood drainage to create more space for real estate. This influx of capital is enabled by close dealings with politicians from the ruling Cambodian People's Party (CPP), whose entrenched leadership and power increasingly circumscribe opposition parties. Money politics filters down to the street level, rendering everyday interactions with police unpredictable. Cambodia's evolution from the years of conflict that followed Vietnamese invasion at the end of the 1970s and the collapse of the Khmer Rouge, which had come to power in the middle of that decade, saw a peace settlement in which the state was awarded a monopoly on the bearing of arms. Although private security guards are abundant around shops, condominiums, and offices in downtown Phnom Penh, they are equipped only with batons, and not even all with these. At the time of our fieldwork, Cambodian law permitted the police and military to be hired by private firms and entities. This yields a distinctive securityscape, where the key state security apparatus is available for hire. We began our work in April 2012 when Phnom Penh was hosting the twentieth summit of the Association of Southeast Asian Nations (ASEAN). At the closing of the April summit (the first of two annual summits), Prime Minister Hun Sen had declared that Cambodian sovereignty is not for sale in a contentious exchange with journalists about China's influence in the country. However, the sale and enclosure of Cambodian land and property have yielded both profit and widening tensions. These relate to a security-scape that reflects and weaponizes the wider political and economic landscapes, symptomatic of the wider relationship between state and capital in Cambodia.

Chapter 4's dispatch from Kurdistan departs from the capital city focus of the Maputo and Phnom Penh sites in venturing beyond the city of Erbil to spaces to its north occupied by the insurgent PKK, and to its south and west into what were termed disputed territories (disputed, that is, between the Baghdad-based Iraqi central government and the government of the Autonomous Kurdistan Region). With the emergence of Dā'ish in mid-2014, it became clear that we needed to look at the region as a multilayered territorial setup tightly secured by a variety of forces, caught up, as in other contests over territorial status, "as contingent products of an ongoing series of connections between people, discourses and objects" (Jones and Merriman 2012, 937). In Kurdistan, we transect securityscape interfaces with sovereignty and territory.

CHAPTER 2

Maputo's Fractures

Colonial Mozambique began as an elongated territory of enclaves. Portugal's empire was originally a maritime and not territorial institution, and when Lisbon needed to demonstrate "effective control" to gain a place at the late nineteenth-century imperial bargaining table when Africa was being portioned out among the European powers, great swathes of Mozambique were leased to private companies. Capitalized by Britain, France, Germany (until World War I), and South Africa, these had para-sovereign rights: issuing their own currencies and postage stamps, recruiting administrators and police, and imposing levies, including through forced labor (Alexopoulou and Juif 2017; Vail 1976). Only in the 1940s was a unified colonial state established. Two decades later, organized anticolonial insurgency began. In 1975 Portugal left, having signed an accord (on 7 September 1974 in Lusaka) for a transition of power to Frelimo, with independence set for 25 June 1975. The new government promptly declared—from its newly inherited capital city far from the sites of anticolonial insurgency—that they were embarking on a transition to socialism.

Frelimo could draw on multiple templates and allies. From the 1950s to the 1980s, many cities in the Global South were shaped by socialism—this transcended those postcolonies that adopted communism or were, like the Ba'athists in Iraq, deemed by Moscow to be "states of socialist orientation." Łukasz Stanek (2020) sees this as part of a project of "socialist worldmaking," challenging the idea that the globalization of architecture can be simply equated with Westernization. Stanek's research "draws attention to the contributions of architects, planners, engineers and construction companies mobilized in state-socialist networks to worldwide urbanization processes after the Second World War" (2020, 166). Their impacts were wide. But the influence of socialism became most legible (with Chinese, Soviet, and Eastern European guidance and weapons) following a series of coups and revolutions in the 1960s and 1970s bringing socialist governments to power.[1] Africa saw more of these than any other continent. M. Anne Pitcher and Kelly M. Askew (2006, 1) note, "Just as 'democracy' today has become a common idiom of political parlance, so too might 'socialism' be considered for Africa an idiom of the 1950s to the 1980s. During that time, no fewer than thirty-five countries out of fifty-three proclaimed themselves 'socialist' at one or other point in their history." From the mid-1970s to end of the 1980s, Frelimo was prominent among these socialist regimes. When the revolutions of 1989 swept away the Eastern European and Soviet role models that had informed socialist strategy in postcolonial Mozambique, constitutional revision jettisoned the rhetoric of socialism. However, as Pitcher and Askew (2006, 3) go on to argue, the erasure of the socialist moment from national narratives in places like Mozambique neglects and devalues the ways historical memory and discursive continuities still shape responses and resistance to changes in the postsocialist present: "Instead of 'postsocialism,' the language of 'neo-liberalism,' 'democratic transition' and 'civil society' dominates discussions of Africa's recent transformations. It looks forward to a presumed rosy and successful future, rather than looking backwards to a failed socialist past. And it prevails because its many advocates—development experts, multinational representatives, foreign consultants, NGOs, and the current African elite—dictate its key terms. They assume and assert that the collapse of socialism has left a 'blank slate' on which the story of 'free market democracy' can be written." For Mozambique, the "socialist" decade and half after independence and the longer period since can also be interpreted as a series of *ruptures* and structural continuities that reconstituted citizenship, property, power, and statehood. As elsewhere (see Lund 2016), when studying these, especially where they have involved violent contests, the dialectic of continuity and change and their capacity to create political subjects and social relations needs to be analyzed (Dinerman 2006; Sumich 2018, 2021; Sumich and Nielsen 2020).

Our primary means of encountering and vantage point into what became of that socialist moment are transects encountering key sites of colonial and postcolonial power in Mozambique in the *cidade de cimento* or "cement city" of central Maputo. We walk, talk (with those we meet on the way, usually in the lingua franca of Portuguese), and write about Maputo, mindful of how its sociospatial transformations are mediated through securityscapes. Our transects through central Maputo were conducted between 28 July and 4 August 2009. When James had first visited Maputo—twenty years earlier—it was cut off from much of its hinterland by the Mozambican civil war, an ideological and power conflict waged largely in rural areas. This confounded attempts at socialist transformation in Mozambique, while also being partly mired in the wider regional and local resistance to these transformations. Maputo (the formerly named Portuguese colonial city of Lourenço Marques) has experienced a succession of transformations since independence. Portuguese colonial power collapsed unexpectedly and abruptly in 1974 and 1975, following the 25 April 1974 coup d'état in Lisbon enacted by disgruntled Portuguese military officers who recognized that the growing anticolonial insurgency in Portugal's African territories could not be quelled. Frelimo had been waging a guerrilla war in rural Mozambique, operating from bases in Tanzania, where they had established a proto-state from the mid-1960s (Panzer 2013), albeit riven by factionalism and Cold War divisions and subject to surveillance by Portugal's intelligence service, the Polícia Internacional e de Defesa do Estado (Kaiser 2017; Opello 1975; Roberts 2017). After 25 April 1974, Frelimo found themselves quickly having to assert their authority across Mozambique amid a collapsing colonial state. However, in the decade after independence Frelimo's socialist mobilizations were beset by domestic and regional resistance and sabotage and hamstrung by internalized colonial norms of governance, as Benedito Luís Machava (2011, 593) notes: "Frelimo's quest for hegemony and its obsessive aim of building a state-nation under the project of 'socialist revolution' led to harsh intolerance of all that was considered a hindrance to these objectives." More recently, John Saul (2020a, 2020b), a veteran and generally sympathetic observer of Frelimo, has commented on the history of subterfuge and inner-party violence, as well as heroism, that were present from the outset. The conflation of internal and external security threats in Mozambique was compounded within just a few years of independence by civil war—beginning in the center of the country in 1977, then spreading to all provinces by the early 1980s—between Frelimo and the rebel Renamo (Mozambican National Resistance). There were auxiliary forces on both sides (Jentzsch 2017), and the conflict became deeply intertwined with regional and Cold War dynamics.

Renamo were fostered at first by Ian Smith's white minority regime in Rhodesia and then by the apartheid government and security forces in South Africa. For more than a decade, Frelimo were unable to control rural swathes of territory, though all the cities and many key transport routes remained in their hands (Finnegan 1992; Hall and Young 1997; Sidaway 1992). A comprehensive peace agreement in 1992 ended the war and led to the brief deployment of a UN peacekeeping mission.[2] In October 2009, three months after our transects, Frelimo won another five-year term of office in the fourth national presidential and parliamentary elections. Indeed, Frelimo—since the early 1990s a firmly procapitalist and business-orientated party, though retaining some of its mass base—have remained continuously in power, also winning elections for a fifth and sixth time in 2014 and 2019. From 2013 to 2019 Renamo renewed sporadic insurgency, mostly in central Mozambique and on a much more confined scale than the civil war of the 1980s and early 1990s. Justin Pearce (2020, 788) argues that to understand this return to arms, we "need to bring the insights of earlier scholarly debates on different phases of recent Mozambican history into our understanding of the present . . . debates over the multiple origins and fractious character of Mozambican nationalism . . . and the lack, particularly in central Mozambique, of a post-war state distinct either from society or from Frelimo." In an account of what she calls "pernicious polarization" in Mozambique, M. Anne Pitcher (2020, 472–73) notes how "formative rifts" endure:

> Rejection of Frelimo's embrace of Marxism and its associated modernist condemnation of "tribes," "tradition," and "obscurantism" provided the ideological justification for Renamo's opposition to Frelimo, especially after 1980. But these elements of Renamo's resistance were never fully articulated, and at any rate, Frelimo abandoned most of these ideas when it adopted the 1990 constitution 2 years prior to the signing of the peace accord. Rather, the differences that fueled (and continue to fuel) polarization between Renamo and Frelimo are in some ways more intractable than ideology. Some are foundational and rooted in the succession crisis following the 1969 assassination of the founder of Frelimo, Eduardo Mondlane, which resulted in the expulsion of the heir apparent, Uriah Simango, from the party; the selection of his rival, Samora Machel, as the new leader; and Simango's subsequent disappearance and presumed murder by Frelimo. Layered onto the cleavage generated by this early crisis are regional, ethnic and religious tensions.

At the time of the transects in 2009, studies on policing and power in rural Mozambique pointed to the mobilizations of rural vigilantes by Frelimo and Renamo (Kyed 2007a, 2007b, 2009). The subsequent (2013–19) Renamo insurgency was in central Mozambique, far from Maputo. As that latest phase of Renamo insurgence was winding down, the past few years have seen revolt in the coastal zone of northern Mozambique by Swahili Sunna, described in chapter 1. However, our 2009 transect encounters were not with these fractures. We focused on how power is expressed in downtown securityscapes in the city that the Portuguese left behind. We traversed the central core of Maputo, where most of the built environment dates from the mid-twentieth century.

In a mixture of links (top-down and bureaucratic governance) and breaks with the colonial epoch, Maputo's housing stock and most urban property were nationalized in 1976, reallocated to Mozambicans by the newly established Frelimo party-state (Sidaway 1993; Sidaway and Power 1995). In the decades since, the binary divisions between the colonial-built cement city and the surrounding *cidade de caniço* or cane city housing the majority further blurred. The late colonial state had struggled to uphold the divides (Morton 2018). Since Frelimo came to power, changes in legal codes, building materials, and flows of people and capital have yielded hybrid urban spaces (Bertelsen, Tvedten, and Roque 2014; Jorge 2020; Roque, Mucavele, and Noronha 2016). However, the former colonial core remains a locus of postcolonial authority and its articulation with the world beyond. As David Morton (2019, 7) notes, "In local languages, this area continues to be called Xilunguíe, which means 'place of the whites,' even though the vast majority of the European population left Mozambique around the time of independence."

Two Transects, One City

29 JULY 2009

Our first transect was conducted on 29 July 2009, starting at ten forty-five in the morning at the open-air food court in the Maputo Shopping Center, a mall known for amenities closely bound to an elite and middle-class urban lifestyle (such as big supermarkets, restaurants, cafes, a cinema, and various shops). The ribbon-cutting for the mall had been performed by Mozambique's president three years before our transect. The year after our transect, its owner, Mohamed Bachir Suleman, would be named by the U.S. Treasury as leading narcotics trafficking and money laundering—though his links to Frelimo have rendered him "legally untouchable" (Sumich 2018, 131). Although the mall did not quite fulfil all the criteria of cleanliness and the feelings of *Geborgenheit* (shelter/safety/comfort) (Hutta 2009) associated with these kinds of private sanitized enclaves elsewhere, it embodied most aspects of a typical mass private property (see Houssay-Holzschuch and Teppo 2009; Raco 2003; Shearing and Stenning 1983, 1985; von Hirsch and Shearing 2000; Wakefield 2003). A limited number of entrances makes the site easy to secure and makes it easy to control entry and exit if necessary, and the mall has tight private security measures in the form of guards and CCTV cameras. In addition, some shops have their own security—wandering through the mall, we observed guards from five different security companies.[3] As we stood in the entrance portal of the main building, ten CCTV cameras could be counted. However, compared to attractive depictions of similar mass private property elsewhere, this mall does not seem to be projected as a meeting point for young and old, or as a venue where people might spend their leisure time (Wakefield 2003, 20). For example, in describing the Victoria & Albert Waterfront mall in post-apartheid Cape Town, Myriam Houssay-Holzschuch and Annika Teppo (2009) note how it had become a fixture of urban life, where socially diverse people go to relax and enjoy the "shoppertainment," with or without the intention of spending a significant amount of money. In Maputo Shopping Centre, the ratio of customers to non-shopping visitors was striking; some of the shop assistants even seemed to be asleep in their chairs. The only place that was busy on that Wednesday morning was the supermarket on the ground floor and to some extent the open-air food court. The second attribute is that, compared with most people on the streets outside, many patrons of the mall clearly belonged to a different class, as judged by their dress and especially the large cars they drove up in. In Maputo as in many other cities, the provisions made for private automobiles generate tangible sociospatial division. Frequently, vehicles themselves become a secure space at the cost of wider insecurity for those without regular access to them, embodying what Don Mitchell (2005) has called "the S.U.V. model of citizenship." As studies from Luanda (Pitcher and Graham 2007) and Managua (Rodgers 2004) have illustrated, highways and traffic partition urban space to allow fast, secured transit for those with vehicles and render it insecure for those without.

As we left the mall through the southern gate, the first car bearing the logo of a private security company came into sight. As we progressed eastward, several construction sites and new condominium complexes caught our attention. On the waterfront we passed the Ministério dos Negócios Estrangeiros e Cooperacão—the Ministry of Foreign Affairs and Cooperation, one of the largest ministerial buildings in Maputo. Further on, the walk led past the construction site of the new Ministério das Pescas (Ministry for Fisheries), which was directly followed by the local Ernst & Young office. All these buildings had their own security. In particular, the Ernst & Young office had a strong presence of G4S guards on the corners of the property, eyeballing every person passing by. Turning south toward the sea, the walk went past several old and new governmental buildings. Except for some limousines with a police escort, few security measures were visible around these official complexes. Turning around the next corner, however, it became clear that photographing ministerial offices could not escape notice. As we tried to leave the area, a marine from the barracks stopped us. After a short warning about not taking photographs and several apologies, the transect could be continued further west toward the colonial fortress situated next to the Praça 25 de Junho. On the short walk along the Rua Marquês de Pombal, which was approximately two hundred meters, three armed response vehicles from different private security companies came our way.

Entering the Praça was the first time we encountered crowded urban spaces. There was an immediate change in atmosphere, activities, and people: street vendors selling fish on the sidewalk, people enjoying their lunch in the park, and informal workers washing parked cars for tips. As it was already noon, we tried to find a spot to relax away from the sun and update our notes. The only free spot in the cool shade was the generously designed stairs of a Portuguese bank, so we decided to rest there, but seconds after sitting down a security guard chased us away. Forced to continue, we were led by the transect along Rua Consiglieri Pedroso and Rua do Bagamayo (the colonial Rua Aráujo) that runs one block to the south. Here, just a few meters into the road, we passed a police station. Looking at the two officers guarding their own station with AK-47s, we realized these were the first police officers we had seen so far. We had walked past countless security guards and at least five armed response vehicles, but (not counting the police escort at the ministry and a customs car near the harbor) had not seen a single police officer patrolling in the public space. Still thinking about this observation, we continued the walk past several banks and shops. Every single bank, as well as at least every second shop, had a security guard outside, standing or sitting on the sidewalks. As we walked deeper into the center of the city, this impression was confirmed repeatedly. Any shop that smacked just a little of money had its own guards, but it was not only the uniformed guards that caught our attention. When we walked around the big apartment blocks in the inner city that were built by the Portuguese in the 1960s and 1970s, it struck us that all of them had a man or a group of men sitting in the entrance. To begin with we did not make much of it, but after a while we realized that they were also some form of private security, which we later confirmed in interviews. However, as these guards wore plain clothes and often sat in groups it was difficult to quantify them in any way.

We soon ended up at the Praça dos Trabalhadores, a massive roundabout with a big statue erected by the Portuguese regime in remembrance of the fallen of World War I, one of whose fronts was the border area of northern Mozambique with the German colony of Tanganyika. At the other end of the Praça is the Central Railway Station, a distinctive domed building that still claims a place among the must-see stations of the world. Inside, however, the station was almost empty. One of the two main platforms was blocked by a train that belonged in a museum (a museum would be established there in 2015), while the other platform did not give the impression of being much busier. Except for a few scattered people, the only other persons in the station were G4S guards who were willing to chat with us. From the station we walked up Avenida Guerra Popular, through the Mercado Central (central market), and across Avenida Karl Marx to the Jardim Botanico Tunduru (botanical garden). Again, this route took us past several different guards, where it was often not clear what exactly they were securing. Sometimes, guards from different companies stood together chatting; sometimes a firm with several guards seemed to secure a whole block with shops, and sometimes they almost seemed to be keeping an eye on the sidewalk. We went past the second group of police officers in front of a bank (at this point we were already over three hours into our walk). During the whole day we saw only two more police officers: one in the Jardim Botânico Tunduru and another one next to a G4S-protected, Chinese-owned hotel apartment complex, which also offered all sorts of amenities like a supermarket and restaurants (we went in to inspect the room rates on offer). After a short detour to the construction site of the new headquarters of one of the leading mobile phone companies in Mozambique (where we were also chased away by a guard who objected to us lingering), this new Chinese-owned complex marked the end of this first transect at four thirty, after almost five hours.

30 JULY 2009

Our second transect, on Thursday 30 July at one in the afternoon, started outside the hotel where we were based during the research. This midrange hotel was typical of its kind from a security point of view. It had guards who were watching both sides that were open to the street twenty-four hours a day and had on display the compulsory warning signs of the same security company's armed response service with their slogan "we secure your world" (and a graphic of a globe that had a locked chain around it). Very soon, our transect led us to Avenida 24 de Julho. It was immediately obvious that this transect would be rather different from that of the day before. Right on the corner of Avenida Salvador Allende and Avenida 24 de Julho was a cafe with many white guests who were being watched over by a security guard. As we walked down the street and later Avenida Eduardo Mondlane, this racialization was repeated. Whereas the public sphere of the sidewalks is predominantly African, in the restaurants here the proportion of whites is much higher and the food and ambiance remain significantly Portuguese.

The fine line between the pedestrian area and the space occupied by the outside seating of restaurants was always carefully minded by a security guard usually equipped with a baton and a two-way radio. The changing character of city precincts was visible not only in the increase in street vendors and cafes but also in such surveillance and security measures. Walking toward Avenida Julius Nyerere, for example, a bank was secured by the police and a private company. When we asked two police officers and a G4S guard about this, they did not see a contradiction. One officer simply said that public and private security are *amigos* and that a bank obviously needs good protection. This, we note later, epitomized a wider situation in Mozambique.

On Avenida Julius Nyerere were several top-end hotels, restaurants, condominium complexes, and a shopping mall. Also, the first of several embassies came into sight. The number of guards around this area increased immediately. Turning around in the middle of the street we could count employees of at least seven different security companies. Furthermore, the number of police officers on the street was significantly higher than on the day before. However, their duty did not seem to be to patrol the public space but rather to secure buildings that hosted banks or other financial institutions.

Walking north up Julius Nyerere, we soon entered the spaces of concentrated power, including the elite Hotel Polana and the palatial presidential residence that was secured by gray bunkers and soldiers. No one can walk past here; we had to cross the road and walk on the other side. We also walked past the residential area of Sommerschield, where some of the wealthy elite lived. In this quarter were many embassies and offices of international organizations, all lined up on Julius Nyerere, especially between Rua de Kassuende and Avenida Kenneth Kaunda, and on Avenida Kenneth Kaunda up to Avenida Kim Il Sung. Soon after passing the American embassy, which had several G4S guards in and around its property as well as police road blocks, we turned into Avenida Kim Il Sung and walked past numerous uniformed private security down to the Hospital Central de Maputo, Mozambique's main public hospital.

After the transect we retreated to the nearby Jardim dos Professores (Teachers Garden) situated in an affluent neighborhood near our hotel. In the original terms of psychogeography, as representing the "effects of the geographical environment, consciously organized or not, on the emotions and behavior of individuals" (Debord [1955] 2006), this garden is utterly different from the Jardim Botânico Tunduru along our first transect. The Jardim Botânico Tunduru has run wild: there are lianas climbing and circling everywhere, and in the tops of the trees rest giant bats waiting for darkness before they swarm out. It is an open space, accessible to everyone. The Jardim dos Professores, although also formally a public garden, has been overhauled by a nearby hotel from a once rundown park into one of the city's green and ordered spaces. In the process, however, the hotel has also established its own cafe within and erected a high fence around the garden. The park itself is now secured by the hotel's security company, which includes an armed response service. Having invested in the park and built an expensive cafe, the hotel exerts a right to dictate terms of entry. This means, for example, that the bigger of the two gates will be closed in the evening, after which the only open entrance is secured by at least one guard. Although we did not see any person or group being actively denied entrance, exclusivity is mirrored by the visitors to this park. Many are white and almost all are more affluent than most Mozambicans. Sitting in the park for a while, one might observe maids with children, a private birthday party attended to by a waiter wearing white gloves, or a school class being taught in the new open-air classroom. Overall, it is a very calm, harmonious atmosphere, though with a slightly staged, even sanitized, feel. This park is not the hectic, sometimes disorderly, Maputo on the other side of the fence. Together with elite Mozambicans, we relaxed there; the Jardim dos Professores becomes, like hotels, landed property and offices, a node in the network of secured sites of power and sanctuary.

Maputo's Securityscapes

One of the most striking observations during transects concerned the police presence. Although Mozambique does not struggle with as high a crime rate as neighboring South Africa, the postsocialist trajectory yielded wide social inequality. As Joseph Hanlon (2007, 2009, 2010) argued, the scale of inequality— particularly evident after Frelimo's socialist project was abandoned in the early 1990s—and ensuing grievances and insecurity became a potent mix. Accompanying the worsening inequality was the increase in opportunity as reflected in the conspicuous consumption and wealth accumulation on the part of a minority. By the 1990s, the city was also full of ex-combatants and weapons were readily available, an "aggravating factor" in the growth of criminality in Maputo as the civil war wound down, according to Fabrice Folio, Carlota Marlen, and Luisa Mutisse (2017, 262). In their "Safety and Security" advisories on

Mozambique at the time of our transects, the British Foreign and Commonwealth Office (2009) warned, "Robbery, often using knives and firearms, is prevalent on the streets of Maputo." The travel and safety warnings from the U.S. Department of State and the German Federal Foreign Office also referred to violent crime (Auswärtiges Amt 2009; U.S. Department of State 2009). In 2008 and again in 2010, Maputo saw short-lived popular uprisings linked to protests about rising food prices. Up to half a dozen deaths resulted on both occasions when the police were quickly overwhelmed and resorted to firing live ammunition. The revolt in Maputo and a provincial capital in central Mozambique, with smaller-scale repetitions 2013 and 2014 (protests by street vendors in 2020 were more localized), were the first instances since independence that government forces had, albeit temporarily, been unable to take control in major cities. Significantly, Bjørn Enge Bertelsen (2016, 43) notes that during the 2010 uprisings "the discarded politics of populist socialist rhetoric—such as *o povo* [the people] and *poder popular* [people's power]—re-surfaced as a politico-cosmological framing for the protests and their organization."

Yet the visible police presence in Maputo has long been markedly uneven. Over the six hours of our first transect, we sighted only three officers on foot and three police cars, but even those were busy escorting a minister or guarding a bank. Discussing this later with friends residing in Maputo, we got a different take: a police presence (particularly at night) is less likely to be reassuring than produce fears of being stopped and pressured to pay a bribe. Even those ensconced in private vehicles feel easily targeted as having money and being unobtrusively pulled over by police. The U.S. Department of State (2009) caution to their citizens was couched in diplomatic language (and ironic, given the frequency of violence and shootings by police in America): "Mozambican police are not at the standard U.S. citizens are accustomed to in the U.S. and visitors should not expect the same level of police service." The German Federal Foreign Office was more direct: "one cannot count on an effective police protection" (Auswärtiges Amt 2009). While attention has tended to focus on large-scale conspicuous corruption, street-level or habitual corruption has become a pervasive element of daily life in Maputo, and elsewhere in Mozambique.[4]

Yet, at the same time, a relative lack of visibility of police in public space punctuated by acts of violence—described in accounts of policing and law enforcement in Mozambique by Bruce Baker (2003), Fabrice Folio, Carlota Marlen, and Luisa Mutisse (2017), Helene Kyed (2017, 2020), and Ana Leão (2004)—creates what others writing about what "weak states" or "transitional democracies" have termed a "security vacuum," in which citizens, commercial agencies, NGOs, as well as the state apparatus rely on other forms of authority and security providers (Dupont, Grabosky, and Shearing 2003; Shearing and Kempa 2000). These can encompass "traditional" forms of security organized in communities or vigilante groups as well as private security providers that are our interest.[5] Such pluralization of policing has been described elsewhere, usually of Western contexts (Jones and Newburn 2006; Loader 1999; Yarwood 2007) and as part of a wider critical sociology of security (Balzacq et al. 2010). While similar trends were found in Maputo, they were slow to equate to the evolving variety of large-scale production of new gated urban spaces and "expanses of privately owned space concentrated in the hands of relatively few corporate interests, which are nevertheless generally open to the public to visit" (Kempa, Stenning, and Wood 2004, 566) that were first described in North American cities (Blakely and Snyder 1999; Shearing and Stenning 1983, 1985). These have since provided a template for "a remarkably diverse range of investigations into the importance of urban space as the locus, medium, and tool of security policies, and into the critical influence of surveillance and securitization strategies with regards to the transformation (splintering, fortification, and privatization) of the contemporary urban environment" (Klauser 2010, 327–28).

In Maputo, there is a piecemeal, more ad hoc, and frequently informal fragmentation of security and space. While a sorting of society "through gates" (Shearing and Kempa 2000, 207) and guards can be observed, a highly individualized and microscale model of urban security is evident in central Maputo. Along both transects, hundreds of private guards were working at a wide range of entrances, buildings, and shops. However, the job of this uncountable number is only to secure a specific object (uncountable because of the sheer numbers, but also as it is not always possible to identify the low-end and freelance security in plain clothes). This opens the question of who polices public spaces. There are police (and soldiers) on the streets. We saw, for example, at streets that led into and out of the center checkpoints with several officers, some of whom were armed with AK-47s or wearing helmets. We also encountered a night patrol late one evening (next to the British High Commission) of at least five police officers with AK-47s. However, given their lack of visibility during the day, this seemed to be more a performance of power than of policing. We observed a higher concentration of police on the second transect, especially on Julius Nyerere between Avenida 24 de Julho and Avenida Mao Tse Tung, and on Kenneth Kaunda between Julius Nyerere and Kim Il Sung, but these are visibly places of state power and capital. Here the police do not have to patrol the public space but protect symbolic institutions and fonts of power. And, as one police officer had remarked, they are there to secure the bank with their *amigos* from the biggest multinational security company G4S.

More often, however, if the police are called for in an emergency, they can take hours to arrive, sometimes even on foot. The state thus uses its police force primarily to secure itself and to safeguard capital and foreign representatives. In Maputo, however, it is evident that most security services are provided as commodities by private entities to other private (household or business) consumers. Their primary role is not to protect the community or public space but to secure private urban enclaves.

During our discussions with security guards, we asked them whether and how they would intervene if they witnessed a crime taking place in public space. Only one guard from one of the bigger Mozambican companies claimed that it is the policy of his company to intervene, and even to send their own armed response. Another guard pointed out the risks of interfering with the public because they will be made responsible if something goes wrong and someone gets shot, whereas if they shoot to kill on their assigned private property, there are fewer problems. All the other guards who work for bigger firms told us that they would intervene either in line with their work ethos as security personnel or as their human responsibility. Nevertheless, the policing of the public is clearly not their duty, least of all for the freelance security personnel in plain clothes. One man we spoke with, who worked twenty-four-hour shifts with twenty-four-hour breaks in between, told us straightforwardly that he knows that bandits are armed and bandits know that he is not. He was, understandably, not willing to risk his life for the equivalent of fifty dollars a month. For a low-paid informally employed guard, such a stance becomes rational as part of the wider context in a Maputo where, in Ilda Lindell's (2008, 1898) terms, "unstable and fluid governance is juxtaposed with a pervasive informality of urban living that is underlined by great economic and social uncertainty and where many urban citizens rely on provisional identities, shifting loyalties and collaborations to access opportunities and survive in the city."

In a morphology that considers the urban legacies of colonial spatial logic and the increasingly contested livelihoods of street vendors in another postcolonial African city, Denis Linehan (2007, 35) describes how "the urban archipelago dilutes the public sphere and fragments rights and legal status. Its spatial form is reflected in the slum, the gated community and the private fortress and its geography is a patchwork system of bounded and secured neighborhoods and highly regulated forms of movement and mobility. Nairobi is consequently a city of walls and boundaries, a city of enclaves, a fortress city—a model of urban development repeated throughout the continent."

Such characterizations have cropped up in other critical studies of postcolonial African cities, albeit also with evidence of considerable creativity and agency on the part of the citizenry (Gandy 2005, 2006; Simone 2006). And nearly three decades ago, David Simon's (1992) survey traced such fragmentation in numerous African cities. In the case of central Maputo, a complex patchwork of security enclaves is evident. The terms *patchwork* and *enclaves* are usually used on a much bigger scale (such as free trade zones) or in a rural setting (such as mines and plantations) (Ferguson 2007; Reyntjens 2005; Sidaway 2007a). Here they appear at the microscale. Morten Nielsen, Jason Sumich, and Bjørn Enge Bertelsen (2021, 890) have recently described Maputo as "a veritable repository of instances of enclaving understood as an aesthetics of imagination that circulates, unmoored and with the capacity to alter horizons and practices."[6] This is not simply the gated community, long common across the border in South Africa—epitomized by what Lipman and Harris (1999) termed "Fortress Johannesburg"—and described elsewhere, from Brazil (Caldeira 2001) to Indonesia (Leisch 2002), postcommunist Poland (Gąsior-Niemiec, Glasze, and Pütz 2009), and the United States (Low 2003). Indeed, few areas in the cement city are physically gated, but they are secured. Elsewhere, bigger gated communities frequently involve a strong notion of (exclusive) community and a high level of organization. This is generally not the case in central Maputo, where secured enclaves usually encompass single private homes and are highly individualized.[7] The forms of security at such enclaves vary with the economic status of the residents and range from a uniformed professional service, which can include guards and an armed response service in the case of an emergency, to an untrained look-out person in plain clothes.

Here the transfer from public to private spaces does not necessarily (or only) mean the production of new private spaces and the privatization of former public property. Except for a few cases of new malls, it describes a trend whereby more affluent citizens withdraw into their secured residential spaces and circulate between these and other secured private spaces such as restaurants, clubs, or offices. In this context the high number of sport utility vehicles (SUVs) on the streets of Maputo would suggest that one does not have to leave comfort/security even when traveling between enclaves (almost all SUVs have an automatic locking mechanism that keeps the driver secure from the outside only seconds after starting the motor).

Security companies often perform roles that supplement the existing state-directed policing in what is sometimes called multiagency (Yarwood 2007) or plural policing (Jones and Newburn 2006), blurring lines between the public and the private (Rigakos 2002). In Maputo this kind of network policing is less evident than the varied types of private security, reflecting wider modes of uneven development. Even in the affluent precincts that we traversed, state displacement from the public sphere was evident on many levels. There is, for example, the quality of the roads: throughout the city, roads and sidewalks are scarred with potholes of all sizes. After a fifteen- to twenty-minute drive outside the city center, the asphalt road stops completely and continues in the form of a dirt track. Even in the suburbs close to the Costa do Sol or on the northwest edge of the city, which is home to some of the affluent elite including a Frelimo minister, the roads are not much better. Basic tracks can be lined with luxury villas (also explaining the high numbers of autolocking SUVs). Furthermore, some of these newer development areas are not served by a piped water supply or linked to the city's sewage system, nor do they all have a collective refuse collection or a formal postal address.

When the elite retreat behind fences and armed response units, the cement city becomes an enclave patchwork. While discourses and practices of security and development are frequently deeply connected (Duffield 2007), the Mozambican case indicates the deep contradictions in the capital city of a state that—at the time of our transects—was being counted among the success stories of democratization, peace, and transition. However, such contradictions were not new in Mozambique. The colonial era rested on a series of disjunctures and exclusions, notwithstanding the geopolitical rhetoric about Portugal and its territories as a *pluricontinental* and multiracial harmony (Sidaway and Power 1995). Frelimo inherited the colonial-settler capital city and wider colonial state, embarking on a transformation articulated through the rhetoric of building socialism. This too was invariably full of contradictions (Wuyts 1989), resembling those evident in many other postcolonial socialisms (Post and Wright 1989). Difficulties were compounded by an economy that remained peripheral, dependent, and poor, within a polity faced with immense internal and externally directed resistance. The rapidity with which that socialist rhetoric was replaced with one of capitalist transition and development—and with which ruling factions repositioned themselves to leverage a new phase of commoditization and privatization and business—is striking. This has been accentuated by sociospatial disparities that relay and rework enclaving at urban and periurban scales (Roque, Mucavele, and Noronha 2016) and beyond. Reflecting on what they designate as "the complicated interrelationship between economic enclaves, their associated security practices and the formation of national citizens in Mozambique," Lars Buur and Jason Sumich (2019, 1579) go on to describe how these processes articulate with Frelimo's current political project:

> Frelimo has progressively narrowed its focus from grand, utopian ideas of transformation to the reproduction of the current structures of power and the relationships upon which they rest. These relationships are situated in the shifting terrain of the frontier between legality and illegality, with its insistence on law under the shadow of violence. Understanding such processes involves an exploration of the relationship between investments and concepts of citizenship as a dynamic process of inclusion and exclusion, coercion and softer forms of producing national subjects. This provides a view of the complex reality in which citizen-subject relations emerge and are produced through disciplinary practices under the ever-present spectre of violent action by the various security forces.

In the conclusions to an earlier landmark study of socioeconomic and political shifts in Mozambique, Pitcher (2002, 264, our emphasis) described how "the threads of the past are stitched into the fabric of the present in Mozambique. . . . At a structural level, former state officials have taken advantage of the tumultuous changes to become bank directors and chief executive officers. Social networks comprised of old and new elites have captured resources and former state institutions have redefined their roles in order to retain their power. . . . Transformation in Mozambique begins and ends with the vibrant, complex *interaction* of the state and social forces, but it is an interaction *bound by history.*"

This dispatch has sampled that history, binding, and interaction through transect encounters with Maputo's security and space and a series of discussions and digressions along the way. More widely, Maputo faces macrofragmentation through privatization of public realms, fortification of the individual and the household, and the purchase of security in multiple private and semiprivate micro spaces. Following independence, streets in central Maputo were promptly renamed after Mozambican heroes and revolutionary leaders from around the world (Castela and Menses 2016; Igreja 2008). Our transects took us along or near avenues bearing the names of Kim Il Sung, Vladimir Lenine, Karl Marx, and Ho Chi Min, lined with business and security guards. Describing the art and culture of the Mozambican revolution, and its contested aftermaths, Polly Savage (2019, 262–63) notes that "FRELIMO has actively sought to erase its historical relationship to Maoism. Still running through the centre of Maputo, however, is Mao Tse Tung Avenue, stubbornly anachronistic, a monument to the aesthetic and cultural networks the party would prefer to forget." Meanwhile, security in Maputo has become a moveable commodity enabled by a range of providers, ranging from foreign-owned and well-equipped armed response companies to a thinly spread and often arbitrarily deployed police force and the thousands of men who work long shifts as unequipped guards in Maputo's former colonial core.

CHAPTER 3

The Fall and Rise of Phnom Penh

"The city is the frontier of modern Asian society," declares Howard Dick (2003, xvii). "Aggressive urban skylines stake the claim" of huge and speculative investments—the volatile nexus enabling urban real estate booms: "Speculation is like a mold: its spores are always present in markets and are usually benign, but under favorable conditions it can very quickly become rampant and destructive" (466). Indeed, drawing on her fieldwork on built forms and market experiments, Sylvia Nam (2017, 648) affirms, "Crucially, speculation is the vanguard of accumulation in Phnom Penh." Yet, as Dick also notes in *Surabaya, City of Work*, his socioeconomic history of Indonesia's second largest city, there is, in much contemporary writing about cities, a forgetting of the scale and significance of earlier phases of the urbanization of capital—notably in the colonial empires during the 1920s, for example.[1] Such selective history coalesced with restricted geography when work on global cities emerged in the 1980s. Contesting claims that some cities (in a so-called Fourth World) had become structurally irrelevant, excluded from the latest phase of "globalization," Gavin Shatkin (1998, 391) examined "the case of Phnom Penh, Cambodia to demonstrate some ways in which globalization has impacted on cities in least developed countries (LDCs). The intent is not to assert that cities in other LDCs can be expected to experience identical forms of urban development, although it is worth noting the parallels with the experience of Maputo, Mozambique, which has experienced a similar transition from 'peripheral socialism' and intervention by an external peacekeeping force."

By then, both Maputo and Phnom Penh witnessed new phases of state-enabled speculative development. And while core global cities were identified in the 1980s and 1990s as the sites where globalization and turbo-capitalism were especially legible (Sassen 2001), the following decade saw productive calls to bring globalization's dynamics into another focus, via analysis grounded in more "peripheral" cities (Bunnell and Maringanti 2010; Robinson 2002; Roy 2009). However, Phnom Penh's trajectory also foregrounds past and present geopolitical orders in which the urban geography of security and conflict has loomed large. In recent years, the establishment of large-scale textile industries has engendered a female proletariat in Phnom Penh whose significance in labor organization has been interpreted by Sabina Lawreniuk (2020) as an anti-authoritarian "geopolitics from below." However, our dispatch develops two arguments focused on top-down and frequently authoritarian security structures, and their extension into the city's postcolonial core. First, we chart how the legacies of Cambodia's recent past (including the terms of the UN peacekeeping mission in the early 1990s and the transition to a postsocialist economy) have produced a securityscape in which state and private security have been enmeshed. Second, we consider how this securityscape became intricately connected with that of "development." We present these arguments by examining everyday power relations on the streets around and between key sites that embody commerce, development, and geopolitics. The dispatch therefore moves across different scales from superpower geopolitics to city streets where we apprehend their interconnections via transects, supplemented with interviews. The securityscape becomes a domain where these converge.

Writing about *Saigon's Edge* (officially Ho Chi Minh City) in neighboring Vietnam, Erik Harms (2011, 8) draws insights from works on the margins of cities like Beijing, São Paulo, and Hanoi, where "even large-scale trends are always reconfigured by micro-politics, economic maneuvering and identity management of local actors navigating extralocal fields of power." While Phnom Penh has a series of edge-city projects (Paling 2012; Percival and Waley 2012), as with our dispatch from Maputo, we focus on the transnational/local connections in configurations of securityscapes in the city center.

Our initial fieldwork took place in April 2012, between the closing of the twentieth ASEAN summit (and the forty-fifth anniversary of the founding of this regional community) and the opening of Cambodia's first stock market on the forty-second anniversary of the day after the fall of the city to the Khmer Rouge.[2] We continued our fieldwork in two phases over September–November 2012. Rather than dispatches based on single-day transects as adopted in Maputo, in Phnom Penh we rewalked sections of each transect multiple times over several visits. These walks were also conducted at different times—in early mornings, late afternoons, and early evenings—but we focus on the daytime business hours of the city. Since the ASEAN summit was already winding down during the first phase of our fieldwork, the only significant shift from the norm was around the Royal Palace during the third phase of fieldwork, which took place soon after the death in Beijing of the former Cambodian king Norodom Sihanouk. When his body was reposed at the Royal Palace from mid-October 2012 until cremation in early February 2013, this zone was transformed by street closures and placed under high surveillance with hundreds of police and military personnel.

Our transects were complemented by eleven semistructured interviews with key informants from private security firms and NGOs. Each interview lasted between thirty and ninety minutes. Thematically, the interviews focused on everyday security in the city as well as on wider and topical issues such as the actions of political and economic elites. Five initial informants were identified from security company websites and contacted via email, and through their networks more informants were identified. We also scrutinized the English- and Khmer-language press, which at the time regularly reported on cases of violence, cover-ups, and inconsistency in law enforcement as well as petty corruption on the part of the Royal Cambodian Armed Forces (RCAF) and the National Police (see summary in Table 1).

TABLE 1. Reports of Violence, Crimes, Cover-Ups, and Corruption Involving the Cambodian National Police and Royal Cambodian Armed Forces (RCAF) Officers in the Local Khmer- and English-Language Press, March–April 2012

Koh Santepheap (publishes in Khmer)	
13 March	The deputy chief of a police station in Tuol Sangke Sangkat, Phnom Penh, was detained by the Khan Daun Penh Royal Gendarmerie for unlawfully firing a gun in public.
22 March	An RCAF First Lieutenant was detained by the Kirivong District Police in Takeo province for threatening people.
30 March	A drunken police officer from Siem Reap province who was tasked with guarding a pig slaughterhouse unlawfully fired gunshots before the visit of ASEAN delegates to Siem Reap province. However, this police officer, the brother-in-law of a local tycoon who is the owner of a garage and slaughterhouse, was not punished, with the details suppressed by the local police.
2 April	A deputy chief of a police station in Prek Achi commune, Kompong Cham province, was charged with killing a local villager while attempting to intervene in local conflicts. The officer had fled after the incident.
3 April	A deputy director of the Local Administration Department, who is also a colonel of the National Police, unlawfully fired a gun in a restaurant to prevent his friends from leaving. The colonel was not punished for his conduct, although his driver was briefly detained.
5 April	Siem Reap Provincial Police confiscated a military truck carrying seven cubic meters of shorea (commercial timbers) to a depot. The truck, belonging to Brigade 99, was temporarily sent to the Forestry Administration for court filing. The soldier driving the truck had paid the guards manning ten checkpoints a total of around 400 dollars.
17 April	A police officer from the Ministry of Interior was on the run after firing shots at a group of people and seriously injuring three.

| 18 April | An RCAF officer was on the run after unlawfully firing a shot to threaten his wife in Daungkor district, Phnom Penh. |
| 26 April | A major general and his three bodyguards brutally assaulted four men in City Hotel, Koh Kong province. The major general and his three bodyguards were placed in custody. |

Nokorwat News Daily (publishes in Khmer)

8 March	A lieutenant general, the head of the Bodyguard Unit to the president of the Senate, filed an appeal to the Supreme Court after being charged with possessing guns and bullets without a license, issuing licenses for gun and bullets to unauthorized individuals, and illegally producing and using public letters by a Phnom Penh Lower Court. He also faced five other charges by the military court including violation of public trust, theft of state property, and illegal distribution of guns.
17 March	Three hundred villagers in Chheu Tom commune petitioned for the dismissal of the chief of Chheu Tom police station who was accused of being involved in a number of corruption cases.
20 March	A gendarme in Khan Sen Sok, Phnom Penh, was charged for robbing foreigners on top of prior theft charges.
24 March	A commander from Border Protection Division 303 was caught illegally transporting prime timber, discovered when his vehicle ran over a landmine, causing the death of his driver.
10 April	An officer of Taprok Commune Police Station in Kompong Cham caused the death of a villager when intervening in local conflicts.
19 April	Officers of the Border Protection Division 204 were suspected of buying illegal timber as well as protecting and facilitating illegal logging and transportation.
26 April	Chhut Wutty, internationally known environmental activist and director of the Natural Resource Protection Group (NRPG), was shot dead by Royal Gendarmerie deployed to protect a timber depot while taking a photo of the site. Another military police officer was also killed in obscure circumstances.

Phnom Penh Post (publishes in English)

26 March	Two military police officers caught with drugs were released without a court hearing. According to officials, this matter would be dealt with internally (Kongkea 2012).
28 & 29 March	Police use force against a peaceful demonstration of factory workers. The follow-up story noting that the police had denied these allegations carried the picture of a hospitalized victim (Nimol and Worrell 2012).
4 & 6 April	Officers were chased out of a press event by villagers who accused the police of not adequately protecting them against crime. The follow-up reported the villagers' unsuccessful attempt to launch a petition demanding that the police guarantee their security.

Cambodia Daily (publishes in English)

2 April	A police officer was on the run after killing a villager with an assault rifle (Soenthrith 2012a).
3 April	A military officer and a police officer were arrested for illegally discharging their weapons in public under the influence of alcohol (Soenthrith 2012b).
4 April	Three police officers were given life sentences for shooting a moneychanger at point-blank range (Sovuthy 2012).

In Cambodia, public and private security landscapes are intertwined, and an influential policing body emerges out of this, connected with capital and political power. Policing mostly focuses on loci of elites and corporations, leaving the wider city unevenly policed. Our dispatch echoes other critical accounts of Cambodia, exploring how this nexus of private capital and profit-driven state interests plays out at different scales and shapes sociospatial interactions. The section below contextualizes Phnom Penh's securityscape, drawing on a secondary literature, press coverage, and interviews with key informants, considering first police and the military, then private security companies, before documenting their interactions.

Phnom Penh in Context

Unable to preserve Cambodia's neutrality as the Cold War conflagration over the future of Indochina expanded from Vietnam in the mid-1960s, combat, revolution, and invasion would overwhelm Phnom Penh in the 1970s. The halt to decades of war in Cambodia in the 1990s was the endpoint of these Indochina conflicts that dated from decolonization coinciding with the Cold War. Yet, when peace arrived in Cambodia, violence and displacements resumed, operating in different modes behind the scenes, largely away from the world's media eye. Describing more than a decade of "land grabbing" by local tycoons and senior politicians, and of thousands of evictions of the poor in Phnom Penh, Simon Springer (2011, 2567) notes how a politics of exclusion and patronage that "predate Cambodia's encounter with neoliberal ideas" have "become inextricably bound-up in processes of neoliberalization." Calling for "further grounded empirical research" attentive to "actually existing neoliberalisms," Springer sketched a patronage system that "has allowed local elites to co-opt, transform, and (re)articulate neoliberal reforms through a framework which asset strips public resources . . . [via] corruption, coercion, and violence" (2554).

Although predatory resource exploitations characterized (post–UN Transitional Authority in Cambodia [UNTAC]) Cambodia in the 1990s (Cock 2010; Le Billon 2002; Levy and Scott-Clark 2008; Milne and Adams 2012), the use of violence and fear and the powers of patronage as modes of governance had deepened since on multiple everyday fronts for communities living near areas marked out for "grabs" (Schoenberger and Beban 2018). Phnom Penh is the seat of highly centralized power and capital and where attendant consumption and privilege are particularly visible. As Caroline Hughes (2003, 213) argues, the control of central Phnom Penh "represents an attempt to impose the kind of control over land and resources, both material and symbolic, that has been used across rural Cambodia. The logic of the new political economy of power in Cambodia turns on the ability to gain and defend control of land and the landscape, both as the basis of the subsistence economy in the countryside and as the space for conducting protests that will be visible nationally and internationally in the cities."

Hughes (2003) and Springer (2010) also describe how the reorganization of urban space since the 1990s has shadowed Prime Minister Hun Sen's consolidation of power, which has continued to the present. The city was "beautified," as Harms (2012) also termed the aesthetics and politics of similar moves in Ho Chi Minh City. Squatters were moved and parks rehabilitated, and along the way the municipal administration was recast as an appendage of the ruling CPP. Hughes (2003, 211) further notes that "the more profound impact of the beautification scheme is the reassertion of governmental control over public space vis-à-vis the more radical political challenge offered by urban protest movements of the 1990s." This (political, development, and security) order has been superimposed on and reworks prior ones produced under successive colonial, monarchical, republican, and revolutionary political orders in Cambodia. The layering of these—the cultural-political imbrications of which were richly dissected by Penny Edwards (2007)—is largely beyond the scope of our dispatch here. However, Cambodia has long been read through a lens of security: the geopolitics of the Cold War deemed its control strategic, with dire consequences on the ground, where thousands of American bombs impacted as the country became embroiled in the wider conflicts over Indochina. When the Communist Party of Kampuchea's Khmer Rouge cadres marched into Phnom Penh in 1975, they forced its population into the countryside in pursuit of a famously disastrous and deeply authoritarian agrarian revolution. Work on this period has revealed a complex picture, whereby during their brief ascendency in the second half of the 1970s the Khmer Rouge had used the city as a control-and-command node. James Tyner and colleagues (2014, 1889) show that the city "was not randomly nor completely destroyed and abandoned. Instead, party officials made deliberate calculations as to those land uses that were to be continued or converted, depending on the specific economic task at hand." By early 1979 the Khmer Rouge had been forcibly deposed, and Cambodia was occupied by the Vietnamese army (Morris 1999). As Gabriel Fauveaud (2014) has mapped, in the scramble for land and property in a repopulating Phnom Penh that accelerated through the 1980s, political connections with the post–Khmer Rouge government were key to who got their hands on what and where. This has endured and deepened. When Vietnamese forces occupied the country (from 25 December 1978) and promptly installed a more orthodox communist government (the Kampuchean People's Revolutionary Party, which became the CPP from 1991, abandoning its rhetorical commitments to socialism), a protracted conflict with remnants of the Khmer Rouge ensued. More than a decade later, the UN-brokered peace was subsequently enforced through thousands of foreign troops under the auspices of a UNTAC peacekeeping mission (1992–93) that oversaw elections. The CPP entered coalition government with another party but effectively seized outright control in July 1997, after a brief period of violent confrontations in Phnom Penh. The CPP has won every election since, albeit against a backdrop of intimidation, bans, and clamps on media coverage for opposition parties.

We came to Phnom Penh two decades after the UNTAC mission, during which recorded violent crimes had declined (Broadhurst 2002; Broadhurst and Bouhours 2009). At the street level, there were police with scooters at major intersections, supplemented by visible gendarmerie stations. The Royal Gendarmerie or military police are under the direct command of the Defense Ministry. However, despite these visible capacities, public confidence in police professionalism is checked by perceptions of susceptibility to corruption, attributing their low salaries, poor training, and mediocre equipment. Roderic Broadhurst and Thierry Bouhours (2009, 184) found that "[in 2005] over half remained positive to police in Phnom Penh . . . (compared to two-thirds in 2001). Despite the significant decline in criminal victimization . . . this was not matched by greater public confidence in the police." However, while they also noted some improvement in perceptions of the extent of petty corruption, the bigger picture involves the role of state "security" apparatus in enforcing the evictions and exclusions that now form prerequisites of much business and power in Cambodia. Thus, Broadhurst and Bouhours state, "The potential emergence of a 'shadow' state and kleptocracy in the context of the rapid development of a market economy is also a significant constraint on the legitimacy of policing institutions" (175).

Our informants also described an institutionalized petty corruption at many levels of the police and gendarmerie, combined with a strong system of patronage. Those who do not have the means to participate in these networks seek to avoid them. Hence the foundation for legitimate policing is fragile at best. As a key informant centrally placed in the security industry put it to us, "You get away with murder if you have money and know the right people." The notion that people try to avoid the police whenever possible was confirmed throughout our research. Chiming with narratives we heard in Maputo, one informant described a scenario where parties in a road traffic accident would first feel out who has better contacts with the state forces before deciding whether or not to call in the police or whether to find other means of mutual resolution. Nonetheless, this does not mean that the police are always superfluous. In emergencies, it is assumed that the mention of money or a degree of (political) connections will speed up the arrival of officers. However, while reports of inconsistent or violent policing are common, it is vital to analyze how these are caught up in overlaps of politics and business that connect Phnom Penh's streets with what Springer (2009, 317) has termed "an extra-local power geometry."

Phnom Penh has a booming private security industry. Uniformed male guards are in front of every mid-level or high-end shop, petrol station, hotel, or restaurant. Their ubiquity at commercial buildings is less evident than at private residences, at which only the more opulent tend to have uniformed guards. Moreover, the terms of the 1990s UNTAC mission and the transformation of the wider security situation accompanying peace talks and agreements required disarmament of the civilian population, including private security firms. In the years after the UNTAC mission, disarmament programs funded by the EU and Japan removed over two hundred thousand guns, leaving Cambodia with relatively few weapons in private ownership (Roberts 2008). The ground rules for all private security companies therefore specify that no firearms can be carried (National Assembly of the Kingdom of Cambodia 2005), limiting their equipment to batons or bamboo sticks, two-way radios, and occasionally handcuffs.

It is patently evident that many private security guards are ill-equipped and untrained. Wearing sandals as footwear is common, as is dozing on duty. It is usual to see these guards washing cars or sweeping property. In effect they enact what electronic surveillance systems do: that is, watching who enters and leaves a property and reporting this to a control room, client, or supervisor. Guards also conduct other functions including opening shop or hotel doors, acting as porters, organizing transportation, handing out parking vouchers, and assisting with parking—in fact, numerous security guards are armed with whistles and red sticks to manage traffic, in place of batons. In these respects, the function of a private security guard resembles that of a concierge, groundkeeper, or door guard, and accords with empirical findings by Jones and Newburn (1998) that the domain of (private) security has expanded to incorporate roles and informal security functions that (in the Western case that informs their study) would be performed by concierges, doorkeepers, attendants, and the like. This trend equates private security with upholding a level of prestige and customer/visitor service for offices and businesses. Moreover, whereas Jones and Newburn (1998) have emphasized how the uniform of security personnel becomes an aspect of the formalization process, private security officers in Phnom Penh can frequently be seen out of their uniforms.

The policing network in the center of Phnom Penh mostly relies on the public police and the weakly professionalized and relatively powerless private security. Since only the police, gendarmes, and soldiers may legally carry arms, "licensed" arrangements have long enabled these state officers to be privately hired by security firms and other enterprises. The Cambodian military long received sponsorship from politically connected elites, who in turn were able to draw on the military units they sponsor to enforce or protect their business as reportage in the *Diplomat* described: "The military had repeatedly protected the business interests of its patrons with violence that included forced evictions" (Hunt 2015). The private hire of the police could be contracted on a longer-term basis—such as for recurring cash in transit (CIT) and the protection of banks—or in a more ad hoc manner whenever armed backup is required, arrangements that security company websites have specified in describing their services: "MPA's license permits our company to work in liaison with the police for armed escort, armed executive protection, CIT operations or crime intervention. . . . Our Rapid Response Teams work together with the police under license to quickly deliver an armed response if required 24-hours-a-day. MPA also has roving inspectors that are randomly inspecting all our sites. All of our management are available anytime to assist you with any security need" (MPA-International 2012a, 2012b). This deployment for commercial needs also extended to contracting the services of the Royal Gendarmerie of Cambodia—the RCAF Military Police responsible for internal order and antiterrorism. At the time of our first transects in 2012, interviewees told us that there were around four hundred police and gendarmes working for private security companies (not including direct hires by other commercial enterprises such as nightclubs or logging companies). As for the practicalities of hiring regular police officers, the security companies issued a contract with the police forces, specifying that they can call (and will pay) if armed police officers are required. The legalities were less clear. What the company website cited earlier presented as a permit "to work in liaison with the police," our informants tended to describe as a process of cooperation and contracting individual "moonlighting" police officers. However, this networking of private security and bought-in police was deployed only for banks, CIT, and other high-target institutions. Shops, most hotels, and all gas stations contracted (unarmed) private security guards, who frequently ended up serving as parking lot attendants, porters, or concierges. When the private security industry purchased the services of police officers, their clients were provided with well-organized expertise and an armed (sometimes military) security force. While this policing outcome traces to terms of the UN-supervised peace settlement, the result was paradoxical: a legally sanctioned state monopoly on carrying arms that simultaneously commodifies and undermines effective policing by making it a condition of wealth, power, and connections. Because the state regulates the private security industry and sets rules for their code of conduct, the opportunity created allowed for (long cash-strapped) state forces to enter the booming security services market and profit from it.

In July 2019, police officers were reminded by the chief of police to seek consent from their seniors before serving as security for tycoons and businesses. Two months later, the RCAF commander in chief, General Vong Pisen, issued a directive ordering soldiers to cease providing private security services to businesses or individuals—though it was not immediately clear if the practice could continue when mandated by senior officers (Sokhean 2019). The altered stance came a year after the CPP had won further elections—having exiled and detained the opposition leadership, on grounds that they were colluding with foreign powers, while the ruling party further consolidated its close relationship with Beijing. Earlier in 2019, in a speech full of references to lessons from the trajectory of Cambodia since the 1950s, Prime Minister Hun Sen reaffirmed that it was the role of the armed forces to support the government. He cited the 1970 seizure of power by Lon Nol—who closely allied Cambodia with U.S. strategy in what would be the last five years of the American wars in Indochina—and an attempted coup in 1994 as examples of what can come to pass when the military is disloyal.[3] In addition to citing the police and armed forces' roles in defending national sovereignty, maintaining social order, combatting crime, ensuing stability, providing disaster relief, supporting the collection of tax revenues, and assisting self-discipline and the welfare of recruits and veterans, the prime minster talked—in the same section of his long speech—about their role to "combat against terrorism, [and] quell in a timely manner attempts to launch color revolution" (Office of the Council of Ministers 2019). The 1994 coup attempt saw Hun Sen briefly detained: events he recounted in the speech. Lee Morgenbesser (2018, 198) notes how, following the coup plot, "Hun Sen became utterly obsessive with his security. Amidst a general reorganization of security forces, which began within months, he turned his own security detail into an elaborate network of 'intervention units.'" With this Praetorian Guard in place, patronage and control was broadened into a "constant circle of protection" (198). July 1994 therefore marked a key moment in Hun Sen's consolidation of power. Another was in 2003 when the police (commanded by a longtime ally) forced the exile of an opponent in the CPP. In 2007, Hun Sen could again rely on the police and paramilitary forces to oust the then ruling coalition and seize power for the faction of the CPP he controlled. In 2009, following the death in a helicopter crash of his police chief (subsequently succeeded by another Hun Sen appointee), he replaced the armed forces commander with another loyalist. The years since have seen power further personalized. Paul W. Chambers (2015, 179) had already described the system as one of "personalized supremacy over security forces through what might be termed 'neo-sultanistic tendencies.'" A few years later Lee Morgenbesser (2018, 198) noted,

> Today, Hun Sen exercises direct or indirect control over the National Counter-Terrorism Special Forces (commanded by his son, Hun Manet) [since then appointed as second in command to the Royal Canadian Armed Forces]; the 2,000-strong Intervention Brigade 70 (led by his ally, Mao Sophan, for two decades), the 4,500-strong Paratrooper Special Forces Brigade 911 (commanded by loyalist, Chap Peakday); the 8,000-strong Gendarmerie Police (deployed nationwide); and a 3,000-strong Bodyguard Unit (the country's best equipped fighting force). Ultimately the most definitive marker of how Hun Sen has personalized power is the wanton transformation of his security detail, which numbered about 60 body-guards in the mid-1990s, into a paramilitary architecture equivalent in size to the national militaries of Senegal, Somalia or Zambia.

For Morgenbesser therefore, Cambodia is a "party-personalist regime," demonstrated by the range of Hun Sen's "unconstrained and discretionary authority" (191). These include gatekeeper to all appointments of high office, the capacity to bestow the honorific *oknha* title (a right reserved for the monarch until 1994) on key supporters, the appointment of relatives to key positions, and what Morgenberger termed "politically auspicious marriages" (197). All six children of Hun Sen and First Lady Bun Rany as well as several of their nieces and nephews are married into favored commercial, military, and police circles. One nephew—Hun To, the son of a provincial governor who is the prime minister's brother—has been accused by Australian media of being a major heroin trafficker but is untouchable by dint of family connection, according to an investigation by Global Witness (2016). This nexus of party, state, and personal interest rests on the appropriation and exercise of violence, control of the juridical system, and key business networks. Our interviews and transects explored aspects of these intersections through everyday street-level security around key sites (hotels, monuments, museums, markets, embassies, and development projects).

After ASEAN: Transect 1

The city is full of flags. We first arrived in Phnom Penh in April 2012, on the afternoon of the last day of the twentieth ASEAN summit, which has been preceded by a visit to Cambodia by China's then president Hu Jintao. The summit is soon closing, evidenced by the diplomatic convoys that halt the traffic moving in the opposite direction to us on the airport road. Later that evening, we walk into the Hotel Cambodiana on Sisowath Quay (Preah Sisovath), an embodiment of postcolonial modernity from the mid-1960s, when Phnom Penh still retained much of the preindependence ambiance of the smallish colonial city of the French protectorate it was until 1953 (Filippi 2012). The Cambodiana therefore dates from just before the American War in Vietnam expanded into Cambodia, a period whose palace intrigues and diplomatic maneuvers, amid relative calm, the Australian diplomat Milton Osborne (1973) richly documented. It was a calm before the storm. By the time Osborne's book appeared, the world it described had already been swept away. Phnom Penh fell to the Khmer Rouge on 17 April 1975. A decade later, writing during Vietnam's occupation of Cambodia, Grant Evans and Kelvin Rowley (1984, 302) noted how power plays between Vietnam, China, Thailand, and the superpowers had produced "a sequence of action and reaction that Machiavelli, well-versed in the problems of new states in early modern Europe, would have understood very well. However, he would have been unfamiliar with the rhetoric of revolution and nationalism in which conflicts between states have become enveloped. That is the mark of the modern era of mass politics. The peoples of Indochina have undergone a particularly traumatic initiation into that era, and there is no sign that the ordeal is over." The CPP consolidated power with Hanoi's support, ideologically seeking to emphasize discontinuity with the Khmer Rouge (Giry 2014). Subsequently, the CPP nominally accommodated themselves to Western narratives about "good governance" and "state building": according to Caroline Hughes and Kheang Un (2011, 2) "this represented a challenge which the Cambodian People's Party has met with élan." Behind such veneers however, which may be misrecognized as "transition" or "democratization," power was translated into patronage and profit.

As we start the transects, by venturing into the privately owned space of the hotel, we pass layers of police and private security guards that complement each other. They have little to do and do not stop us walking into the hotel, through the airport-style metal detector gate. There are several diplomatic cars parked outside, bearing flags, containing bored drivers. The literature on hotels as diplomatic/commercial/social enclaves comes to mind (Craggs 2012; Fregonese and Ramadan 2015).[4] The Cambodiana mirrors the tumultuous postcolonial trajectory of Cambodia. In the words of a travel website,

> The Cambodiana Hotel was conceived in the 1960s as part of Sihanouk's pro-gramme of building ambitious modern structures. . . . It was intended to stand on stilts providing views through to the river as part of a wider cultural and en-tertainment precinct. By the 1970s, Sihanouk had been deposed and the original plans for the site abandoned. Lon Nol's government made the hotel a military barracks . . . until the late 1980s, the Cambodiana was left in virtual ruin . . . res-urrected just in time for the arrival of UN officials, NGO personnel, journalists and international officials presiding over the UN mission. . . . The Cambodiana was the only show in town and everyone stayed here from celebrated journalists to Prime Ministers and Presidents. When foreign governments decided to rees-tablish their embassies in Phnom Penh the Cambodiana was the logical place to get things started. (Rusty Compass 2011)

Today the Cambodiana more often accommodates tourists, but on the night of our first visit the hotel was a site of diplomatic dealing, duly secured by private security. Across the road is the Royal Palace. This enduring center of symbolic and temporal power since its construction under the auspices of the nineteenth-century French protectorate is surrounded by a density of police/gendarmes that makes it relatively distinctive within the wider core of Phnom Penh.[5] Our first transect returned to Sisowath Quay, turning left past the rows of security at the gates of the Cambodiana to the giant traffic circle near Hun Sen Park and four key sites that epitomize power relations—a casino, a Cambodia–Korea Cooperation Center, the Ministry of Foreign Affairs and In-ternational Cooperation, and the National Assembly.

Where Sisowath Quay meets the traffic circle sits the NagaWorld Hotel and Entertainment Complex containing casinos, karaoke lounges, restaurants, and fourteen floors of suites and rooms. On a subsequent visit, we witnessed the outer layer of NagaWorld's private security shove men across the public road in front of the entrance where taxis congregate. NagaCorp is listed on the Hong Kong stock exchange (though registered in the Cayman Islands) and chaired by a former FBI agent, and the website describes its Chinese-Malaysian founder and CEO as an "Economic Advisor to the Prime Minister of Cam-bodia [Hun Sen] and an Advisor to the Royal Government of Cambodia with Ministerial status" (Lewis 2013). The casino is enabled and functions through the close relationship between the state and private capital at different levels.

According to its corporate reports, NagaCorp had a private jet to fly in "VIP customers" and not long after our fieldwork bought two Airbus A320s for this purpose (Morton 2014). Those at the casino floor with piles of hundred-dollar bills were mostly group tours from China (where gambling is banned) and Vietnam (for which the company also has limousines to bring casino visitors from Ho Chi Minh City). More recently, NagaWorld has expanded: the nearby NagaWorld 2 has more than a thousand bedrooms. Already, at the time of our first Phnom Penh transects in 2012, NagaWorld overshadowed the nearby National Assembly. The latter may be part of the state apparatus—classically the entity claiming to bear the monopoly on legitimating the use of violence in a given territory—but it is NagaWorld that had been granted a forty-one-year monopoly casino license covering a two-hundred-kilometer radius. Teri Shaffer Yamada (2017, 743) posits that "NagaWorld's special relationship with politicians can be understood in terms of its status as a new form of 'monopoly revenue farm' within Cambodia's custom of client relations."

The prominence of NagaWorld and the securityscapes that surround it reflect a wider conjuncture in Cambodia. What Sebastian Strangio (2014, 264) called the "narrative of suffering and redemption"—that had accompanied the early 1990s winding down of armed conflict with UN guidance and Western aid—has been overlaid by growing Chinese connections. These offer new motors of development as well as fortifications of "security," buttressing those that have emerged since the 1990s. Two buildings nearby also enable and reflect Cambodia's articulations with the world beyond its borders: the Ministry of Foreign Affairs and International Cooperation, a site where loans and aid deals are brokered, and a Cambodia–Korea Cooperation Center, which rests on over 2.77 billion dollars of Korean investments since the mid-1990s (Sotharith 2010).

Our transect, however, turns away from these sites, past a giant welcoming poster for Chinese president Hu Jintao's visit. On Preah Suramarit Boulevard we pass the police and gendarmerie stations, the latter with a giant advertisement pole in its front yard, around which the gendarmes sit and chat. We turn right into Boulevard Samdach Sothearos, walking toward a monument that symbolizes a key strategic relationship. The Cambodia–Vietnam Friendship Monument blends socialist realist style with a stupa and is the occasional focus of protests.[6] There are several security guards at its base when we approach. There is an incense burner below this monument to what were fraternal socialist regimes. We continue around the Royal Palace, past the offices of the Royal (Bodyguard) Police and development ministries, NGOs, and a private villa that is the residence of the British consul. Outside it a G4S security guard nods at us from his booth, inside of which is a poster depicting how/where to look for bombs under cars.

After walking through commercial and residential neighborhoods lined with private security guards outside most shops and apartments, we are near the Tuol Sleng Museum. Often depicted as a destination associated with "dark tourism" (Hughes 2008; Lennon and Foley 2000; Williams 2004), the museum connects visitors with representations of past violence (Sion 2011; Tyner, Alvarez, and Colucci 2012; Violi 2012). Occupying the site of the former S-21 (or security facility 21), which had once been a primary school, the entry gate opens onto a courtyard and the former cells bear photographic portraits of victims, instruments used for incarceration and torture, and disinterred human remains. The museum has few visible staff. We noticed only a woman at the ticket booth alongside two male security personnel at the entrance of the museum. One of them had the prominent tag "Tourism Police" (in English) affixed to his uniform. Although he was markedly differentiated from the other privately hired security guard at the entrance to Tuol Sleng, it is unclear to what extent the tourism police took on additional responsibilities beyond maintaining order at the museum compound. Leaving Tuol Sleng, we walked toward the Russian market. There are numerous "international schools" along the road. According to Stephen Duggan (1997), by the mid-1990s it was increasingly common to find institutions offering European-certified courses (like the Cambridge A-levels and International Baccalaureate) in tandem with other foreign organizations and capital. These extralocal networks require the constant presence of security officers, and there were several around the schools. Indeed, security guards are found everywhere here: a toy shop we passed had two security guards seated in front. So did a bakery located on the corner of a relatively quiet street. Private security signals prestige/distinction (akin to a brightly illuminated shop or office signage) rather than protection. On a subsequent visit to Phnom Penh, we rewalked this section of the transect in the early afternoon, when again private security outnumbered the lunching police by a ratio of more than four to one.

Nearby there is a concentration of bars and restaurants. At the intersection between Street 63 and Street 302, swanky apartments line the road. As usual, there are security guards. However, no guards were seen at some of the stand-alone bungalows located further down the street—the only visible form of security for these dwellings derived from high gates and walls—a common feature in newer buildings in and around Phnom Penh. Besides such exclusive residential enclaves, Street 302 offers glimpses into the history of international peacekeeping and foreign aid in Cambodia, the geopolitical circumstances for which have been documented by Sorpong Peou (2005, 112–13): "Over the 1992–2004 period, international assistance in Cambodia covered a wide range of human security activities associated with peacekeeping and peace building (namely, international criminal justice, the promotion of electoral democracy and human rights, as well as economic reconstruction) with external actors generally sharing a set of liberal norms promoting security." Street 302 hosts several institutions that embody this security-development nexus: the Australian Volunteers' Association, USAID, and the Office of High Commissioner for Human Rights (Chandler 2007; Stern and Öjendal 2010). As we approached this cluster of development organizations, the number of guards increased. Turning around in the middle of the street, we could count employees of at least three different security companies. Those key organizations involved in human security/development issues must be in turn secured by local security forces. Their collective presence forms a node in the network of secured sites of power, sanctuary, and humanitarianism.

Beneath the "Security-Development" Nexus: Transect 2

Our second walking transect started at Psah Thmey, the popularly dubbed "Central Market." The site embodies and reflects French colonialism. The dome-shaped main market building was erected in 1937, with French capital (in the form of development aid) continuing to play an important role in its refurbishment from 2009 to 2011. Arriving at the north gate of the market, we were greeted by a private security guard who efficiently ushered us to the entrance. The main responsibility of the officer, with only a whistle in hand and visibly devoid of any other security apparatuses (like a baton), appeared to be regulating the flows of traffic/people in order to facilitate ease of access to the market. The market has four wings radiating outward from the domed edifice. It is bustling and one of the few places on our transects with visible security cameras. On the way out we notice armed police. In direct contrast to the private security guard who ushered us in, these state police personnel take on a more active role in watchful surveillance on the compound. Outside, we walked westward onto Street 61. Along the way, almost all commercial establishments (cafes/restaurants, schools, and gift shops) were minded by one or two security guards, usually carrying only a baton and assisting customers with parking and opening doors for patrons.

We turned right onto Street 96 past sites of concentrated power, including the luxury hotel Raffles Le Royal and the U.S. embassy complex. Contrasting with the unevenly tarred streets that we had traversed over the previous few days, this stretch of road had clearly been well maintained. Uniformly spaced trees served as dividers for the broad, two-way traffic lanes; elaborately colored tiles formed the surface of sidewalks. If the American flag hoisted within the embassy ground failed to connote the place as a symbol of power, the high gates and cameras ensure the segregation/security of the property did. At each of the four corners of the rectangular compound, there was a booth that hosted three to four security staff who would scrutinize passing pedestrians and vehicles. However, as with other security officers whom we witnessed, their duty was not to patrol the public space but to secure selected buildings. Posters displayed in front of the main gate warn people against taking photographs/videos of the site. We cannot linger. Once past the embassy, police are again replaced by private security.

Maps still indicated the existence of a lake where we were standing, but Boeung Kak has been drained to enable property development. As we advanced, we were abruptly stopped by a man who was sitting by the access way to the site. Acting like the gatekeeper of the place, he waved us away and asked us not to take photographs. Sensing our reluctance to conform to his demands, he turned around and shouted, summoning the prompt appearance of a uniformed security guard. While we were forced onto an alternative path, it was instructive to witness the interactions between the two men—the "informal" groundkeeper had to rely on hired security personnel to conduct effective policing. As such, mundane details of the uniform and logo of a security firm are imperative in legitimating day-to-day performances of security. The lake was drained by Shukaku Inc., a company closely linked to political power in Phnom Penh. Many of those evicted from the lakeshore had refused to leave the lake region and were protesting their eviction (Chakrya 2012)— we passed a banner. State and corporate powers converge here. A resident directed us to a bulletin board picturing the police role in the evictions. Nearby there was another entrance to the construction site. Although it was "guarded" by another two gatekeepers, their late afternoon napping granted us an opportunity to venture into the reclaimed lake.

Skyscrapers were being constructed beyond the lake. The plan is for more here. The draining of Boeung Kak exemplifies the fusion of capital and political power that secures evictions (involving amply documented violence) to enable "development." The case is highly visible. The role of women activists in galvanizing protest has been critically, yet sympathetically, interpreted by Katherine Brickell (2014, 1256) "as a geopolitical issue, one that leads to innermost incursions into everyday life, one that has spurred on active citizenship and collective action evidencing the injustices of dispossession to diverse audiences, and one that has rendered female activists' intimate relationships further vulnerable." Brickell (2020, 5–6) has since examined Khmer women's struggles over forced eviction and domestic violence in an interconnected account of what she calls "survival-work, bio-necropolitics and precarity, intimate war and slow violence, law and lawfare, and rights to dwell." Boeung Kak looms large in her chronicle. But though the best-known case of forced eviction, by virtue of its location in Phnom Penh and the profile accorded to it in international media coverage, it exemplifies broader processes. Land grabbing and economic land concessions are widespread in Cambodia, producing new forms of displacement, exemplifying how the convergence of security and development that others have traced elsewhere is predicated on insecurity and dispossession for some: accumulation by dispossession (Reid-Henry 2011; Stern and Öjendal 2010). Indeed, it is this security-development nexus that underpins capital accumulation, even as the reality on the ground may be a profusion of alliances and conflicting interests between security-development institutions and local populations, as Sylvia Nam (2017) documents for Phnom Penh, and Chandler (2007), Sarah Milne (2015), Courtney Work (2014), and Eve Zucker (2013) describe elsewhere in Cambodia.

Different claims about security were articulated in Phnom Penh during our fieldwork. When Hu Jintao had stopped in Cambodia for two nights prior to the twentieth ASEAN summit in April 2012, he was on his way home from a meeting of the BRICS community of large emerging markets in New Delhi. The close relationship between Cambodia's government and Chinese economic and political elites (see Sullivan 2011) did not pass unnoticed among ASEAN delegations who were pushing for a joint communique on the overlapping territorial claims between Beijing and ASEAN members (principally the Philippines) in the South China Sea. Cambodia has emerged as both business partner and strategic ally for China's preoccupation with territorial "security" threats posed by an assertive United States, India, and Japan (Garver and Wang 2010). The close relationships between the regime in Phnom Penh and Beijing and Cambodia's refusal to compromise, which marked the first time ASEAN member states failed to agree on a joint communique, caused considerable tensions between Cambodia and other ASEAN members and in 2020 prompted pointed questioning of Cambodia's "agency" in supporting regional interests (even while construction by Chinese companies of the facilities for Cambodia's turn to assume the chairing of ASEAN summits and dialogues in 2022 is already underway in the deep-water port of Sihanoukville, a vital part of China's Belt and Road Initiative; see Ellis-Petersen 2018; Franceschini 2020).[7]

In a press conference after the April 2012 summit, Prime Minister Hun Sen angrily denied that China had excessive influence over Cambodia, saying that the "media should not engage in crazy analysis" and "Cambodia is not goods to be bought by anyone as a sovereign state" (Lewis 2012). Against this backdrop of the ASEAN summit, Phnom Penh became a diplomatic stage. Security was heightened; Phnom Penh was full of police and gendarmes during the state visit and summit. As might be expected anywhere when summits occur, tight control and clearing of "public" space had also occurred at a prior ASEAN summit in Cambodia in 2004 (see Springer 2010, 115–16). Beyond such symbolic events, however, development, power, and "order" are presented as the basis of Cambodia's progress. Prime Minister Hun Sen talks of this development, order, and progress, simultaneously drawing on a historical repertoire, invoking moral authority to construct Cambodia's postconflict developmental trajectory (Norén-Nilsson 2013). It is hard to disentangle these discourses from new and older networks of power or to demarcate the frontiers of international and national power circuits (Davis 2011; Kent 2007; Paling 2012). Such challenges are also evident in many other Asian cities (McKinnon 2011; Roy and Ong 2011; Sarma and Sidaway 2020).

In Phnom Penh, however, security was on the agenda at that twenty-first ASEAN summit in November 2012 (also the occasion for ASEAN leaders to meet counterparts in related summits). Recently reelected U.S. president Barack Obama also arrived for talks, a historic event that the *New York Times* duly reported: "Four decades after American warplanes carpet-bombed this impoverished country, an American president came to visit for the first time. He came not to defend the past, nor to apologize for it. In fact, he made no public mention of it whatsoever" (Baker 2012). Days before the meetings police reportedly had arrested at least eight people who had emblazoned their homes with Obama's portrait alongside a painted "SOS," seeming to ask for his support against their eviction without compensation from housing that was being forcibly emptied in order to create a "security zone" around the airport before foreign and world leaders arrived (Reuters 2012). Those leaders had broader "security dilemmas" in mind, related to the balance of power in the Asia-Pacific (Tang 2009). Away from that gaze, for those being cleared out of the way, however, the grounded meaning of security/insecurity is made flesh.

Some months later, Cambodia's July 2013 general elections saw significant advances by the opposition, who also claimed that electoral fraud had denied them a victory over the ruling CPP. The opposition mounted a series of rallies in Phnom Penh and at first refused to take their seats in the National Assembly. Prior struggles over land rights and displacements, labor struggles (including garment industry strikes), and street protests quickly coalesced with the aftermath of the elections.

Following the Transects

James returned to Phnom Penh several times in 2013–14, by which time the CPP had outmaneuvered the opposition, and the development path of elite enrichment, enclosure, and the nexus of state-party-private power was consolidated. Phnom Penh contains multiple layers and histories of security/insecurity and urbanization, from the royal and colonial crafting of a capital in the century prior to Cambodia's independence, through the real estate boom in the 1960s and war-swelled city in the early 1970s to the subsequent violent displacement (1975), invasion (1979), UN oversight (1992–93), and transformations since.

Representations of Cambodia often place it temporally or spatially alongside or after conflicts and ruptures, for example, as *Sideshow* (Shawcross 1979) to the Vietnam War, as the key subject of *The War after the War* (Chanda 1986), or simply *Cambodia after the Khmer Rouge: Inside the Politics of Nation-Building* (Gottesman 2004). However, attention to grounded, everyday moments/forms of security/insecurity problematizes a narrative that "places Cambodia in a recently invented category of 'post-conflict' countries suffering from pervasive violence and traumatic collective fragmentation, with a certain set of problems requiring a certain set of measures which fit the essentialised understanding of its political culture" (Öjendal and Sedra 2006, 508). That political culture has wider and deeper structures (Gainsborough 2012). As we argue, it is vital to see security/insecurity as complex and multiply determined by intersecting scales, histories, practices, and vernaculars. Meanwhile, security narratives at planetary and regional levels repositioned Cambodia geopolitically. Andrew Mertha (2014, 19) characterized China's relationship with Cambodia under the Khmer Rouge as "complicated, awkward and challenging to conceptualize." Complexity endures, with Beijing remaining a key economic and political ally. A month after the contested 2013 election results, the *Economist* (2013) pointed to other historical ironies. The United States had complained to Phnom Penh about voting irregularities while enhancing its dealings with Vietnam, where there are no competitive elections. The difference "lies in the fact that the Obama administration has chosen Viet-

nam as an ally in America's security 'pivot' towards Asia. . . . It is admirably ro-
bust in standing up to America's new rival, China. . . . Cambodia, by contrast
is China's main ally in the region. . . . Realpolitik, much in vogue in the 1970s,
is back."

Cambodia thereby crops up in new dynamics of great power competition,
accompanying rise of China narratives, with attendant discussions of its place
in "regional security." The CPP won further elections in July 2018, having first
outmaneuvered and then repressed the opposition. They mold the securityscape that enables layers of patronage—an inner circle around Hun Sen, his
relatives and close allies in the armed forces and police, those honored within
the clientelist *oknha* title, which, though still formally conferred by the King,
has become the gift of the CPP (Verver and Dahles 2015) and a mass outer circle, extending far into rural Cambodia, who rely on CPP benefaction and/or
fear the violence that its control over business, force and law confer. The many
on the margins in Phnom Penh and those factions of the urban middle class
outside the main power structures, who might contest the established order of
patronage and power (Eng and Hughes 2017; Nachemson 2018) or supported
the political opposition, now have no ready political outlets. In an update on
the situation in Cambodia accompanying publication in October 2020 of the
Khmer-language version of its 284-page report "Cambodia's Dirty Dozen: A
Long History of Rights Abuses by Hun Sen's Generals," Human Rights Watch
(2020b) noted, "Since the release of the English language report in 2018, Prime
Minister Hun Sen and the ruling Cambodian People's Party (CPP) have continued to benefit from the unquestioning support of senior officials in the
army, gendarmerie and police to effectively eliminate all political opponents
and dissolve the main opposition party, rendering the July 2018 national elections meaningless. Cambodia now has more than 50 political prisoners and
dozens of others facing charges." Press freedoms, which have long been limited in the Khmer-language press, have been further curtailed and indepen-
dent media, including those publishing in English, shut down or fallen under
government sway (Beban, Schoenberger, and Lamb 2020). At the same time,
a "war on drugs," launched in January 2017, shortly after Cambodia hosted
Philippine president Rodrigo Duterte—another strong-man national leader
infamous for a violent anti-narcotics clampdown—has yielded arbitrary de-
tentions, severe prison overcrowding, and police corruption. Thousands of
people have ended up detained for "rehabilitation" in unsanitary centers, without fair legal process or treatment and often subject to violence. Additionally, according to Amnesty International (2020a, 7), "Cambodia's prison population has skyrocketed by 78% since the campaign started, from 21,900 at

the end of 2016 to over 38,990 in March 2020, even though Cambodia's prisons have an estimated capacity of just 26,593. In early 2020, the population of Cambodia's largest prison facility, Phnom Penh's CC1, exceeded 9,500 prisoners—463% of its maximum capacity of 2,050."

Alexandra Kent (2006, 358) has suggested that the ambivalence and complexity of security in Cambodia mean that "it is time to consider the mechanisms by which different discourses and practices of security are, in fact, secured." She describes how "the moral logic of Khmer self-identification, well-being and nationhood" (p. 351) intersects with and mediates persistent structural violence in contexts of what Henk Schulte Nordholt (2011, 401) elsewhere describes (in the Indonesian case) as "a law of the rulers instead of the rule of law."[8] Phnom Penh's securityscape is complex, but its command locus has progressively centered on Hun Sen. By 2014, Sebastian Strangio (2014, 265) thought that "twenty years ago it might have seemed as if Cambodia lay in a democratic slipstream. Now it seems like the dream of a half-forgotten age." It will soon be thirty years since the postconflict transition and UN presence ended in the early 1990s. A decade on from that, in a biography of Pol Pot, the Khmer Rouge leader, Philip Short (2004, 449) had judged Cambodia "fragile." Short thereby closed his book with words adopted from African American spirituals that had also provided a title for James Baldwin's (1963) landmark text on racism in the United States. He wrote that Cambodia "is fragile. It is too weak to make more trouble. The fire next time will be somewhere else."

CHAPTER 4

Kurdistan

The Fire Next Time

In a "history of *spaces/powers*" in Yemen, John M. Willis (2012, 6) asks, "How were both North and South Yemen made possible as bounded political, social and moral spaces? And how do we write the histories of spaces that were themselves inextricably rooted in local and trans-local histories of economy, empire, state formation, religious thought, and resistance?" Willis's strategy is to study roads and security, both in imperial (British and Ottoman) archives and in local and Islamic narratives. As it did early in the twentieth century, and again prior to Britain's departure from Aden in 1967, Yemen continues to generate concerns about security, terrorism, and disorder. In recent years, Yemen has experienced armed rebellion, American drone attacks, aerial bombardment by Saudi Arabia, and consequent massive displacements of civilians and scores of injuries and deaths. Describing Yemen's "free fall into a humanitarian abyss," Waleed Hazbun (2018) argues that complex local and regional dynamics are frequently reduced to simplistic narratives about sectarianism and regime security. Some similar spatial histories, including a resort to a "sectarian master narrative" (Visser 2012), are evident in the context of Iraq. Iraq is also mentioned alongside Vietnam in debates on America's world role, reverberating with what an edited collection about *Vietnam in Iraq* in a series on "Contemporary Security Studies" calls "legacies and ghosts" (Dumbrell and Ryan 2007).

However, rather than dissect external geopolitical security narratives about Iraq, this chapter focuses on ground-level security practices that regulate and frame territory. Geopolitical narratives about Iraq have shifted from the threat posed by President Saddam Hussein's Ba'athist regime (via "weapons of mass destruction") to that of failed states (via sources of dangers beyond the Western purview, e.g., "jihadists"). Such sweeping designations overwrite the complexity on the ground. The term *failed state* suggests an absence of authority.

But that is seldom the case. In fact, such an assumption misrecognizes proliferations, and what Sara Fregonese (2012, 655) calls "coconstituting" of sovereign power by a range of state and non-state actors. Describing the Central African Republic, Louisa Lombard and Tatiana Carayannis (2015, 3) note that "in contrast to the picture of a shapeless, amorphous political space that emerges in most accounts of this 'failed state,' there is instead a hive of competing authorities across the region born of specific historical relationships and dynamics." Attendant to similar complexity, we examine security practices in the Autonomous Kurdistan Region of northern Iraq in the context of the heterogeneous territorial structure of the region. During our research, this fluidity saw the control of the Kurdistan Regional Government (KRG) extend (with Kirkuk reclaimed as Kurdish and largely controlled by the KRG) and the establishment of front lines with Dāʻish.

The complex layers of territory and security here point to intersecting and layered configurations. In the early 1990s, John Gerard Ruggie (1993, 174) argued that "it is truly astonishing that the concept of territoriality has been so little studied by students of international politics; its neglect is akin to never looking at the ground that one is walking on." Although territory has long been an object of scrutiny in political geography (as in the section introductions and essays assembled in Kasperson and Minghi 1970), it has become a theme of lively theoretical discussions in the past decade (Antonsich 2011; Elden 2014, 2015; Murphy 2012; Painter 2010; Sassen 2013). As Stuart Elden (2010, 799) argued in an early key intervention in these discussions, territory "can be understood as a political technology: it comprises techniques for measuring land and controlling terrain, and measure and control—the technical and the legal—must be thought alongside the economic and strategic."

With these approaches in mind, we reflect on the intertwined geography of security/biopolitics/territory that has emerged in northern Iraq. We describe the interactions of territory and securityscapes in Iraqi Kurdistan, focusing on the biopolitical modus operandi of Kurdish security. The dispatch then moves to Kirkuk—before and after its occupation by forces of the KRG—and to the Qandil Mountains, largely controlled by the PKK (Kurdistan Workers' Party). Our conclusions problematize narratives that fold an array of grounded territorial formations into the category of "failed state." As elsewhere, in Iraq this label belies the ways in which territory functions and the complex interface of securityscapes and sovereigntyscapes.

Securing Territory

On 29 September 2013, a bomb shook the KRG capital Erbil, leaving six at-
tackers and six security officers dead and sixty wounded, among them civilians.[1] The attack was carried out by a suicide bomber in a van packed with
explosives, followed by a gunfight. It is notable that this was the first suicide
bombing in Iraqi Kurdistan since 2007. Farther south, in Baghdad and other
Iraqi cities, such bombings were daily occurrences: just a day after the September 2013 bomb in Erbil, for example, thirteen bombs killed at least forty-seven
in Baghdad.[2] The 2007 attack (which resulted in fourteen deaths) had targeted the same building: the headquarters of the Asayish, the KRG's internal security agency. A suicide bombing in 2004 that took ninety-eight lives
had targeted and killed the deputy prime minister of the KRG. Whereas in
much of the rest of Iraq brutal and frequently sectarian war rages and mur-
ders civilians, the handful of bomb attacks in the Kurdish region since the fall
of Saddam Hussein have mostly targeted the apparatus of the KRG, especially
the Asayish.

The victims of the 2004 bombing are commemorated by a monument in an
Erbil city park where there was once an Iraqi army base. The first transect begins near that site and moves into the disputed territories to the southwest and
then to the PKK-controlled area adjoining the boundary between Iraq, Iran,
and Turkey. While our empirical focus is on state and quasi-state security apparatus, this leads us analytically to the relations between sovereignty, territory, and personhood.

Till worked in Kurdistan (with only relatively short periods away) from
July 2013 until his participant observation roles in Syria and elsewhere in Iraq
in 2015. James joined him in Kurdistan in July and August 2013 and again in
September 2014. Till's extended period there and connections as an employee
of a public university enabled a series of key interviews. Although we foreground the transects here, fifteen in-depth interviews with informants connected to security in the KRG also inform our analysis. Nine interviews were
conducted with senior politicians and members of parliament from the Kurdistan Democratic Party (KDP) and the Patriotic Union of Kurdistan (PUK),
two of the three main political parties forming the KRG. Among these interlocutors were a military advisor to the president (from the KDP), the KDP's
advisors for Syria and foreign relations, the minister responsible for the disputed territories (KDP), and the head of the PUK in Kirkuk. Other interviews
were conducted with the head of the central presidency in Erbil, a regional
head of the intelligence service, a Peshmerga (military forces) colonel, and the

manager of a private security company in Erbil. In addition to the more formal interviews, daily encounters and interactions—each stop at a checkpoint and every conversation with members of the security forces—inform the dispatch. In Kurdistan, moreover, the interaction of movement and scale was different from that in Maputo and Phnom Penh. For the transects in Kurdistan we used vehicles, moved beyond key cities, and covered more ground.

Kurdish identity and politics within and beyond Iraq are heterogeneous. Political parties intersect with tribal, linguistic, and ideological cleavages.[3] In Iraq, a bitter contest between the KDP and PUK culminated in armed conflict between 1992 and 1998 (intertwined with a longer struggle with Baghdad and relations with regional and outside powers), ending in an uneasy alliance that still survives.[4] In addition, there are several thousand PKK fighters in the mountains along the Turkish border. These fractures interact with the Turkish, Persian, and Arab majorities of the states whose boundaries cut across a putative Kurdish homeland (Culcasi 2006). Iraqi Kurdistan has been shaped by a long history of ethno-territorial struggle in which the Kurds experienced relative marginality and repression (culminating in genocide carried out by the Iraqi government in the 1980s). Whereas the Iraqi state increasingly defined itself as "Arab" in the second half of the twentieth century, in particular after the Ba'ath Party came to power in the late 1960s (Davis 2005), its weakening in the face of external onslaught and armed struggle by the Kurds has seen the Kurdish territories transformed. Kurdish autonomy in the three northern provinces rests on a securityscape that demarcates insiders (Kurds) and others (Arabs) in ways that invert the former biopolitical logic of the Ba'athist state. Yet while there has been much commentary on Saddam Hussein's security state, the intersections of territory, sovereignty, and security in the Kurdistan region are relatively thinly documented.[5]

Although the Iraqi state had faced a series of challenges since its demarcation by imperial cartographers after the First World War, these have been compounded since the U.S.-led invasion in 2003.[6] At the time of our research, insurgents controlled large swathes of territory and the Kurdistan region was autonomous, with its own government, armed forces (the Peshmerga) and security service (Asayish), and a separate visa regime. Iraq, however, remained the de jure state, and the KRG received 17 percent (about ten billion dollars per annum) of Iraq's total oil and gas revenues. Although the KRG has been seeking its own infrastructure for oil and gas extraction and export to limit this dependence, it has relied on this money from central government coffers, which Baghdad halted from 2014, resulting in heightened tensions between the two governments (Paasche and Mansurbeg 2014). Relations worsened further after the KRG held a referendum on independence in 2017, following which Baghdad sought to impose limits on the KRG's autonomy.

At the time of our research in 2013 and 2014, its high level of autonomy led many scholars to conceptualize the Kurdistan region as a "quasi-state" and focus on disputed territories beyond its formal border with the rest of Iraq (Bartu 2010; Natali 2010; Romano 2007; Wolff 2010).[7] Accounting for multiple territorial layers in and around Iraqi Kurdistan, however, requires consideration of the boundary practices of the KRG, both at the concentrated security spaces of its (contested) external borders and at hundreds of internal checkpoints, as well as through its broader regime of internal surveillance. Thus, the intersection of security and territory in the Kurdistan region is complex. To examine these intersections on the ground, we consider biopolitics, signaling the intersections of a variety of powers: the production, regulation, and control of population in connection with territory (Foucault 2010).[8] Whereas many interpretations of Foucault identify biopolitics with management of life and governmentality with the economy and the production of modern subjectivity, in the context of Iraqi Kurdistan, security and military/police power are their most tangible configurations, shaped by a history of armed struggle, forced migration, and insecurity. While governmentality "has population as its target, political economy as its major form of knowledge, and apparatuses of security as its essential technical instrument" (Foucault 2009, 108), it is that technical instrument that forms our focus here. Security impacts life everywhere in the Kurdistan region at all times. In this context, Kurdish ethnicity becomes a key marker. Arab Iraqis are subject to heightened control. When considering oil export policies or budgets, questions of sovereignty and power in Iraq and Kurdistan are constantly contested. Ongoing power games and lack of clarity on responsibilities and jurisdictions are the source of many disputes. Encountering the biopolitics of security on the ground, however, leaves little doubt about who exercises sovereignty and controls territory.

The main agency responsible for security within the KRG is the Asayish, which is supported by the immigration office and other policing agencies (police and traffic police) and by wide parts of the population. The responsibilities of the Asayish are primarily antiterror but also include serious crime and drug smuggling. It can best be described as a hybrid of secret police, internal intelligence service, and antiterror unit. Established in the mid-1990s by the two main political parties, the KDP and the PUK, the Asayish have offices in every town. Dennis Chapman (2009, 3) notes that although it is legally an agency of the KRG, whose Peshmerga and interior ministries were nominally unified, "the KRG security sector remains divided on a party basis, with the KDP dominating the Governorates of Dohuk and Erbil in the north and northwest portion of the Region and the PUK dominating Sulaymaniyah Governorate in the south. KDP and PUK each maintain parallel Peshmerga, police, Asayish and [internal party] intelligence services in their areas." Little escapes the attention of the Asayish. While the security the agency provides is widely recognized, their authoritarian aura makes casual conversation critical of them almost impossible. Just attempting to talk about the Asayish will end most conversations immediately or make interlocutors noticeably uncomfortable. But when conversation is possible, people leave no doubt that the security agency answers to the two political parties, not the KRG.

The Asayish symbol—the Kurdish flag cupped between two hands, also resembling an eye—is worn by its personnel at checkpoints. Centered on the Asayish, a tight security network spans the KRG-controlled territories, operating on several levels of control and biopolitics. This network has three components that were tightening during the period of our research (which saw the emergence of Dā'ish on Kurdistan's southern and western boundary):

1. *Checkpoints controlling movement.* Every visitor to the region immediately encounters a network of checkpoints at roadblocks between and around towns.[9] This roadblock system within the region makes it impossible to move without being checked by Asayish units that resemble light infantry. Besides a visual scan of the vehicle and observing for suspicious behavior of passengers, the KRG has a colored license plate system that facilitates fast clearance and control: blue plates indicate official vehicles that are rarely checked; red plates are for taxis, which are often pulled over to check the passengers; private vehicles bear white plates and are almost always stopped for the exchange of a few words with the driver. Officers can quickly determine where a driver is from by their accent (or dialect) and thus whether he (women drivers are less frequent) is commuting within the region or is far from home. Since Arabs rarely learn Kurdish, it is also possible to pick out an Arab in a Kurdish car. Vehicles with Iraqi plates from outside the region are invariably singled out and searched for explosives and weapons. Depending on the security threat level, vehicles with Iraqi plates may not be allowed to pass a checkpoint at all. Once vehicles are stopped, the Asayish focuses on ID cards.

2. *Immigration and ID cards.* The KRG has established a separate visa and residency screening system in addition to the national Iraqi ID registration. Acquiring a residency or ID card involves several

steps. Applicants, including Iraqi citizens not already registered in the Kurdish region, need a letter from a sponsor vouching for them. If the sponsor and/or the applicant are unknown to the Asayish, a background check is performed in addition to the more classically biopolitical strategy of blood tests (for HIV, hepatitis, and other infectious diseases). The final stage of the process is an interview at the local Asayish headquarters that includes questions on political orientation, occupation, and family ties.

3. *Surveillance and information gathering.* Plainclothes Asayish officers patrol cities and towns, listening out for accents and checking for anything out of the ordinary. Those deemed suspicious are interrogated. Although not officially declared, it is well known that the Asayish has a network of informants updating them on developments and sentiments among the general population, who, in turn, also report anything out of the ordinary to the agency. A military advisor to the president stressed to us that this extent of cooperation and collaboration is precisely what differentiates the KRG territories from those under the nominal writ of Baghdad. Although many Kurds remember the Ba'ath state's security police, the Asayish tends to be perceived as a protector in the context of the extreme insecurity elsewhere in Iraq. This requires heightened levels of direct control and surveillance that were especially stretched during the period when the KRG acquired new territories. However, biopolitical surveillance is accompanied by narratives of blood and soil, and Kurdish solidarity. We consider their interactions below, in which the blood and soil narrative is foregrounded via transects to Kirkuk and Kurdish solidarity in the securityscapes around Qandil.

Into Disputed Territories: Transect 1

With the research themes of biopolitics, territory, boundaries, and security and our destination in mind, on the morning of 28 May 2014 Till embarked from the offices of the KDP-run Directorate of Kurdish Affairs outside the region of the KRG in Erbil. After a ninety-minute drive, a large colorful sign welcomed visitors to Kirkuk—followed immediately by a landscape of blast walls, Kevlar, and guns. The first stop was the local KDP office to discuss the security situation on Kirkuk's streets. A complex securityscape had emerged that sought to accommodate all ethnicities, despite mutual distrust creating a security vacuum that has sometimes been filled by insurgents. In the six months before Dāʻish and the Peshmerga had advanced on Kirkuk, seventy inhabitants were killed in political violence.

Parts of the Nineveh Governorate, Kirkuk Governorate, Diyala Governorate, and Makhmur District are claimed by both the KRG and the central government in Baghdad. These disputed territories—including Kirkuk, the location of Iraq's second largest oil field—have long been a source of tension, resulting in standoffs between the Peshmerga and the Baghdad-controlled Iraqi Security Forces. Kirkuk has long been a symbol in Kurdish narratives that script it as a cultural capital, although the population is diverse, with Arabs, Kurds, Turkmen, Yezidi, and Christian communities. Historically, the Turkmens formed the majority within the city of Kirkuk, while the Kurds dominated Kirkuk province (Gunter 2011; Stansfield 2013; Wolff 2010). The presence of an ethnic Turkmen population led Ankara to watch developments there closely and threaten intervention if their safety was endangered.

While historically the Kurds and Turkmen had formed the majority, since the Baʻath regime's sustained Arabization campaign around Kirkuk from the 1970s, Kurds were expelled or fled and Arabs became the predominant ethnic group. However, population data have long been used as a statistical tool to justify "arbitrary changes of ethnic categorization by the political power conducting the census ... [as well as] equally arbitrary changes in the political meaning assigned *to* these ethnic categorizations, and to their numerical size" (Dundar 2012, 3, emphasis original). The latest census was conducted in 1957, before Saddam's Arabization campaign (Gunter 2011; Romano 2007). With Saddam's overthrow in 2003, claims to disputed areas by Baghdad and Erbil have been substantiated by both sides citing the numbers of their own ethnic community living there. While the Kurds argue that historically Kirkuk is theirs, the Arabs point to the number of Arabs currently living there. For more than a decade, Kurds have sought to repopulate Kirkuk. The fundamental biopolitical instrument of census continues to be a domain of contest. According to the post-Baʻathist Iraqi Constitution (Article 140), and before that the Transitional Administrative Law (Article 58), the stipulated process for settling border disputes included a "normalization," or undoing the Arabization process, and a census followed by a referendum to be held before 2017. Since this would likely mean that the disputed territories would fall to the KRG, Baghdad had always opposed the process.

Furthermore, the reversal of the Arabization process would mean expecting Arabs who have lived there for some thirty years to willingly surrender homes, a potent recipe for continued insecurity since they would be unlikely to listen and support any leadership that had "surrendered" Kirkuk. The fact that one of largest oil fields in the area lies under Kirkuk complicates the dispute. Kurdish informants, however, more often refer to Kirkuk in terms of blood and soil than oil. Moreover, while the law (in the form of Iraq's constitution) was on the side of the Kurds, the implementation of a referendum that could settle the dispute between Baghdad and Erbil in any case seemed unlikely to settle the tensions of a multifaceted conflict dating back decades and entangled with strategic natural resources (Gunter 2011; Natali 2008; Romano 2007; Wolff 2010). With Baghdad blocking the referendum and the Kurds unwilling to compromise on the status of Kirkuk and any Kurdish politician who supported the handover of Kirkuk unlikely to be reelected, both sides settled for an unstable compromise. While interviewees cited the referendum and Article 140 when asked about the future of the disputed territories, all intimated that no quick solution could be found. An adviser to the president (referring to himself as a private citizen) more boldly proclaimed that it might take fifty, maybe one hundred or more years to resolve, but the Kurds will never renounce their claim.

While the Peshmerga and the Iraqi Army secured different sectors around the city, a multiethnic federal police force and Asayish were charged with Kirkuk's internal security. According to Kurdish officials we spoke with, this is where the problems began. In theory, following President Talabani's (2005–14) reconciliation initiative, all ethnic groups were supposed to organize security collectively within the federal police force, but in practice they did not trust each other. The Kurds regularly accused their Arab counterparts of cooperating with insurgents in the city. High levels of distrust and the leaking of operational details to insurgents created a security vacuum. While international and regional media spoke of "jihadists," Kurdish officials describe them as "Ba'athists" and "Sunni tribes" with deeply rooted antipathy toward the Kurds and the government in Baghdad. One high-ranking member of the KRG stated emphatically in an interview, "Anyone who claims something different does not understand the situation."

The securityscape on the ground in Kirkuk (where different forces and ethnicities seek to control sectors) was replicated on a larger scale across the disputed territories. Poring over a map with a senior KRG official to get a clearer idea of security and control in the disputed territories, he described a chaotic patchwork of different setups and arrangements. While no blueprint has been agreed, the rule of thumb is that where there is a majority of Kurds, the security is Kurdish; if the majority is Arab, the security forces are federal; and in between, Turkmen militias operate in conjunction with Kurdish forces. However, in an ethnoscape shaped by deportation, Arabization, and the resettlement of the formerly deported and where a census conducted by one side can trigger conflict, consensus on majorities will remain continually questioned and can decide life and death. Any movement of troops may trigger violent responses.

The disputed territories are a liminal space for both the KRG and Baghdad, but one that both claim. Adding to the complexity, one party to the contest is formally part of the other—the KRG is part of the Republic of Iraq, and Kurdish parties also form parts of the central government, and there are some Kurdish members of the Iraqi Security Forces. While the disputed territories can be clearly mapped in legal terms, on the ground there has long been a more fluid border demarcating territory controlled by the Peshmerga and territory under the control of the Iraqi Security Forces. Thus, the disputed areas depicted on maps are not empty uncontrolled border space subject to (re)negotiation but filled with thousands of soldiers. In some parts each side has established their presence; at others they converge and continually renegotiate the boundary on the ground. One of few exceptions to the fluid border could be found in the security trench around Kirkuk, reached by driving through the city and past the vast oil extraction, refining, and storage infrastructure to Kirkuk's outskirts where it begins. While looking across to an Iraqi Army post complete with their U.S.-supplied armed vehicles, the Peshmerga explained how the trench separates nearby Arab settlements from Kirkuk, by cutting off access via all small roads and tracks so that insurgents and vehicles loaded with explosives cannot enter the city unnoticed. With the installation of the trench, all vehicles must pass through an Asayish checkpoint on the main roads that remain open. The wall was the KRG's first line of defense. Subsequent events made it only one of many Kurdish security rings around the city. While the drive into Kirkuk, like any trip through the undisputed KRG territories, involved short stops at a regular series of checkpoints, the return from the disputed territories traversed an international-border-like infrastructure, where the Asayish searched all vehicles and questioned drivers and passengers to prevent weapons, insurgents, and explosives from reaching Erbil.

Till revisited Kirkuk and the frontline/new Kurdish boundaries twice, the first time on 15 June 2014, five days after Mosul fell to Dā'ish and four days after the Peshmerga took Kirkuk and all of its surrounding area. The second visit was a week later when the Kurds had begun to fortify their positions around their newly controlled territory. Arriving from Erbil on 15 June at around lunchtime, there was no atmosphere of a victory celebration near the center of Kirkuk or at the fortified complex hosting the PUK's headquarters despite the dramatic events that had taken place just days before. The Iraqi flag was still flying on official buildings, and federal police (bearing Iraq's flag on their sleeves) were on the streets doing their jobs in the usual manner. At the PUK headquarters both the local party head as well as Ala Talabani, a member of the Iraqi National Assembly federal parliament (and President Jalal Talabani's niece), were keen to confirm the reports in regional and international media that the Iraqi Army stationed around the city had withdrawn before Dā'ish arrived at the outskirts of the city (indeed, later that day, the sight of Iraqi uniforms strewn in the desert outside the barracks indicated this). To prevent Dā'ish from taking over Iraqi Army positions, the Peshmerga moved in, seized all equipment left behind, and took over the positions to secure all of Kirkuk. When asked if federal police would still be seen on the streets in the future, and infer that Baghdad had now officially lost control and influence over the Kurds, the head of the PUK forces grinned but responded diplomatically with "we will see," also reiterating that the changed situation symbolized the implementation of Article 140, or the aspiration that Kirkuk would now remain Kurdish.

Leaving the building after the interview, the street was full of heavily armed security forces including KRG police officers (the unmarked militia that act as close protection details) and Asayish. The PUK provided an armed convoy for the drive to the new Peshmerga positions west of the city that marked the front line. Although Dā'ish were only five hundred meters away, the atmosphere was calm enough to wander around and take pictures of the Peshmerga and Kurdish flags over Humvees and bomb blast walls still carrying the Iraqi flag. Later Till joined a spontaneous press conference given by the general of the First Division stationed in this section of the front. Inside a shipping container, over cold sodas, hot coffee (to toast Peshmerga success), and baklava, the general explained that they were building defenses, including what he called a "wall of protection," to prevent any force from outside from entering the newly Kurdish-controlled territories. Later he specified that all areas under Peshmerga control "are Kurdish to us." With the chaotic withdrawal of the Iraqi Army, the Peshmerga was filling a security vacuum to prevent Dā'ish moving in. More significantly, without fighting Baghdad's forces, the Peshmerga was able to seize control of those parts of the disputed territories that the Kurds long considered theirs. The conflict that began soon after was with Dā'ish, not Baghdad: hundreds of thousands of Arabs, Turkmen, and others fled into Kurdish-controlled territories as these were the only spaces considered safe.

On 15 June, bulldozers were starting to fortify Peshmerga positions along a canal that marked the new border of Kurdish territory. A week later, the landscape was already dominated by high earth walls and an old T-55 tank dug in with its barrel facing Dā'ish positions. An improvised position had quickly acquired an air of permanence. The seizure of Kirkuk had a revanchist dimension—Kurds reclaiming a city that had been progressively and often violently Arabized since the 1970s. A brutal war waged further south. But our Kurdish interlocutors knew exactly what territory they wanted, and what they were content to leave to the Iraqi Army (and its tactical allies) and Dā'ish to contest. In terms of biopolitics, boundaries, and territory, the KRG's aim was to deepen control and hold fast. It was not to last, and the KRG lost much ground to the Iraqi Army when Dā'ish started to collapse here in 2016. The articulation of securityscape and territorial control had shifted again, as we detail in the closing section of this dispatch. In the meantime, the transect research took our work northward, toward the interstate border with Turkey.

To the Qandil Mountains: Transect 2

While Western media discussions of territory in Iraqi Kurdistan have tended to focus on the disputed territories and the ideological-territorial project associated with the declaration of a caliphate straddling the borders of Iraq and Syria, the case of Qandil shows that the idea of Kurdistan's "undisputed territories" does not really hold what it promises. The situation on the ground in Qandil is more complex than the language of statehood, monopoly of violence, and boundaries may readily encompass. Despite three decades of intense violent conflict between the PKK and the Turkish state (claiming about forty thousand lives), analytical literature on the PKK's ideological evolution remains relatively small.[10]

There are few accounts of the PKK's base in the Qandil Mountains that straddle the borders of Iraq, Iran, and Turkey. The discourse about Qandil, however, includes the realization that the PKK cannot straightforwardly be beaten by military means, Turkey's large standing army notwithstanding (Bacik and Coskun 2011; Bengio 2011; Larrabee 2013). The PKK began retreating into Iraqi territory from the outset of its armed struggle in the 1980s. While the Ba'athist state was acutely hostile, Saddam Hussein's regime was preoccupied by the conflict with Iran and the Iraqi Kurds. The KDP and the PUK both operated farther south and thus produced a buffer between the PKK and Saddam's forces. At the same time, the terrain was ideal for a guerrilla force, and a zone emerged that was controlled by the KDP and, around Qandil, increasingly by the PKK. The foundation for this arrangement was a deal struck in the 1980s between PKK and KDP leaders Abdullah Öcalan and Masoud Barzani, giving the PKK the right to use what was then KDP-controlled territory along the Iraqi-Turkish border to set up camps and launch operations inside Turkey. Without this, the PKK would have had to operate in hostile territory from the outset. Although the Turkish military soon started attacking the PKK camps in northern Iraq, it could not wage anti-guerrilla warfare there as effectively as it could within Turkey and was limited to aerial bombing, occasionally supported by ground troops.

Responding to Turkey's objective to decimate the PKK and Baghdad's lack of control, Ankara and Baghdad negotiated a deal in 1984 permitting Turkish forces to enter Iraqi territory as far as five kilometers inside the border. Marcus (2007) suggests that one of the reasons for Baghdad to agree to this was the hope that Turkish forces would also hit KDP camps. When this occurred, relations between the PKK and KDP were strained, but the PKK was soon entrenched around Qandil and could neither be eliminated by the Turkish or Iraqi armies nor expelled by the Peshmerga. The PKK's expulsion from bases in Syria in 1998 both fostered ideological innovation and reinforced the value of its Qandil base (Paasche 2015). When U.S. forces arrived in northern Iraq in 2003, they too did not seek to occupy this area, although they did establish checkpoints on the roads leading to it (Brandon 2006).

When pressed about the KRG's inability to exercise control over its "undisputed" territory in Qandil, the KDP's head of foreign relations suggested a visit to the area to understand the situation better. Since there is no office one can call, Till first headed to Qandil in November 2013, unsure of what reception awaited him. After a forty-five-minute drive up to the mountains from Soran (halfway between Erbil and the Iranian border), he turned off the main road, stopped by the last Asayish checkpoint, and first entered territory where grounded security is wholly in PKK hands.

Till returned to Qandil with James in September 2014. This time, after discussions at the last Asayish checkpoint, it took about ten more minutes, through a small village, before we came to a checkpoint run by the PKK. Several well-armed guerrillas in combat dress, flags of the PKK and affiliated organizations, and a large portrait of Öcalan made it clear who was in charge here. Asking to talk with PKK representatives, we were invited into the checkpoint post and offered hot tea, cigarettes, and chocolate pralines while one of the guerrillas held a series of walkie-talkie conversations. Within an hour a PKK commander arrived. Having completed the usual round of introductions, he accompanied us to Qandil though an area that, according to the PKK, has been under their military control for fifteen years. There are no Peshmerga here. Yet when transecting PKK-controlled territory, we saw the KRG's flag flying over a large building. While the PKK holds the monopoly of organized violence on the ground (though not overhead, where Turkish drones and planes frequently overfly) here, the KRG remains responsible for providing services for the villagers who are still registered as residents of the KRG. The flag we spotted was flying over one of its schools, around which armed PKK members wore the red star on their brassards. Whereas a KDP politician suggested we visit Qandil to appreciate the terrain that makes it impossible for outside forces to easily evict the guerrillas, around Qandil it is evident that some KRG state apparatuses are present, but its forces are not securing the area. Hence an autonomous region with its own security force had ceded security to a guerrilla force that has used this territory to support attacks on a neighboring state (Turkey), while the central government in Baghdad largely ignored the whole arrangement. Discussing this with representatives from the KRG and the KDP and Peshmerga commanders revealed clear security/control boundaries but fluid ones when it comes to state service provisions, including education. Within the complex network of biopolitics, territory, and boundaries, issues of Kurdish solidarity and mutual support soon emerge. Our original questions about "hosting" or "tolerating" the PKK did not yield responses, until one interviewee explained why he did not comprehend the question: "The PKK are Kurds, this is Kurdistan, and they are at home. We [the KRG] are not in a position not to tolerate or not to host them despite struggles that in the past led to intra-Kurdish fights."

However, this does not mean that the Peshmerga representatives or political advisors unilaterally support the PKK, its tactics, and its ideology. For the KRG, the situation in Qandil does present a complicating factor in their relations with Ankara. KRG officials seek to minimize this by advocating a stand for a peaceful solution and no active support for the PKK, although there are splits along party lines related to wider cleavages among the PKK, KDP, and PUK that have been reinforced by the former's close alliance with the Kurdish-led movement in northern Syria (Bozarslan 2014). Given the fact that the PKK is not confined to the mountains but is in control of several villages that are provided public services by the KRG, the question of what constitutes "active support" posed a challenge for most interviewees, the most direct answer, from an adviser to the president, being specified as financial aid and weapons deliveries. Inquiries about what would happen when wounded PKK fighters show up in a KRG-run hospital went unanswered. Yet while some interlocutors have no problem with the issue, citing pan-Kurdish solidarity, others refer to Ankara or Baghdad when it comes to the responsibility for dealing with them. Officially the KRG follows a line of facilitating peace talks and containing the PKK, although the idea of containment is not clearly defined. KRG representatives suggest that the PKK is only temporarily in Qandil, indicating that the PKK is explicitly concerned with Kurdish issues in Turkey and that they will leave once the issues are resolved.

Over the years, however, the PKK has shifted from the aspiration to establish a Kurdish nation-state in eastern Anatolia toward modes of organization avowedly outside the state, its boundaries, and its institutions, following what Öcalan calls *democratic confederalism* (conceived as a form of grassroots democracy influenced by anarchist thought). Outlining the principles of democratic confederalism, Öcalan (2011, 34) is very explicit about the anti-statist logic as well as the targeted spaces of this paradigm: "Democratic confederalism in Kurdistan is an anti-nationalist movement as well. It aims at realizing the right of self-defence of the peoples by the advancement of democracy in all parts of Kurdistan without questioning the existing political borders. Its goal is not the foundation of a Kurdish nation-state. The movement intends to establish federal structures in Iran, Turkey, Syria, and Iraq that are open for all Kurds and at the same time form an umbrella confederation for all four parts of Kurdistan."

The aspiration is not only to transcend international boundaries but also to build democratic confederalism across a broader Kurdistan and to defend it by all means necessary—including armed force. The war in Syria enabled the model to be replicated in parts of Rojava (as the majority Kurdish areas of northeast Syria are known) by the Kurdish Democratic Union Party (or PYD), affiliated with the PKK via the shared creed of democratic confederalism. Rojava's revolution however was contained to the north by Turkey and to the south and west by Dā'ish and the remnants of the Syrian Ba'athist state (Gunter 2014; Paasche 2015; Schmidinger 2018). The dynamics between top-down and bottom-up power in Rojava and its relationship to Qandil are complex and contested. The connections and contrasts between Kurdish movements in those insurgent spaces and parties that form the backbone of the KRG are read by Joost Jongerden (2019, 62) as less about ideological differences over state forms than "those who maintained the state-idea as ultimate objective and those who rejected it, attempting to articulate a form of non-state government."

The PKK has no intention of beating a retreat from a swathe of territory in northern Iraq of between ten and forty kilometers wide and around two hundred kilometers long. At Qandil, a memorial to fallen cadres that over-looks a PKK military cemetery adds to the sense of permanence.[11] When we arrived in September 2014, there were fresh graves. And as one of the PKK's cofounders and a member of the Executive Committee explained to us in an interview, Qandil "embodies democratic confederalism," while adding that the KRG's vital oil pipeline runs through PKK-controlled land. However, refer-ring to a map of the area, he qualified that the level of control varies. In some areas, PKK cadres are confined to the mountains, but civilian areas have be-come depopulated due to past fighting. However, in spaces like Qandil where the PKK has established a grounded monopoly on violence (except for Turk-ish attacks from the air), the KRG's police cannot be involved in disputes and would not be allowed entry. Instead, it was claimed that democratic confeder-alism is based on a committee structure and organizing daily life through un-derstanding and reconciliation rather than through police, rules, and repres-sion. Rhetorically, the PKK emphasizes that military affairs and civilian issues are strictly divided and do not interfere with each other.

When discussing the PKK-controlled spaces, it is challenging to find the right terminology, given their formal disavowal of boundaries and national territorial aspiration and their relationship with the KRG that defies easy sum-mary. Things have become more complex since 2014, when the PKK's forces joined the Peshmerga at the front lines with Dā'ish, operating far from Qandil or Turkey. Whereas many narratives about Iraq have been focused on these front lines and discuss state failure/fracture, these categories may obfuscate the complex intersections of biopolitics, security, sovereignty, and territory. For Damien Doyle and Tristian Dunning (2018, 538), Iraq comprises "multi-ple competing, collaborating and overlapping state and non-state actors [that] wield political authority, claim legitimacy and deploy violence to achieve po-litical, economic and/or security goals. Many armed actors occupy a grey area between 'state' and 'non-state,' a situation of hybrid political authority that is both a product of, and a contributor to, fragmented sovereignty."

Of course, for decades historical and comparative sociology has wres-tled with the slipperiness of sovereignty. Philip Abrams (1988, 58) famously claimed that "the state is not the reality which stands behind the mask of po-litical practice. It is itself the mask which prevents our seeing political practice as it is." A few years later, in the opening to what became another much-cited paper, Timothy Mitchell (1991, 77) argued that "the state has always been diffi-cult to define. Its boundary with society appears elusive, porous, and mobile. I argue that this elusiveness should not be overcome by sharper definitions, but explored as a clue to the state's nature." From a related angle, Nikolas Rose and

Peter Miller (1992) argued that much work on the state and government elided how they are artifacts of power—and so a more appropriate analytical focus should be problematic of governmentality—the governance of conduct.

But we can learn more about the sovereign "fragments" that are said to characterize Iraq from writing on other recent cases of precarious articulations of sovereignty. Drawing on the trajectory of armed conflict in Sri Lanka and describing the strategies of the ethno-separatist Liberation Tigers of Tamil Eelam, Bart Klem and Sidharthan Maunaguru (2017, 630, emphasis added) advance that "insurgent movements are not merely vying to be assimilated into the community of sovereign states. They are also capable of subtly *rearticulating the way sovereignty is understood and practiced*. Rebel movements with state-like ambitions are not simply lagging behind purportedly normal states, struggling toward some fixed yardstick of sovereignty. They are better thought of as laboratories of sovereign rule that actively transform the way sovereignty is practiced and understood." Reflecting on the ground of another site usually interpreted through the lens of state failure, and building on accounts there of governance without government (Menkhaus 2007), Alice Hills (2014, 91) notes that while Somalia has become the paradigmatic failed state to many observers, "in fact, Somalia is managed by a variety of security and administrative entities that are linked ethnically and economically but have different levels of stability and styles of governance." In other words, rather than a fixation on violence and conflict and state failure, critical analysis equally needs to consider how, as in Marika Sosnowski's (2020, 1395) account of "Negotiating Statehood through Ceasefires," "order is constructed, promulgated, and utilized in sovereign contests." Our transects in Kurdistan negotiated similarly variegated arrangements.

Following the Transects

Although the motives for it will long be debated (Hinnebusch 2007), one key backdrop to the American-led invasion of Iraq in 2003 was a narrative about security (Sovacool and Halfon 2007). However, as we noted in the introduction (p. 17), it is vital to ask whose security as well as to approach security "not as some kind of universal or transcendental value but rather as a mode of governing or a political technology" (Neocleous 2011, 26), "that imbues itself on all social relations and attaches itself to almost all commodities" (Rigakos 2011, 63). As Ali Bilgic (2014, 261) insists, in writing about former Yugoslavia, another site of conflict and Western intervention, "Ideas about what security means, for whom security can be sought and how security can be achieved are constitutive to ideas about how individual and collective identities are constructed." Our dispatch points to an array of Kurdish territorial structures and in many ways echoes what others have described elsewhere as a plural field of security power brokers (Côté-Boucher, Infantino, and Salter 2014; Jeursen and van der Borgh 2014; Schomerus and de Vries 2014). Beyond encounters with this plurality however, the transect journeys we report additionally mirror an aspect of territorial control, specifically over networked mobility. Although many checkpoints in Iraqi Kurdistan appear semipermanent (with well-built barriers and kiosks like those found at parking lots or toll booths elsewhere), others may signal temporary power shifts as Peshmerga and PKK (and Dā'ish) travel. In the fluid situations of Iraq (and Syria), power and security hinge on the regulation and exercise of mobilities. In October 2014, images of Peshmerga convoys and weapons being cheered by thousands of other Kurds circulated widely. Ankara acquiesced to the Peshmerga crossing Turkish territory as they moved between KRG territory in northern Iraq and Dā'ish-besieged Kobane in northern Syria. These events, together with wider struggles around Kirkuk and Kobane, became symbolic sites in the vexed and long-standing interactions of Kurdish territory, security, and space (Gourlay 2018).

For a moment during the Dā'ish summer offensive in 2014 and later the Battle of Mosul (October 2016–July 2017), the securityscape was overwritten by an existential threat that saw former enemies and longtime competitors working together. PKK combatants came down from Qandil to fight with the different Peshmerga factions. The Iraqi Army first sought refuge in the Kurdistan region and later launched parts of their assault on Mosul from there. The PKK's Iranian wing, the Kurdish Free Life Party (PJAK), was fighting with the Shia militias. U.S. special operations forces moved through territory that was under control of the Iranian military advisers of the al-Quds Brigades. Technically the PKK and Turkish forces both fought the same enemy in Mosul. One could see veteran fighters from different factions shaking their head in disbelief over the relative harmony between disparate forces, expressing careful hopes that this unity could continue into the post-Dā'ish era and stabilize the region. Those hopes were shattered as soon as Dā'ish were dislodged from Mosul in July 2017. While the fires in what remained of eastern Mosul were still smoldering, Iraqi Security Forces as well as Shia militias moved toward Kirkuk. Under the pretext of eliminating remaining Dā'ish pockets, entire armored divisions and brigades of Iraqi Special Operation Forces and thousands of Shia militiaman were deployed in around Kirkuk.

Much had already changed since the first transect there in mid-2014, when the Peshmerga had filled the security vacuum left by the hastily retreating Iraqi Army. Although many of those spaces later became heavily contested, at the time of our transect the Kurds in Iraq had managed to secure all of those disputed spaces they historically claimed to be Kurdish. Trying to capitalize on the historic moment, Masoud Barzani, president of the Autonomous Kurdistan Region, announced plans for an independence referendum. In a critical examination of the disjuncture between Barzani's stated and private motives, Hawre Hasan Hama (2020) notes how dissatisfaction and internal protests against the KRG had spread since 2015, compounded by KRG corruption, stalemate over proposed constitutional changes (from a presidential to a parliamentary model—opposed by the KDP but supported by most other political parties), and a fiscal crisis triggered by deteriorating relations with Baghdad, falling oil prices, and the war against Dā'ish.

Regional and international actors as well as the other Kurdish parties advised against the referendum. But Barzani pressed for the independence referendum. Hama (2020, 122) considers that unilateral independence was not in reach, given united opposition from Baghdad, Iraq's neighbors, and outside powers. Hence, motivations for staging the independence referendum "included the KDP's need to maintain its hegemony in Kurdish politics, the desire to continue Barzani's presidency indefinitely, and the need to shift public opinion away from the political and economic failures of the Kurdish leadership." After being postponed several times, the poll was finally held on 25 October 2017. The vote for independence was over 90 percent, though with uneven turnout. But this was a symbolic result: no state recognized the referendum. Almost immediately, Iraqi forces backed by Shia militias assaulted Kirkuk and other disputed territories. Being vastly outnumbered and outgunned, the Peshmerga hastily retreated to the undisputed parts of KRG territory. After almost two weeks a fragile ceasefire was agreed, although sporadic fighting continued for weeks. With discontent increasing among his former supporters and despite a ramped-up Asayish, Masoud Barzani had to leave office. Realizing their regained strength, Baghdad imposed sanctions on the KRG and retook border posts in Kurdistan including Erbil International Airport. In less than two weeks the Kurds lost a significant source of crude oil revenues, much of the contested territory they took from Dā'ish, and the right of visitors to enter the region directly without a visa issued by the Iraqi authorities. Intra-Kurdish tensions were reanimated, with the two main parties accusing each other of treachery.

Farther north, the PKK presence in Qandil continues, though—in a decisive resumption of military means—Ankara has repeatedly bombarded Qandil since June 2015, restaging the Turkish republic's "traditional fears of disintegration and the culture of insecurity" (Kösebalaban 2020, 335). Having already abandoned a brief path of accommodation/talks with the PKK more than a year before, following a coup attempt against him in July 2016, Turkish president Recep Tayyip Erdoğan redoubled condemnation of PKK (and his opponents reportedly behind the coup plot) as *terör örgütü* (terrorist organizations). Despite his antipathy toward many of the secular principles of the republic founded by Mustafa Kemal Atatürk in 1923, Erdoğan and his allies "endorsed the century long state policy [variously of assimilation and repression] towards the Kurds . . . the very same discourse and tactics employed by their [secularist] predecessors" (Gurses 2020, 315). Meanwhile, in April 2016, Iranian Kurdish parties allied with the PKK and present in Qandil had resumed insurgency in Iran.[12] Iranian drones, missiles, and artillery have periodically targeted Qandil since—sometimes in apparent coordination with Turkish forces.

Dā'ish were displaced from most of Iraqi Kurdistan in 2017 after an arduous struggle on the part of a broad alliance of forces. However, compounding regional uncertainties, in October 2019, President Trump suddenly announced a withdrawal of most U.S. forces from northern Syria. This simultaneously buttressed the Turkish state, which moved their armed forces and militias deeper into Rojava, and Damascus, which gained enhanced leverage over the Kurdish forces. The following January saw five missiles launched from Iran hit a base housing U.S. troops near Erbil airport (following a U.S. drone strike that killed the senior Iranian general Qasem Soleimani near Baghdad airport). The base was again targeted by six rockets launched from inside Iraq in October 2020. Iraqi Kurdistan currently hosts over a million people who are either refugees or classified as Iraqis internally displaced by conflict. Thousands of Dā'ish fighters, who had little or no agency or ideological affiliation with Dā'ish, and their family members, including many children, are detained. Noting that "ISIS recruited some children by force or coercion, while other children joined because of peer or family pressure, financial need, to escape family problems, or to gain social status. These factors mirror the drivers of child recruitment in most armed conflicts around the world. Multi-country research has found that ideology is rarely the primary force motivating children's association with violent extremist groups," Human Rights Watch (2019, 8) describes how these victims become suspects and confessions are often coerced. Securityscapes in Iraqi Kurdistan remain fraught and contested.

CODA

The World Does Not Exist
for Our Theories

Methodological Reflections

When, over twenty years ago, James walked sections of the Portuguese-Spanish border to engage with its geopolitics, he did not conceptualize his fieldwork as a transect. The transecting of securityscapes, however, had its beginnings in those purposeful steps and as a method of engagement in the historic naval city of Plymouth, evolving through joint research with his return to Maputo and subsequently in Phnom Penh and Kurdistan. Based on the experiences that yielded *Transecting Securityscapes*, yet mindful of and attentive to their limits, we contend that transects offer productive strategies for studying power. When purposely engaged during transects, every conversation, every turn and pause forms part of the record, instead of being just a chat or break while waiting for something else. Each transect demanded careful reflection on objectives, treading the fine lines between confidence, collaborations, reflexivity, sighting, talking, reading, and witnessing. Lines of sight shift according to who walks, when, and how. Questions about their suitability to answer research questions are partly addressed by asking how transects might repose such questions. Situated in this way, transects are rewarding—though they may require a willingness to justify the method to often skeptical reviewers or colleagues, who may perceive "just walking" (Kowalewski and Bartłomiejski 2020) as less rigorous than discourse analysis, surveys, or interviews. We hope that *Transecting Securityscapes* might enable others who push critical geopolitics, still often theory-led and discourse-bound, into other terrains of the everyday. Transects may be combined with a range of other methods and modes of encounter. These may be more formal, as we did via interviews, or involve the kinds of collaborative map making that Bruno Lefort (2020, 11) develops in a study of Beirut, whereby "a detour by a micro, ethnographic approach enables us to shed light on gaps, particular situations in which frictions with the dominant forces are visible. These frictions have to be taken seriously. . . . Ultimately, analysis of these micro-situations shows the necessity to reconsider the relation between the city and war beyond the dominant focus on destructive forces and anxious urbanism. Urban spaces, far from merely symbolizing and reproducing conflicts, are also the place where mundane practices and imaginations reinvent the social fabric."

Other tandem modes of encounter include collaborations with journalists (Paasche 2016), and what Natalie Koch (2018) describes as "event ethnography," which similarly draws on the serendipity of "contingent encounters." Reflecting on the challenges and value of research in sites coded as "red zones" by insurers and diplomats, where insecurity is "seen from above—that is, from Paris, Washington or London," Sten Hagberg (2019, 14) contrasts the colorful maps produced by offices in the Global North with the insights of researching security/insecurity "from below" in Burkina Faso and Mali. According to Hagberg, this bottom-up perspective demands methodological pluralism in places where "the ethnographic study of insecurities is badly needed, while being difficult to carry out in practice" (14). We concur and would include transects within Hagberg's description of "a need to mobilize a whole array of methodological and conceptual practices (auto-ethnographies, media analysis, teamwork, interlocutors' own observations and field notes, underground tracts, social media, archives, etc.)" (15). Similarly, when bearing witness from conflicted sites in Sudan, Audrey Macklin (2004, 78), whose reflections on security as a utility were cited in the introduction (p. 3), spoke of "'connecting the dots,' between commerce, war and gender." We find inspiration from Macklin's writing and consider that transects may similarly offer a means to make connections. In common with her account of "militarized commerce, armed conflict and human security in Sudan," *Transecting Securityscapes* "is not purely analytical; it is also inflected with concerns about methodology about my [in this case, our] positioning" (78). Other writings from southern cities articulate similarly open methods of encounter (Simone 2019). A similar move by a group of scholars associated with a Beirut-based Summer Institute on Critical Security Studies in the Arab World is "interested in engaging and experimenting with research and pedagogical practices that centre on the active dynamics of translation, and how these concepts and frameworks used to mark a 'critical' agenda travel, mutate and sometimes fail to capture the relationships and experiences one may wish to understand or express" (Abboud et al. 2018, 276).

Walking sections of the Iberian border to encounter and narrate its geopolitics and the walk this sparked in Plymouth was not envisaged as a replacement

FIGURE 2. Meccan securityscape, 7 January 2020. Photograph by James D. Sidaway.

for other textual or interview-based study. Yet transects have become something more than a supplement. When the two of us went to Maputo in 2009, we did not envisage a decade of transecting and narrating securityscapes. Nor did we then have a clear idea of possible further case studies. However, a combination of finding transects rewarding, a desire to continue work in other places, personal interests and connections, and more mundane issues such as the availability of research funding and academic positions have enabled us to continue to work together. We continue to experiment with the potential of transects as a mode of encounter and narrative strategy. In addition to the work in Yangon (Sarma and Sidaway 2020), James has been mapping securityscapes in Mecca (Figure 2). The role of surveillance and policing in and around the al-Masjid al-Ḥarām, enclosing the holiest place in Islam, more widely mirrors that at mass private and public spaces in Saudi Arabia, where profit, biopolitics, and belief intersect (Alhadar and McCahill 2011). Mecca is simultaneously mundane and exceptional. In the words of Saudi artist Ahmed Mater (2016, 576), whose larger-than-life visual works capture this, "Like few cities on earth, Mecca, 'Makkah' bristles under the weight of its own dramatic symbolism. It is a hallowed site revered by millions and yet at the same time a point of perpetual immigration. This has been the case for centuries. Yet over the past few years the city has been recast, reworked, and ultimately reconfigured."

The scale of this reworking, linked to Saudi and international capital flows into new malls, new hotels, and an extension to and remodeling of the Great Mosque itself, has elicited critical comment—though it scarcely registers in comparative urban studies. Mater's richly photographically charted account of Mecca "as a living city" rests on a mode of transecting the city that draws on some of the material on urban walking that also inspired for our transects. Mater (2016, 577–79) records a process begun in 2008, after his first pilgrimage to Mecca since early childhood: "I began a series of deliberately experimental and meandering journeys within the spiritual center of the Islamic World: Mecca. In many ways these expeditions—by foot, by car, rarely covering the same route twice and at all times open to creative happenstance—have their roots in psychogeography . . . yet my explorations also go beyond what is usually implied by psychogeography in terms of their relational dynamic . . . that encompasses socially and politically instrumental events, collective dreams and ideologies."

While James was last in Saudi Arabia in January 2020, a U.S. drone strike killed Iran's top security and intelligence commander, Major General Qasem Soleimani, near Bagdad airport. Viewing a wall-mounted TV in a Holiday Inn, James watched CNN's coverage of Iranian counterstrikes, directed at an American military base in Erbil (screen shot in Figure 3). While those mediascapes about security/insecurity progressed, news broke of the crash of Ukraine International Airlines Flight 752. None of the 176 passengers and crew aboard survived when the three-year-old Boeing 737 went down soon after takeoff from Tehran. Following initial media talk of technical failure, it transpired that the Tehran–Kiev flight had been accidently shot down by a short-range surface-to-air missile. As we swapped messages, amid recollections of flights into and out of Iraq and discussion of airpower and missile systems, the long history of civilian aircraft as targets—and weapons—came to mind (Sidaway 2012). In subsequent days, ad hoc memorials appeared in Kiev and Tehran, resembling the kind of temporary street memorials that James had photographed around the World Trade Center site soon after 9/11 (Figure 4), much like those that appeared at the junction of Chicago Avenue and East Thirty-Eighth Street in Minneapolis following the killing there of George Floyd in May 2020 by a po-

FIGURE 3. Screenshot of CNN coverage of Iranian missile strikes on American military targets in Iraq, 8 January 2020. Photograph by James D. Sidaway.

FIGURE 4. Informal memorial at the wire fence surrounding the World Trade Center site, New York, April 2002. Photograph by James D. Sidaway (first published in Sidaway and Mayell 2007).

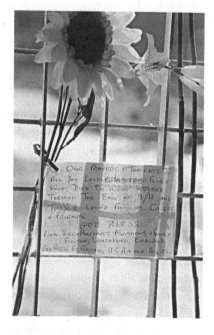

lice officer. A video of George Floyd's death, filmed by a member of the public, soon circulated worldwide. Floyd's repeated pleas of "I can't breathe" as a police officer knelt on his neck became a leitmotif for protest and mobilization against systemic police abuses and institutionalized racism. Such temporary, informal memorials to lives lost and those cast in stone (more often "for the fallen" or "heroes") and the events around them reflect claims on and distill contests around life, memory, order, security, and worlding. These "truth spots" are local castings but may resonate nationally and elsewhere. What and who are memorialized in installations and narratives about loss (as well as lives erased or forgotten) frequently articulate with national-scale scripts. Hence, also, the momentum around takedowns of Confederate symbols and Columbus statutes. Across northern metropoles in the context of BlackLivesMatter (in the wake of George Floyd), there have been numerous ad hoc celebratory memorials, in tandem with the toppling/removal of statues of memorialized individuals like Edward Colston (toppled and pushed into the harbor of the English port city of Bristol by protestors on 7 June 2020), which like that of Cecil Rhodes in Oxford had long been contentious (a Rhodes statue in Cape Town was removed on 9 April 2015), in recalling and normalizing the trauma of unnamed individuals and the insecurity of those in the present.

Speaking to the British journalist Ed Vulliamy (who himself had covered the Bosnian War and first Gulf War and returned to Iraq in the following decade) twenty-three years on from the publication of *Dispatches*, Michael Herr recounted, "I was always being asked to go to Vietnam and to functions and reunions. I never went. They invited me to the dedication of the Vietnam memorial in Washington DC, and I declined. I later went by myself and found it dynamic and very, very emotional—always someone there in sun or snow, day or dead of night, pointing out the name of an uncle to some kid" (cited in Vulliamy 2000). That "pointing out" signals how both the informal, ad hoc, temporary memorials that spring up after traumatic or violent loss and the naming of individuals on state-commissioned memorials lend themselves to a range of readings, connections, and what Charlotte Heath-Kelly (2020, 282) has called "grammars of commemoration."

Convergence versus Heterogeneity in Securityscapes

All three dispatches in *Transecting Securityscapes* focused on urban elite power centers; only in Kurdistan did we venture beyond. Of course, Maputo, Phnom Penh, and Erbil also connect with fences and bunkers at state borders (Miller

2019) and other, even more distant, sites of enclosure and extraction, but each is part of an internationally connected network of cities. Maputo and Erbil (bar a period of suspension when Dāʿish drew close) both have direct flights to Europe (before COVID-19 groundings). Phnom Penh is also a day from Europe, via a stopover elsewhere in Southeast Asia or the Persian Gulf. For most of the past fifteen years or so, it has also been possible to fly between any of these three cities in a long day, through Asian or Middle Eastern hubs. These cities too, and the areas of them we transected, are sites where what Leslie Sklair (2005) described as a "transnational capitalist class" is visible. According to Sklair (2005, 485), "The TCC consists of people who typically have globalizing as well as (rather than in opposition to) localizing agendas. These are people from many countries who operate transnationally as a normal part of their working lives and who more often than not have more than one place that they can call home. This reflects their relationships to transnational social spaces and the new forms of cosmopolitanism of what I have conceptualized as generic globalization." Sklair sees four factions within that class: a corporate sector who own and/or control major transnational corporations and their local affiliates, a state faction of globalizing politicians and bureaucrats, a technical faction of professionals, and a consumer-oriented faction of merchants and media. In fact, there are often overlaps between the factions, which are also configured around family links, lineage, and political party (the two-party system of the KDP and PUK in Iraqi Kurdistan) and the dominant, former communist ruling parties of the CPP and Frelimo in Cambodia and Mozambique. The securityscapes in each city are profoundly configured by this process of class domination, and the core of each nodal city resembles other such places elsewhere more than it does the respective surrounding territory. All invoke/imitate what Asher Ghertner (2015, 6), writing of iconic projects necessitating mass demolitions in Delhi, refers to as *Rule by Aesthetics*, a "mode of governing space . . . in which intensely political decisions about who and what belongs in the city took place primarily on the basis of codes of appearance" in pursuit of an image of the urban sanctuary presenting as a world-class city. However, our dispatches also indicate that beyond this connectivity and convergence in appearance are relatively heterogeneous securityscapes. Here, Saskia Sassen's (2001) response to criticisms of her model of *global cities*—which posited London, New York, and Tokyo as the exemplars of a process of global city formation increasingly legible in many other cities (arguably pioneered in leading postcolonial cities like Singapore)—remains pertinent. Sassen (2001, 348) notes that "a common critique asserts that the global city model posits convergence and homogenization among those cities. The development of global city functions in different cities across the world does indeed signal convergence of something. But this is a highly specialized, institutionally differentiated process."

Such institutional differentials feature in our three case studies. This echoes Benoît Dupont, Peter Grabosky, and Clifford Shearing's (2003, 341) observation that "[security or policing] assemblages should not be based on a unique 'one-size-fits-all model,' but should instead value pluralism and accommodate the diverse contexts, cultures and knowledges found in weak and failing states." Our research has negotiated diverse securityscapes, embodying what Jaideep Gupte (2017, 204) has called "the granularity in security outcomes in cities." Categories of state, non-state or hybrid, and formal/legal and informal/illegal do not always travel meaningfully in space and time. In colonial ventures, Micol Seigel (2018, 74) reminds us, private policing had often preceded public versions: "Europe's classic colonizing companies (the British South African Company, the Royal Nigerian Company, the Imperial British East Africa Company, and the East India Company) all had their own proprietary police." Others have propounded that the distinctions between public/private securities are ideological rather than ontological. So, like the other reifications—such as internal/external, exception/normality, pre-/post-9/11, state/market, and informal/formal—they are problematic binaries (Johnston 1992; Neocleous and Rigakos 2011). Their overlaps exceed their differences. Beyond recognizing what is at stake in such binaries, however, we should also be reluctant to generalize about urban security in the contemporary Global South. Even terms and categories, such as "police" and "security guard," have varied associative meanings depending on the context, yielding a "crowded terrain" as Martin Murray (2020, 52) has recently described in the case of security governance in Johannesburg. Comparing the police or gendarmerie in Phnom Penh to the Asayish in Kurdistan reveals detailed functions, responsibilities, and histories that are hugely different. We are inclined to add an exclamation mark to Dupont, Grabosky, and Shearing's (2003) words, reflecting diversity in how particular notions, apparatus, and spatializations of security come into being and how each variant of security creates a space for itself in relationship with contending framings of risk, insecurity, precarity, and danger.

Other Securities

We introduced the securityscapes concept with reference to the interfaces with other techno, finance, and sovereignty scapes. This entanglement saw security invoked in Mozambique when, since our work there, over two billion dollars were lent to the country by Swiss and Russian banks in order to finance a vastly overpriced tuna fishing fleet and armada of patrol boats to secure, so it was said, fishing grounds. Firms based in Israel, Germany, Russia, and Switzerland were implicated, along with Mozambique's State Security and Intelligence Service (Serviço de Informação e Segurança do Estado). In the background were prospects for offshore natural gas extraction in Mozambican waters next to the northern Cabo Delgado province (Hanlon 2017; Macuane, Buur, and Monjane 2018). Consequently, in 2013, the IMF stopped all payments to the Mozambican government, foreclosing the "success story" narrative they had produced over the previous decades, which fell apart when Standard & Poor's downgraded the country's long-term rating from a B to a B-minus. Reporting the scandal as a stink, the *Economist* (2015) noted that "much of the money would end up being spent on security equipment, not fishing boats." A German NGO described the scandal as "a textbook example of how grand corruption operates: the scheme built on long-established elite networks underpinned by corruption, capitalized on by government decision-making behind closed doors, distorted public policymaking and involved the complicity of international business" (Shipley and Jenkins 2019, 2). Since then, several Mozambican journalists, reporting on fresh tranches of high-level corruption related to the natural gas concessions and the sequence of violence (by insurgents, police, armed forces, and private security firms) and displacement in Cabo Delgado, have been assaulted and killed. The Maputo offices of the newspaper *Canal de Moçambique* were torched in August 2020. Amnesty International (2020b, 3) described how intruders "poured fuel on the floor, furniture and equipment, and threw a Molotov cocktail. According to witnesses, the explosion, which reduced the office equipment, furniture, files and archives to ashes, was heard several kilometres away. The attack occurred four days after *Canal* had published, on 19 August, an investigative piece on what the paper alleged to be an unethical procurement process involving senior officials at the Ministry of Mining Resources and Energy, and the governing party elites."

In the light of such shenanigans, the temptation here is to join those who refute security as a fetish—to advocate instead anti-security, as in the claim that "the more we succumb to the discourse of security, the less we can say about exploitation and alienation; the more we talk about security the less we talk about the material foundations of emancipation; the more we come to share in the fetish of security, the more we become alienated from one another and the more we become complicit in the exercise of police powers" (Neocleous and Rigakos 2011, 15). Certainly, security frequently remains a master signifier, whose power lies in its links with other social relations, and at different scales. We need to be critical about those powers and wary when they are invoked by the powerful or problematically linked to the scale of the status quo "national," overwriting other scales. For instance, Inderpal Grewal (2006, 36) recalls how the homeland security discourse that had come to pervade the United States early in the twenty-first century "inverts the politics of domestic violence by suggesting not that home is [all too often] a site of patriarchal violence but that the home must be protected against it—thus taking on nationalist discourses of protection by externalizing danger."

Tellingly, before we could finish *Transecting Securityscapes*, confronted by the dramatic and rapid advance of Dā'ish in 2014, Till, then in Kurdistan, quickly had to redefine security in some other everyday ways. Security was no longer simply a promiscuous concept or marketable commodity, or the intellectual domain of study that had earned him a doctorate and led the two of us to Maputo, Phnom Penh, and Kurdistan. While the region filled with refugees, all around students, colleagues, and friends were losing loved ones who were in the Peshmerga. Some of the complex political layers and spaces of security faded. Former competitors over space and political influence rushed to the front together. Differences were put on hold. Iranians, the PKK and its various affiliates, Christian fighters, tribal militias, and old Peshmerga, armed with even older rifles, tried to plug the holes in the front lines to protect their families. Till was deeply challenged. While he was collecting his monthly academic salary of crisp hundred-dollar notes in thick brown envelopes and poring over the twists and turns in the scholarly literature on security, children with terror in their eyes asked Till, the security "expert" representing the West (by virtue of his German nationality), "Why are you not helping us?"

In this state of emergency, Till decided to act, meaning to join as an international volunteer with the Kurdish People's Protection Units (YPG), which at the time had even less support than the Peshmerga. Days later, hanging on to an AK-47 manufactured in 1965, Till was holding the completely overstretched front with Kurds, Arabs, and other international volunteers. During those days, security was the number of bullets in your chest rig. Security was having a last grenade to hold to your chest when being overrun, to make sure your family did not have to watch your gruesome death on the internet. Security was having enough food for the energy to stay awake indefinitely since there was no relief. Security came from energy drinks that kept your eyes open during the wolf light in the morning, the time Dā'ish liked to attack. Security was the sixteen-year-old machine gunner who set the dry grass on fire with his tracers so that the enemy could be seen crawling. Security meant the U.S. jets that suddenly appeared to support those on the ground. Imagine you lie in a trench at night, Dā'ish bullets zipping by your head and their fighters shouting out *takbirs*. Imagine your friend's whisper, "Tonight we are going to die." Then imagine the deep roar of an AC-130 gunship coming toward your front line. Over your position the American war machine deploys angel wing flares in the night sky. Soon follow the constant thumping sounds of the gunship's mighty cannon. Security simply meant surviving the night. Being temporarily away from the front line in a well-guarded base, security was the absence of omnipresent insecurity, so mind and body could relax for a short while.

Months later, after Till's unit had liberated Tel Abiat and connected the Kobane and Jizira cantons, his unit was attacked by a vehicle-borne improvised explosive device: a bomb on wheels. Many friends got sliced open, killed, and burned. When he closes his eyes at night, Till sometimes still sees the burned, black body of a friend, the young Heval Akif, which two other friends carried to a pickup. The only other color in that disturbing image is of the blood still welling out of his eyes, running down his cheeks like tears. In mined cities where every step could be your last, insecurity is the absence of medics, ambulances, and medical supplies. Till then went back to Europe and trained as a medic. Together with other international volunteers he set up a combat medic unit just ahead of the battle for Manbij beginning in May 2016.

The battle for Manbij had one of the highest casualty rates in the war against Dā'ish, second only to that sustained in the defense of Kobane. It was also first time U.S. and British special forces entered the battle on the side of the Kurds and their allies who had formed the Syrian Democratic Forces (SDF). Between the first offensive operations against Dā'ish in northern Syria in May and June 2015 and the Manbij offensive in May 2016, the only foreign special forces that had been active around the front lines were the French, who sent small teams after the attacks in France for which Dā'ish claimed responsibility. Those French teams coordinated airstrikes from the front lines and secured advancing Kurdish forces from suicide bombers in armored trucks with Javelins (modern anti-tank guided missiles) and surveillance drones.

In early June 2016, the first convoys with support from U.S. forces left their bases in Rojava and rolled past cheering civilians toward the front lines. Unlike the well-embedded small and covert French teams, the Americans made no secret of their arrival or presence. In fact, Till witnessed how U.S. special operations forces used their own location as well his team's ambulance as bait to lure the best Dā'ish fighters out into the open, to be taken down by a loitering F-18. For weeks, Kurdish and affiliated Arab units tried to breach the Dā'ish defenses around Manbij: the city was surrounded by a minefield and a trench, and in the suburbs, snipers waited in ambush positions. Between sniping and ambushes, Dā'ish fighters moved through a network of tunnels connecting their positions, where they had food and water to fight for weeks. When an SDF unit made it past the defenses and got close enough, suicide bombers in trucks hiding in wait behind the many gates would speed out toward them. At sunset, when new SDF units of about forty fighters would mount up on their Toyotas to attack the city, Till and his medics would get ready too. Sometimes half of that unit would be brought to the medics within hours, some still alive, some dead, but most somewhere in between.

In days when there was no SDF attack on the city, Dā'ish would punish fleeing civilians. Snipers would hunt young girls, whose bodies rolled in carpets or blankets would lie next to Till's ambulance, their small feet sticking out, their parents wailing. With SDF and U.S. special operations forces overwhelmed by the escalating casualties, Kurdish commanders attached Till's medic team to the U.S. and British special forces teams that were always with SDF frontline commanders. Together with the special forces' medics, Till's team would stabilize casualties and evacuate them through the desert and over the partially blown-up bridge to the field hospital on the eastern banks of the Euphrates. The command post was the central hub for the northern front line of the battle where intelligence came together, Kurdish commanders and foreign special forces made war plans, and units that pulled out of the fight rotated with new units entering the battle. Here, ancient Soviet-made armored personnel carriers dropped the wounded. In the relative absence of journalists, and thus largely screened from the wider world (though see Rojava Information Center 2019), Till also encountered what might be conceptualized as a mode of alter-geopolitics, or what Sasha Davis (2015, 3) characterizes elsewhere as *affinity* geopolitics: "Instead of politics being a game of determining which group gets to enjoy security through achieving hegemony, affinity-based approaches borrow heavily from anarchist and feminist perspectives and insist that power be deployed to destroy hierarchies and insider/outsider dichotomies, thereby bringing security to all." The scenes resembled the recollections of a fleeting episode in *Anarchy's Brief Summer*, Hans Magnus Enzensberger's (2019) compilation account in 1972 of the Spanish Civil War (based on personal testimonies and interviews with survivors, documents, and memoirs). Describing the anarchist republican forces connected with the charismatic figure of Buenaventura Durruti (1896–1936) and a self-governed Catalonia, *Anarchy's Brief Summer* reconstructs an extraordinary five days when justice and fairness became animating codes despite the wider war. In 2016, Till was witness to a revolutionary moment of radical gender equality and restorative justice—ironically, mediated by the protection of the most powerful war machine that has ever existed and near a front line with Dā'ish—when some U.S. special operations forces effectively took instructions from battle-hardened Kurdish women without questioning their authority. Members of the Women's Protection Units (YPJ) within the SDF danced before battles to music blasted from car speakers while the American soldiers sipped sweet chai and nodded their heads to the rhythm. Some American soldiers even wore the insignia patch of the all-female YPJ, the red star prominent on the sleeves of their multi-camo uniforms: no invented claims of weapons of mass destruction, no deals with murderous warlords, but a sense of standing in solidarity on topographic and moral high ground. Keeping watch over this spontaneous camaraderie and hoisted revolutionary flags, American jets and drones circled.

Although the battle was punishing, the presence and commitment of foreign special forces left no doubt that Dā'ish would eventually be crushed. Yes, while security is invoked within modes of domination and entangled with capital, class, patriarchy, and imperial and racialized powers, it still could be reimagined as a common good, shared and treasured. Manbij was one of the least secure places on earth during those weeks, but the combatants besieging the city fought against Dā'ish not simply to replace them with the usual status quo of nepotism, patriarchy, and tribalism, but to overcome historic injustices with a progressive commitment to direct democracy. Everyone sensed that they were part of something extraordinary; one of those fleeting and fragile, but unforgettable, moments when liberation was in the air.

* * *

The alliance with U.S. forces in the face of a common enemy was a conjuncture that could not endure. In October 2019, the United States hastily withdrew most of its forces from Rojava. The *Economist* (19–25 October 2019 edition) ran a cover story leader under the title "Who Can Trust Trump's America? The Consequences of Betraying the Kurds." With the thousand-strong U.S. trip wire force packing up, militias and other armies operating under the sovereign flags of (or backed by) the governments in Ankara, Damascus, Moscow, and Tehran soon carved up territory and around two hundred thousand people fled (Belkaïd 2019). Writing in the *Atlantic*, Peter Wehner (2019) noted that among the senior Republican figures who questioned the wisdom of the U.S. president's decision (seemingly made during Trump's 6 October telephone conversation with Turkish president Recep Tayyip Erdoğan), onetime Trump ally senator Lindsey Graham said it would enable the "ethnic cleansing" of the

Kurds. Nine months later, announcing plans in July 2020 to deploy federal security forces in American cities, President Donald Trump remarked,

> In recent weeks, there has been a radical movement to defund, dismantle, and dissolve our police departments. Extreme politicians have joined this anti-police crusade and relentlessly vilified our law enforcement heroes. To look at it from any standpoint, the effort to shut down policing in their own communities has led to a shocking explosion of shootings, killings, murders, and heinous crimes of violence. This bloodshed must end. This bloodshed will end. Today, I'm announcing a *surge* of federal law enforcement into American communities plagued by violent crime. We'll work every single day to restore public safety, protect our nation's children, and bring violent perpetrators to justice. We've been doing it, and you've been seeing what's happening all around the country. We've just started this process, and, frankly, we have no choice but to get involved. (White House 2020, emphasis added)

Trump's predecessors had also adopted the term *surge* when talking about security. First in January 2007, George W. Bush announced a *surge* in military deployment in Iraq, in the face of growing resistance to the American-led occupation. In December 2009, Barack Obama adopted the term, albeit talking about "a civilian surge," in tandem with plans to augment the U.S. military presence in Afghanistan. Whether consciously or otherwise, in July 2020 Trump invoked the language associated with America's overseas wars and attendant counterinsurgencies when talking about American cities. In contrast, Jelani Cobb (2020, 15)—a professor at Columbia Journalism School and staff writer for the *New Yorker*—called the protests following the killing of George Floyd an "American spring." Consciously subverting American exceptionalism, Cobb thereby asks his readers to *reconsider* conventional American geopolitical narratives and their mapping of order/disorder and security/insecurity:

> Consider for a moment how the events of May 25th through June 9th—the days of democratic bedlam in the streets, bracketed by the death and burial of George Floyd—would appear had they occurred in some distant nation that most Americans had heard of but might not be able to find on a map. Consider that, in the midst of a pandemic whose toll was magnified by government incompetence, a member of a long-exploited ethnic minority was killed by the state, in an act defined by its casual sadism. Demonstrators pour into the streets near the site of the killing, in a scene that is repeated in city after city. The police arrest members of the media reporting the story. The President cites a threat to law and order, and

federal agents as dispatched to disrupt protests in nation's capital, using tear gas and a military helicopter. These acts further erode his already tenuous position, prompting church leaders to rebuke him, and decorated generals to question his fitness for office.

In such a scenario, the lines of conflict gain new clarity, the abuses more unqualified horror. American commentators would compare the successive nights of protest to the Iranian uprisings of 2009 and the Arab Spring of 2011. The U.S. State Department, depending on its allegiances, might surreptitiously aid the protesters. We would all recognize the moment as the product of a traumatized society.

Such traumas will not be cured through reaching backward into repertoires of imperial and sovereign security. Securing the future necessitates another path.

NOTES

INTRODUCTION. SITUATING SECURITYSCAPES

1. Judith Bovensiepen (2009) also considers how East Timor's landscape becomes dangerous for those returning home (after the forced displacement and violence of Indonesian occupation from 1975 to 1999) given returnees' concerns about the disruptive spirits of those killed during the conflict who could not be accorded customary funerals.

2. In numerous contexts, however, visibility for Islam portends state surveillance, danger of assault, or worse. The turn to Hindutva ideology under right-wing governments in India and the anti-Rohingya pogroms in Myanmar are prominent examples of the reanimation of such anti-Muslim violence and insecurity. In Western contexts, surveillance multiplied after 9/11, whereby Muslims become suspect communities (Nguyen 2019) yet were concurrently terrorized by anti-Muslim hatred (see https://tellmamauk .org).

3. Dexter Fergie's (2019, 644–45) historical account traces how now commonplace meanings of (national or state) security supplanted meanings associated with economic recovery and the insecurities wreaked by the Depression. According to Fergie, this semantic shift signaled a momentous turning point: "National security heralded a novel way of imagining the world, one in which a permanently prepared United States would confront seemingly omnipresent threats. It marked the re-thinking and re-making of U.S. power abroad and at home."

4. For a review and application of securitization theory, see Uriel Abulof (2014). The journal *Security Dialogue* has been a key forum for case studies, theoretical reflection, and sometimes contentious debates about securitization theory's limits and merits.

5. In many sites, for states and subjects, discussion of crime and criminality lies at the heart of vernacular security—which, in turn, according to Jean and John Comaroff (2016, xiii), becomes "the vernacular through which politics are conducted, moral panics voiced, and populations ruled."

6. Given the fraught representational politics in references to the Islamic State and the variety of acronyms used to describe it (ISIL, ISIS, IS), we adopt the term Dā'ish (derived from the Arabic abbreviation for the group), which was used by all our interlocutors in Kurdistan. On that ideological–territorial project, see Ali Hamdan (2016). For a judg-

ment on Dā'ish having "strayed from Islam" and the necessity of fighting them, see Al-Yaqoubi (2016).

CHAPTER ONE. TRANSECTING SECURITYSCAPES

1. The urbanization of capital is summed up elsewhere in his work as the "evolution of a special kind of production realization system which defines new roles for economic agents. *Landowners* receive *rent*, *developers* receive *increments in rent* on the basis of improvements, *builders* earn *profit of enterprise*, *financiers* provide money capital in return for *interest* at the same time as they can capitalize any form of revenue accruing from use of the built environment into a *fictitious capital* (property price), and the *state* can use *taxes* (present or anticipated) as backing for investments which capital cannot or will not undertake but which nevertheless expand the basis for local circulation of capital. These roles exist no matter who fills them" (Harvey 1982, 395, emphasis original).

2. See too Harvey's (1985) essay "The Geopolitics of Capitalism."

3. For example, drawing on a wide literature on cities, violence, infrastructure, and interview narratives in a southern Indian city and paralleling the work on personal, community, and gendered securityscapes considered in our introduction, Ayona Datta and Nabeela Ahmed (2020, 67) "adopt an expanded notion of infrastructure that is mutually constitutive of gender-based relations of power and violence from the home to the city. Developing the rubrics of gendered safety and urban violence, [they] argue first, that lack of access to infrastructure is a form of intimate violence and second, that this violence is experienced and constituted through multiple scales, forms, sites and temporalities of infrastructural absence."

4. A useful review of Shehadeh's *Palestinian Walks* is offered by Ahmad Qabaha (2019).

5. The practice and potential of walking as a method geographical "fieldwork" that negotiates cities, culture, history, and capital has received renewed attention (see Richardson 2015 and Smith 2010) under the label of "psychogeography" (Debord [1955] 2006), which now has an expansive literature. Alastair Bonnett (2009, 46) locates this as part of a wider "'psychogeographical turn' that can be identified in British literary culture and avant-garde." Detailing the roots and practice inspired by the French Situationists and a plethora of writings, mappings, and activities, Bonnett goes on to note that "over the past two decades, psychogeography has re-emerged and been re-worked. It has not simply been inherited and continued but re-imagined in ways that reflect the changing nature of the relationship between radicalism, history and geography" (47). For a reading of Situationists as strategic thinkers, see Stevphen Shukaitis (2014). For our work too, Bradley Garrett's (2014) conversion of psychogeography into "urban exploration" is suggestive, though it has faced critique that it needs to take much fuller account of masculinity, privilege, and marginalization (Mott and Roberts 2014).

6. Our wording here adapts Nadia Atia's (2019, 1069) critique of Judith Butler's (2004) *Precarious Life: The Powers of Mourning and Violence*: "While Butler and other critics based in the Western Academy have in the last twenty years questioned whether brown, and especially Muslim brown, bodies can possibly have been accorded human status when they are so easily allowed to die, and so rarely mourned, a corpus of Iraqi literature

and artistic practice . . . has tackled the same questions, but necessarily from the perspective—for which Butler strives but cannot embody: that of a subject stripped of their human precarity in Euro-American discourse." So while Butler describes, according to another engagement with her work, "the political decisions and social practices through which some lives are protected and others are not" (Lorey 2015, 18), she is less effective in foregrounding words of those rendered as precarious others. For a productive and grounded rereading of Butler from Kabul, critical of American and other narratives in which Afghans are categorized as either perpetrators or victims, see *The Carpetbaggers of Kabul and Other American-Afghan Entanglements* by Jennifer Fluri and Rachel Lehr (2017). It is worth reading their book in tandem with Mike Martin's (2014) *An Intimate War: An Oral History of the Helmand Conflict* and Jonathan Steele's (2011) *Ghosts of Afghanistan: The Haunted Battlefield*. In ways that echo Nadia Atia's observations about who writes about Iraq and the subjectivities they embody, Nile Green and Nushin Arbabzadah (2013, xv) point out that "in spite of the huge growth of commentary on Afghanistan since the fall of the Taliban, studies continue to rely on an astonishingly small number of source materials, of which an even smaller proportion were written by and for Afghans themselves."

7. The year 1984 was also the first time that one of us visited majority-Kurdish areas of southeastern Turkey. The following year, in the vicinity of the Turkish-Iraqi border, James met Kurdish intellectuals linked to the PKK. Over two decades later, James's acquaintances among the refugee Kurdish community in Plymouth, England, also offered initial contacts for our work in Iraqi Kurdistan.

8. Writing from Indonesia in early April 2020, Rohana Kuddus's reportage is indicative of the riskscapes informing many responses from elsewhere to the COVID-19 epidemic: "When news about the COVID-19 outbreak began to proliferate in January, the general attitude in Indonesia was nonchalant. As neighbouring countries—the Philippines, Malaysia, Australia—began to report mounting cases in February, public officials continually described the virus as a foreign phenomenon that would not penetrate our borders" (2020, 35). Soon afterward, however, this proved otherwise, and, again part of a wider trend, state responses saw an "expansion of executive powers, development of surveillance infrastructure and restrictions on freedom of movement and association [that] will outlast the virus itself, perhaps affecting Indonesian political life for months and years to come" (41).

9. As Rivke Jaffe and Tessa Diphoorn (2019, 911) stress, "In Europe and North America, professional, centralized public police forces were formed largely in the late eighteenth and early nineteenth centuries. These new institutions took shape not just simultaneously with, but in relation to, efforts to maintain order in colonial territories. . . . By emphasizing this relational development of police forces across the empire, such research troubles the popular division between 'repressive colonial' and 'consensual domestic' models of policing." Derek S. Denham (2020) has referred to contemporary forms of this as a "colonial boomerang," and there is also a long trajectory of critical reflection on "ghettos" as a form of "internal colony" (Cowen and Lewis 2016), but we prefer Julian Go's (2020, 1193) reference to a process of "imperial feedback," which "occurred as a result of imperial importers, many of them veterans of America's imperial-military apparatus, who constructed analogies between colonial subjects abroad and racialized

minorities at home." While its origins may be traced to the projection overseas of the American frontier (during the late nineteenth-century conquests of Hawaii, Cuba, and the Philippines and then the Pacific War and occupation of Japan), the Cold War saw a new phase, in finessing what Stuart Schrader (2019, 71) calls an "imperial circuit" of police practices, training, and technologies. This accompanied domestic struggles over civil rights and a politicized War on Crime, established by President Johnson in 1965, that would prove more enduring than Johnson's 1964 declaration of a War on Poverty, itself framed by white anxiety about putatively unruly and threatening Black populations (Hinton 2017) and administered by for-profit contractors (Offner 2019). In 1971 President Nixon added a War on Drugs, which saw the erstwhile War on Poverty morph into more of a war on the poor. None of these combative programs had decisively come to an end when their racialized and militarized feedback loops were reactivated after 9/11 by the War on Terror. See too Nikhil Pal Singh (2019) and our reflections in the coda on the #BlackLivesMatter mobilizations of the spring and summer of 2020.

10. Recent work on the decolonization of Mozambique in wider Indian Ocean and comparative frames has also begun to reposition the historiography of Mozambican independence in richer postcolonial frames. See Pamila Gupta (2018), Pamila Gupta and Estienne Rodary (2017), Sheila Khan, Maria Paula Meneses, and Bjørn Enge Bertelsen (2019), and Marcus Power (2020). As Michel Cahen (2015) indicated, work on Mozambique's civil war, some of which we draw on in setting the contexts in chapter 2, is as yet unevenly integrated into such frames.

CHAPTER TWO. MAPUTO'S FRACTURES

1. On early Soviet and Eastern European contacts with Frelimo, see Natalia Telepneva (2017), who points out how Frelimo used this to eclipse other nascent Mozambican national liberation movements.

2. See Paul Higate and Marsha Henry (2009) on the *Insecure Spaces* of peacekeeping. Though their book does not contain a case study of the early 1990s UN deployment in Mozambique, their account of how UN peacekeepers (in Haiti, Kosovo, and Liberia) perform security through their daily professional and personal practices casts light on and informs our account here of contradictory mixes of peace and security. We briefly return to the impacts of UN peacekeeping in chapter 3's treatment of the fall and rise of Phnom Penh.

3. At the time of our fieldwork, Maputo's telephone directory listed thirty-three security companies in the city. A quick online search in 2020 yielded a dozen, mostly multinational firms.

4. This matches insights from the interview study by Anna Persson, Bo Rothstein, and Jan Teorell (2010, 16, emphasis original) on the failure of anticorruption reforms in Kenya and Uganda: "The closer to the top you find yourself in the hierarchy, the more likely it is that you are going to benefit in *absolute* terms from engaging in corrupt practices, perhaps even in the long run. . . . [Among] ordinary citizens, and especially the poor segments of society . . . corruption is not actively supported, but rather pragmatically accepted for the simple reason that it facilitates life, either by maximizing efficiency in achieving objectives which would otherwise be out of bounds, or by minimizing risks,

such as avoiding trouble with, for instance, the police or the courts. In both cases, corruption is used as a means for bypassing unpredictable (or predictably inefficient) institutions."

5. The role of these authorities, who often invoked supernatural powers as well as resorting to weapons, has been documented in rural Mozambique with reference to the resistance to Portuguese colonialism, the liberation war, and the civil war of the 1980s and early 1990s and its disruptive aftermath (Rodgers 2008; West 1997, 2001; Wilson 1992). Work on the civil war continues to explore the complex of motivations and links between violence, counterresponses by Frelimo and Renamo, and the wider national and regional strategic picture (Cahen 2015; Morier-Genoud, Cahen, and Rosário 2018). Although Bjørn Enge Bertelsen (2009) offers a valuable study from and around the provincial city of Chimoio, and Harry G. West (2005) on the northern Mueda plateau, examination of spiritual security/insecurity and power in the cities and periurban areas of Mozambique—along the lines of Adam Ashforth (1996, 1998, 2005) on Soweto, South Africa—is lacking. The brief remarks about community policing of "witchcraft matters" in periurban Maputo by Fabrice Folio, Carlota Marlen, and Luisa Chicamisse Mutisse (2017, 273) and Linda van de Kamp's (2016) accounts in *Violent Conversion: Brazilian Pentecostalism and Urban Women in Mozambique* signal the agendas and articulate the spiritual ontologies of (in)security with which we opened *Transecting Securityscapes*.

6. Similar microscale (in)securities and enclaves are described from Mumbai by Jaideep Gupte (2017, 216) in terms of "highly localised, time-sensitive and spatial characteristics, like for example which street or even which floor of a building you reside in, are the vernacular characteristics of violent urban spaces that challenge our broader understanding of urban safety. They dismantle state-centric characterizations of urban security as a uni-directional relationship between the state as the provider, and urban citizens as the beneficiaries, and yet, are dominated by state and military-centred terminology."

7. Near to Maputo, new gated communities have appeared along the coast and in the nearby town of Matola, where land prices are lower and larger gated enclaves can be more easily established. These are beyond our focus here. The next dispatch, on Phnom Penh, is attentive to mega-developments and the feel and security enveloping speculative capital and the role of Chinese investments. These are/were also present in Maputo but have become more prominent in the decade since the transects, in particular through the activities of the (construction-, engineering-, and mining-focused) Anhui Foreign Economic Construction Company (Wang and Moody 2014).

CHAPTER THREE. THE FALL AND RISE OF PHNOM PENH

1. Now Indonesia's second largest city, Surabaya was in the early twentieth century one of Asia's leading ports, featuring on globes and world shipping maps alongside Calcutta, Hong Kong, Singapore, and Shanghai. See Robbie Peters (2013) for a compelling account of (in)security and power in Surabaya.

2. The exchange is a joint venture of the Korean Stock Exchange and the Ministry of Economy and Finance. It is on the twenty-fifth floor of the landmark Canadia Tower, in an area where new skyscrapers are evident. Although a dozen brokerages (half of which are from other Asian countries) are licensed, at the time we finished the work in Phnom

Penh they traded in only one company: the Phnom Penh Water Supply Authority, which was partially privatized via an initial public offering on the exchange's opening day.

3. This period—told from the vantage point of U.S. diplomatic history—is recounted by Kenton Clymer (2004).

4. Hotels, as sites of gentrification, colonial power, violence, and "security," are also foregrounded in subsequent work with walking transects in Yangon (Sarma and Sidaway 2020). Likewise, writing a decade after our Maputo transects, João Sarmento and Denis Linehan (2019, 276) analyzed the Grande Hotel that opened in 1955 in Mozambique's second city of Beira, seven hundred kilometers north of Maputo, thus: "By converging a relational reading of both violence and architecture, we reconstruct through the excavation of archival and related materials, the processes present in the histories of the hotel and city at large, to unmask how they acted as spaces of slow violence." The Grande was never profitable and, after Frelimo took possession of it following Mozambican independence, eventually fell into disrepair and became dilapidated and occupied by squatters.

5. Penny Edwards (2007, 44) notes how "the desire to increase the 'appearance' of power would prove a central preoccupation of the protectorate, which, like the French protectorates of Tunisia and Morocco, sought to bolster its own superimposed order in Cambodge by buttressing what it considered to be 'traditional rituals, spatial patterns, and architectural ornament.'" The innovative construction in the 1860 of a palace in Phnom Penh, and its subsequent modifications and alterations, mirrored the interactions and constructions of Khmer style in conjunction with those of French colonial modernity. In turn, these provided part of the basis for the constructions and reimaginations of Khmerness (see also Peycam 2010).

6. As Grant Evans (1998) showed in neighboring Laos, rituals and memorials by the post-1975 communist regime were quickly enfolded with prior cultural structures from the preceding monarchy.

7. At an October 2020 roundtable panel, these remarks of Bilahari Kausikan, outspoken career diplomat and former ambassador-at-large and permanent secretary of the Ministry of Foreign Affairs in Singapore, ostensibly speaking in his personal capacity, were widely reported in regional media (Strangio 2020) and elicited outraged responses from Cambodia and Chinese officials: "Speaking about a year after the 2012 debacle in Phnom Penh where Asean for the first time failed to agree a Joint Communique because the then Cambodian Foreign Minister refused any compromise on the South China Sea, Hun Sen said supporting China was 'Cambodia's political choice.' . . . To state things bluntly, I see Cambodia and Laos teetering precariously on the edge of making a parallel mistake as that which led to very tragic results for their countries in the late 1960s and 1970s. . . . We shall see. They have some difficult choices to make. And if they should make wrong choices, they will confront Asean as a whole with difficult choices. We may have to cut loose the two to save the eight" (Kausikan 2020).

8. Kent (2006, 351) also adds that "a key notion for understanding this logic is the Khmer concept *sok*, which translates roughly as well-being or peace of mind. The word *sok* is derived from the Pali term *sukkha*, which means the absence of suffering or, better, the absence of 'unsatisfactoriness' (*dukkha*). According to Buddhist thought, *dukkha* is overcome by transcending the passions and desire, and by practising virtue. Accordingly, well-being comes to mean not simply the abolishment of suffering or uncertainty—since

these are inevitable in life—but rather the ability to limit desire and transcend unsatisfactoriness, both for oneself and for others. The Khmer term *sok* therefore draws upon a system of meaning that goes beyond our [as conceptualized in most work on security studies] notion of security and is inextricably tied to Buddhist understandings of virtue." She notes that a Khmer-English dictionary records four hundred words with *sok* as a root. Other work from Cambodia on these vernacular ontologies of security/insecurity includes Beban and Work (2014), Bennett (2018), Davis (2016), Guillou (2017), and Kidron (2020).

CHAPTER FOUR. KURDISTAN

1. Erbil is sometimes rendered as Arbil or Irbil. In Kurdish it is known as Hewlêr or Hawler.

2. Iraq Body Count keeps a tally of this dreadful toll: www.iraqbodycount.org.

3. See Mohammed Ahmed (2012), Mahir Aziz (2011), Mohammed Ahmed and Michael Gunter (2007), and Faleh Jabar and Hosham Dawod (2006)—especially the chapters therein by Bozarslan, van Bruinessen, Dawod, and Stansfield. All these structures are experienced through gender, given the patrilineal structure of Kurdish societies whereby sovereignty, masculinity, and identity are deeply intertwined (Alinia 2013; Begikhani, Gill, and Hague 2015; Clark 2013; King 2008, 2014; Mojab 2004). Challenges to this patrilineal structure in areas controlled by the PKK and PYD have reworked these gender relations but are beyond our scope here.

4. See David McDowall (2004) for a history up to the American-led invasion of 2003. On Iraqi Kurdistan and the United States, see Douglas Little (2010). Although relations between the Kurdish political parties are not our focus, as we note on the Asayish, it continues to be run on party lines, which articulate with lineage in complex and dynamic ways (Ross and Mohammadpour 2018), adding a further twist to security/territory interface. This interface is also intimately tied to accumulation: the business of petrodollars, commodities, real estate, contracts, patronage, and corruption. In the same year that a valuable primer on these appeared (Leezenberg 2006, since supplemented by Leezenberg 2019), confidential sections of a U.S. diplomatic cable from the Regional Embassy Office (REO) Kirkuk on "Corruption in the Kurdish North" stated that because "formal government [the KRG] is subordinate to the party [KDP and PUK] . . . loyalty became the paramount value; competence and honesty were dismissed. Once in power, party leaders took their rewards; their followers emulate them. Ignorance and ever-present worries about Baghdad also help to keep people's eyes shut to the problem. Thus, in Kurdistan corruption spread from the top down" (U.S. Department of State 2006, para. 3). However, the REO cable goes on to indicate something more like a top-down/bottom-up dialectic in which security is a hinge: "The core of the corruption in both [KDP and PUK controlled areas] i.e., 'the godfathers' as one interlocutor termed them, lies with those who control the security forces. They keep the game running because controlling the guns means they can enforce their illegal contracts. Security forces, and thus corruption networks, depend on their patrons and thus seldom cross party lines, i.e. companies that do business in Erbil do not do business in Sulaymaniyah and vice versa. This extends even to the cell phone industry" (para. 4).

5. The classic (though controversial) account is Kanan Makiya (1998). See Brands and Palkki (2012) for the Ba'athist regime's security-threat conceptions and Martin Dimitrov and Joseph Sassoon (2014) for a comparative study of the single-party security states of Communist Bulgaria and Ba'athist Iraq. The development of a national security state in Iraq is placed in regional contexts by Roger Owen (2014) and Charles Tripp (2013).

6. Although focused on the insurgency that challenged the British mandated state in 1920, Abbas Kadhim (2012) is an instructive short survey. Malik Mufti's book (1996, 9, emphasis original) "tracing the *evolution* of 'stateness'" in Iraq and Syria is also helpful. Both books also problematize the notion of an Iraq conjured up ab initio by the British. Equally, through an account of the development of ideological and nationalist movements prior to the Ba'ath, Johan Franzén (2011) examines the evolution of the Iraqi state, its detractors and development, and Eric Davis (2005) provides a valuable survey of state power and historical memory drawing on a survey of Iraqi sources. Usha Natarajan (2011) stages a suggestive comparison of sovereignty in Mandate (1914–32) and Coalition-occupied (2003–11) Iraq. On opening wider Kurdish histories, see the special issue of *Iranian Studies* guest edited by Djene Bajalan and Sara Zandi Karimi (2014). See Sherko Kirmanj (2014) on Kurdish history textbooks produced by the KRG.

7. A frequent narrative about the Kurds represents them as a nation without a state, as in the English-language version of an influential edited collection, *People without a Country: The Kurds and Kurdistan* (Chaliand 1980). However, as Diane E. King (2014, 234) asks, "What does it mean for an ethnic group to 'have' a state? Does it mean dominating the state, or simply constituting the majority of its citizens? For several hundred years before the European colonial powers created state boundaries throughout the Middle East in the early twentieth century, no ethnic group other than the Turks and Persians 'had' (dominated; constituted the majority in) a state. . . . However, a number of different ethnic groups, including the Kurds and Arabs, 'had' small-scale polities with dynastic leadership governing under loose Ottoman control . . . they were at least very statelike, and at some points in their history had a great deal of autonomy. Kurds may therefore have 'had' more states than many of their ethnic neighbors."

8. Facing the vast literature on biopolitics, we follow Thomas Lemke (2011, 2) in recognizing that "defining biopolitics and determining its meaning is not a value-free activity that follows a universal logic of research. Rather, it is an integral part of a shifting and conflicting theoretical and political field."

9. Drawing on the work of Mat Coleman and other critical scholarship on policing, David Correia and Tyler Wall (2018, 89) describe the checkpoint as "among the most routine and everyday police practices, as is the fear and insecurity it instills." Checkpoints with barrier gates are often outsourced to private security. In the hands of military, checkpoints can become key expressions of power, accompanied by flags and other signs of sovereign claims. On checkpoints as foci in contested postcolonial sovereigntyscapes, see Sidaway (2003). On U.S. counterinsurgency in Iraq and checkpoints, see Gregory (2019). For an analysis from Peshawar, Islamabad, and Lahore, see Maximilian Lohnert (2019) and Alexandra Rijke (2019) on occupied Palestinian territories. Drawing on the Sri Lankan case, Pradeep Jeganathan (2004, 75) describes checkpoints as "located not at the boundary of the state, but at its shifting fluid margins." He points also to their locations "at the boundaries of a target. . . . If the logic of the anticipation of violence creates

a plethora of shifting targets . . . then the checkpoint is an attempt by an agency of the state to control that flickering movement . . . [that] configures practices of anticipation in a double way. On the one hand, to pass through a checkpoint is to remember why checkpoints exist—it is to recall the possibility of a bomb. The few who are, in fact, carrying or have some knowledge of a bomb would also, I imagine, anticipate its explosive impact. But on the other hand, there is another kind of anticipation—that of soldiers checking the flow of traffic and people, asking questions. They are anticipating violence in another way" (69). It is also instructive to compare and contrast the modus operandi of discipline at checkpoints with both the ways that "military technologies and approaches to security 'crossover' into civil and commercial spheres" (Nguyen 2015, 8) elsewhere and the carceral mobilities through which prisoners are moved (Moran, Piacentini, and Pallot 2012). Studying these (in the case of imprisoned asylum seekers in the United Kingdom, some of whom would be Kurds), Nicholas Gill (2009, 195) points to "the politics of mobility not only as an outcome but as part of a process of representation."

10. For accounts of the PKK's ideological trajectory to the mid-2000s, see Aliza Marcus (2007) and Abdullah Özcan (2005). In its earlier years, PKK notions of and claims on territory mirrored those of the Turkish state that it was struggling against. Both saw territory in zero-sum ways, as essentially Turkish or Kurdish, seeking to overwrite each other's and third-party presences (Törne 2015, 28n7). On the subsequent evolution of and influences on the PKK and PYD territorial and political strategy, see Michiel Leezenberg (2016), Marlies Casier and Joost Jongerden (2012), and Jongerden (2019). It is instructive to read these in tandem with the account of Anatolian Kurdish disavowals of the state in Wendelmoet Hamelink and Hanifi Baris (2014), and what Brendan O'Leary (2012, 515) calls "Kurdish strategic adaption, to remake both Iraq and Turkey in their interests."

11. See Nicole Watts (2012) for an account of biopolitics/governance of martyrs and memorials at another site in Kurdistan.

12. On dynamics of the Iranian state project and Kurdish resistance, including cross-border labor, see Kamal Soleimani and Ahmad Mohammadpour (2020a, 2020b) and Shahram Akbarzadeh et al. (2020).

REFERENCES

Abboud, S., O. S. Dahi, W. Hazbun, N. S. Grove, C. P. Hindawi, J. Mouawas, and S. Hermez S. 2018. "Towards a Beirut School of Critical Security Studies." *Critical Studies on Security* 6 (3): 273–95.

Abrahamsen, R., and M. Williams. 2011. *Security beyond the State: Private Security in International Politics.* Cambridge: Cambridge University Press.

Abrams, P. 1988. "Notes on the Difficulty of Studying the State (1977)." *Journal of Historical Sociology* 1: 58–89.

Abulof, U. 2014. "Deep Securitization and Israel's 'Demographic Demon.'" *International Political Sociology* 8 (4): 396–415.

Ahmad, M., and R. Mehmood. 2017. "Surveillance, Authoritarianism and 'Imperial Effects' in Pakistan." *Surveillance & Society* 15 (3): 506–13.

Ahmed, M. M. A. 2012. *Iraqi Kurds and Nation-Building.* London: Palgrave Macmillan.

Ahmed, M. M. A., and M. M. Gunter, eds. 2007. *The Evolution of Kurdish Nationalism.* Costa Mesa, Calif.: Mazda Press.

Akbarzadeh, S., C. Laoutides, W. Gourlay, and Z. S. Ahmed. 2020. "The Iranian Kurds' Transnational Links: Impacts on Mobilization and Political Ambitions." *Ethnic and Racial Studies* 43 (12): 2275–94.

Alexopoulou, K., and D. Juif. 2017. "Colonial State Formation without Integration: Tax Capacity and Labour Regimes in Portuguese Mozambique (1890s–1970s)." *International Review of Social History* 62 (2): 215–52.

Alhadar, I., and M. McCahill. 2011. "The Use of Surveillance Cameras in a Riyadh Shopping Mall: Protecting Profits or Protecting Morality?" *Theoretical Criminology* 15 (3): 315–30.

Alinia, M. 2013. *Honor and Violence Against Women in Iraqi Kurdistan.* New York: Palgrave Macmillan.

Al-Yaqoubi, S. M. 2016. *Refuting ISIS: Destroying Its Religious Foundations and Proving It Has Strayed from Islam and That Fighting It Is an Obligation.* 2nd ed. Herndon VA: Sacred Knowledge.

Amnesty International. 2020a. *Substance Abuses: The Human Cost of Cambodia's Anti-Drug Campaign.* London: Amnesty International. https://www.amnesty.org/en/documents/asa23/2220/2020/en/.

———. 2020b. *Media Freedom in Ashes: Repression of freedom of Expression in Mozambique*. London: Amnesty International. https://www.amnesty.org/en/documents /afr41/2947/2020/en/

Antonsich, M. 2011. "Rethinking Territory." *Progress in Human Geography* 35 (3): 422–25.

Appadurai, A. 1990. "Disjuncture and Difference in the Global Cultural Economy." *Theory, Culture and Society* 7 (2–3): 295–310.

Ashforth, A. 1996. "Of Secrecy and the Commonplace: Witchcraft and Power in Soweto." *Social Research* 62 (4): 1183–34.

———. 1998. "Reflections on Spiritual Insecurity in a Modern African City (Soweto)." *African Studies Review* 41 (3): 39–67.

———. 2005. *Witchcraft, Violence and Democracy in South Africa*. Chicago: University of Chicago Press.

Atia, N. 2019. "Death and Mourning in Contemporary Iraqi Texts." *Interventions* 21 (8): 1068–86.

Auswärtiges Amt, Federal Republic of Germany. 2009. "Mosambik: Reise-und Sicherheit shinweise" [Mozambique: Travel and Safety Information]. https://www.auswaertiges -amt.de/de/aussenpolitik/laender/mosambik-node/mosambiksicherheit/221782.

Ayling, J., and P. Grabosky. 2006. "When Police Go Shopping." *Policing* 29 (4): 665–90.

Aziz, M. A. 2011. *The Kurds of Iraq: Nationalism and Identity in Iraqi Kurdistan*. London: I.B. Taurus.

Bacik, G., and B. B. Coskun. 2011. "The PKK Problem: Explaining Turkey's Failure to Develop a Political Solution." *Studies in Conflict and Terrorism* 34 (3): 248–65.

Bajalan, D., and S. Z. Karimi, eds. 2014. "The Kurds and Their History: New Perspectives." Special issue of *Iranian Studies* 47 (5): 679–855.

Baker, B. 2003. "Policing and the Rule of Law in Mozambique." *Policing and Society* 13 (2): 139–58.

Baker, P. 2012. "Obama, in Cambodia, Sidesteps Ghosts of American Wartime Past." *New York Times*, 20 November. https://nyti.ms/RScqp9.

Baldwin, J. 1963. *The Fire Next Time*. New York: Dial Press.

Balzacq, T., T. Basaran, D. Bigo, E.-P. Guittet, and C. Olsson. 2010. "Security Practices." In *The International Studies Encyclopedia Online*, edited by R. A. Denemark, 1–30. Oxford: Wiley-Blackwell.

Barker, K. 2015. "Biosecurity: Securing Circulations from the Microbe to the Macrocosm." *Geographical Journal* 181 (4): 357–65.

Barnett, C. 2015. "On the Milieu of Security: Situating the Emergence of New Spaces of Public Action." *Dialogues in Human Geography* 5 (3): 257–70.

Bartu, P. 2010. "Wrestling with the Integrity of a Nation: The Disputed Internal Boundaries in Iraq." *International Affairs* 86 (6): 1329–43.

BBC News. 2010. "Deadly Riots in Mozambique over Rising Prices." 1 September. https:// www.bbc.com/news/world-africa-11150063.

Beban, A., L. Schoenberger, and V. Lamb. 2020. "Pockets of Liberal Media in Authoritarian Regimes: What the Crackdown on Emancipatory Spaces Means for Rural Social Movements in Cambodia." *Journal of Peasant Studies* 47 (1): 95–115.

Beban, A., and C. Work. 2014. "The Spirits Are Crying: Dispossessing Land and Possessing Bodies in Rural Cambodia." *Antipode* 46 (3): 593–610.

Beckett, L. 2020. "'All the Psychoses of US History': How America Is Victim-Blaming the Coronavirus Dead." *Guardian*, 21 May. https://www.theguardian.com/world/2020/may/21/all-the-psychoses-of-us-history-how-america-is-victim-blaming-the-coronavirus-dead.

Begikhani, N., A. K. Gill, and G. Hague. 2015. *Honour-Based Violence: Experiences and Counter-strategies in Iraqi Kurdistan and the UK Kurdish Diaspora*. Farnham: Ashgate.

Belew, K. 2018. *Bring the War Home: The White Power Movement and Paramilitary America*. Cambridge, Mass.: Harvard University Press.

Belkaïd, A. 2019. "Turkey and Russia Redraw the Map in Northeast Syria." *Le Monde Diplomatique*, November. https://mondediplo.com/2019/11/02turkey.

Bengio, O. 2011. "The 'Kurdish Spring' in Turkey and Its Impact on Turkish Foreign Relations in the Middle East." *Turkish Studies* 12 (4): 619–32.

Bènit-Gbaffou, C., S. Didier, and E. Peyroux. 2012. "Circulation of Security Models in Southern African Cities: Between Neoliberal Encroachment and Local Power Dynamics." *International Journal of Urban and Regional Research* 36 (5): 877–89.

Bennett, C. 2018. "Living with the Dead in the Killing Fields of Cambodia." *Journal of Southeast Asian Studies* 49 (2): 184–203.

Bennett, J. R. 2010. "Cambodia: Military, Inc." ISN Security Watch series, 16 August. Centre for Security Studies, ETH Zurich. https://www.ethz.ch/content/specialinterest/gess/cis/center-for-securities-studies/en/services/digital-library/articles/article.html/120178.

Bertelsen, B. E. 2009. "Sorcery and Death Squads: Transformations of State, Sovereignty, and Violence in Postcolonial Mozambique." In *Crisis of the State: War and Social Upheaval*, edited by B. Kapferer and B. E. Bertelsen, 210–40. New York: Berghahn Books.

———. 2016. "Effervescence and Ephemerality: Popular Urban Uprisings in Mozambique." *Ethnos: Journal of Anthropology* 81 (1): 25–52.

Bertelsen, B. E., I. Tvedten, and S. Roque. 2014. "Engaging, Transcending and Subverting Dichotomies: Discursive Dynamics of Maputo's Urban Space." *Urban Studies* 51 (13): 2752–69.

Bevins, V. 2020. *The Jakarta Method: Washington's Anticommunist Crusade and the Mass Murder Program That Shaped Our World*. New York: PublicAffairs.

Bilgic, A. 2014. "Exploring 'What's Good about Security': Politics of Security during the Dissolution of Yugoslavia." *Journal of Balkan and Near Eastern Studies* 16 (2): 260–78.

Bishara, F. A. 2020. "The Many Voyages of *Fateh Al-Khayr*: Unfurling the Gulf in the Age of Oceanic History." *International Journal of Middle East Studies* 52: 397–412.

Björkdahl, A. 2013. "Urban Peacekeeping." *Peacebuilding* 1 (2): 207–21.

Blakely, E. J., and M. G. Snyder. 1999. *Fortress America: Gated Communities in the United States*. Washington, D.C.: Brookings Institution Press.

Bonnett, A. 2009. "The Dilemmas of Radical Nostalgia in British Psychogeography." *Theory, Culture, and Society* 26 (1): 45–70.

Boria, E. 2008. "Geopolitical Maps: A Sketch of a Neglected Trend in Cartography." *Geopolitics* 13 (2): 278–308.

Botterill, K., P. Hopkins, and G. Sanghera. 2020. "Familial Geopolitics and Ontological Security: Intergenerational Relations, Migration and Minority Youth (In)securities in Scotland." *Geopolitics* 25 (5): 1138–63.

Bovensiepen, J. 2009. "Spiritual Landscapes of Life and Death in the Central Highlands of East Timor." *Anthropological Forum* 19 (3): 323–38.

Bozarslan, H. 2014. "The Kurds and Middle Eastern 'State of Violence': The 1980s and 2010s." *Kurdish Studies* 2 (1): 4–13.

Brady, B. 2010. "The Cambodian Army: Open for Corporate Sponsors." *Time*, 9 June. http://www.time.com/time/world/article/0,8599,1995298,00.html.

Brandon, J. 2006. "Mount Qandil: A Safe Haven for Kurdish Militants—Part 1." *Terrorism Monitor* 4 (17): 1–3.

Brands, H., and D. Palkki. 2012. "'Conspiring Bastards': Saddam Hussein's Strategic View of the United States." *Diplomatic History* 36 (3): 625–59.

Brickell, K. 2014. "'The Whole World Is Watching': Intimate Geopolitics of Forced Eviction and Women's Activism in Cambodia." *Annals of the Association of American Geographers* 104 (6): 1256–72.

———. 2020. *Home SOS: Gender, Violence, and Survival in Crisis Ordinary Cambodia*. Chichester: John Wiley.

Bridger, A. J. 2013. "Psychogeography and Feminist Methodology." *Feminism & Psychology* 23 (3): 285–98.

Brigden, N., and M. Hallet, eds. 2021. "Fieldwork as Social Transfomation: Place, Time and Power in a Violent Moment." Special issue, *Geopolitics* 26 (1).

Broadhurst, R. 2002. "Lethal Violence, Crime and State Formation in Cambodia." *Australian and New Zealand Journal of Criminology* 35 (1): 1–26.

Broadhurst, R., and T. Bouhours. 2009. "Policing in Cambodia: Legitimacy in the Making?" *Policing and Society* 19 (2): 174–90.

Browne, S. 2015. *Park Mothers: On the Surveillance of Blackness*. Durham, N.C.: Duke University Press.

Bubandt, N. 2005. "Vernacular Security: The Politics of Feeling Safe in Global, National and Local Worlds." *Security Dialogue* 36 (3): 275–96.

Bunnell, T., and A. Maringanti. 2010. "Practising Urban and Regional Research beyond Metrocentricity." *International Journal of Urban and Regional Research* 34 (2): 415–20.

Butler, J. 2004. *Precarious Life: The Powers of Mourning and Violence*. London: Verso.

Button, M., and T. John. 2002. "'Plural Policing' in Action: A Review of the Policing of Environmental Protests in England and Wales." *Policing and Society* 12 (2): 111–21.

Buur, L., and J. Sumich. 2019. "'No Smoke without Fire': Citizenship and Securing Economic Enclaves in Mozambique." *Development and Change* 50: 1579–1601.

Buzan, B. 1983. *People, States, and Fear: The National Security Problem in International Relations*. Chapel Hill: University of North Carolina Press.

Byler, D. 2019. "China's Hi-Tech War on Its Muslim Minority." *Guardian*, 11 April. https://

www.theguardian.com/news/2019/apr/11/china-hi-tech-war-on-muslim-minority
-xinjiang-uighurs-surveillance-face-recognition.

Cachinho, H. 2014. "Consumerscapes and the Resilience Assessment of Urban Retail
Systems." *Cities* 36: 131–44.

Cahen, M. 2015. "Review of Stephen A. Emerson *The Battle for Mozambique: The
Frelimo-Renamo Struggle (1977–1992)*." *H-Luso-Africa, H-Net Reviews*, January.
https://www.h-net.org/reviews/showrev.php?id=42879.

Caldeira, T. P. R. 2001. *City of Walls: Crime, Segregation and Citizenship in São Paulo*.
Berkeley: University of California Press.

Campbell, D. 1998. *Writing Security: United States Foreign Policy and the Politics of Identity*. Rev. ed. Minneapolis: University of Minnesota Press.

Carbone, G. M. 2005. *"Continuidade na renovação?* Ten Years of Multiparty Politics in
Mozambique: Roots, Evolution and Stabilisation of the Frelimo-Renamo Party System." *Journal of Modern African Studies* 43 (3): 417–42.

Casier, M., and J. Jongerden. 2012. "Understanding Today's Kurdish Movement: Leftist
Heritage, Martyrdom, Democracy and Gender." *European Journal of Turkish Studies*
14: 1–10. http://ejts.revues.org/4656.

Castela, T., and M. P. Menses. 2016. "Naming the Urban in Twentieth-Century Mozambique: Towards Spatial Histories of Aspiration and Violence." In *Urban Planning in
Lusophone African Countries*, edited by C. N. Silva, 215–24. Abingdon: Routledge.

Chakrya, K. S. 2012. "Cops Ejected from Boeung Kak Press Event." *Phnom Penh Post*, 4
April. https://www.phnompenhpost.com/national/cops-ejected-boeung-kak-press
-event.

Chaliand, G., ed. 1980. *A People without a Country: The Kurds and Kurdistan*. Translated
by M. Pallis. London: Zed Press.

Chambers, P. W. 2015. "'Neo-sultanistic Tendencies': The Trajectory of Civil-Military Relations in Cambodia." *Asian Security* 11 (3): 179–205.

Chanda, N. 1986. *Brother Enemy: The War after the War*. New York: Harcourt.

Chandler, D. 2007. "The Security-Development Nexus and the Rise of 'Anti-Foreign Policy.'" *Journal of International Relations and Development* 10 (4): 362–86.

Chapman, D. P. 2009. "Security Forces of the Kurdistan Regional Government." USAWC
Research Project. Carlisle, Pa.: U.S. Army War College. https://apps.dtic.mil/dtic/tr
/fulltext/u2/a510826.pdf.

Chazkel, A., M. Kim, and A. N. Paik. 2020. "Worlds without Police." *Radical History Review* 137: 1–12.

Chen, B., S. Marvin, and A. While. 2020. "Containing COVID-19 in China: AI and the Ro-
botic Restructuring of Future Cities." *Dialogues in Human Geography* 10 (2): 238–41.

Chester, E. T. 2001. *Rag-Tags, Scum, Riff-Raff and Commies: The U.S. Intervention in the
Dominican Republic, 1965–1966*. New York: Monthly Review Press.

Clark, J. H. 2013. "'My Life Is Like a Novel': Embodied Geographies of Security in Southeast Turkey." *Geopolitics* 18 (4): 835–55.

Clymer, K. 2004. *The United States and Cambodia, 1969–2000: A Troubled Relationship*.
London: Routledge.

Coaffee, J. 2004. "Rings of Steel, Rings of Concrete and Rings of Confidence: Designing

Out Terrorism in Central London Pre and Post September 11th." *International Journal of Urban and Regional Research* 28 (1): 201–11.

Cobb, J. 2020. "An American Spring of Reckoning." *New Yorker*, 22 June. https://www.newyorker.com/magazine/2020/06/22/an-american-spring-of-reckoning.

Cock, A. R. 2010. "External Actors and the Relative Autonomy of the Ruling Elite in Post-UNTAC Cambodia." *Journal of Southeast Asian Studies* 41 (2): 241–65.

Cohn, C. 1987. "Sex and Death in the Rational World of Defense Intellectuals." *Signs* 12 (4): 687–718.

Coleman, M. 2016. "State Power in Blue." *Political Geography* 51 (1): 76–86.

Collins, A., ed. 2012. *Contemporary Security Studies*. Oxford: Oxford University Press.

Comaroff, J., and J. Comaroff. 2016. *The Truth about Crime: Sovereignty, Knowledge, Social Order*. Chicago: University of Chicago Press.

Condos, M. 2017. *The Insecurity State: Punjab and the Making of Colonial Power in British India*. Cambridge: Cambridge University Press.

Correia, D., and T. Wall. 2018. *Police: A Field Guide*. London: Verso.

Côté-Boucher, K., F. Infantino, and M. B. Salter. 2014. "Border Security as Practice: An Agenda for Research." *Security Dialogue* 45 (3): 195–208.

Cowen, D. 2014. *The Deadly Life of Logistics: Mapping Violence in Global Trade*. Minneapolis: University of Minnesota Press.

Cowen, D., and N. Lewis. 2016. "Anti-Blackness and Urban Geopolitical Economy." https://www.societyandspace.org/articles/anti-blackness-and-urban-geopolitical-economy.

Cowen, D., and A. Siciliano. 2011. "Surplus Masculinities and Security." *Antipode* 43 (5): 1516–41.

Craggs, R. 2012. "Towards a Political Geography of Hotels: Southern Rhodesia, 1958–1962." *Political Geography* 31 (4): 215–24.

Crawford, A., S. Lister, S. Blackburn, and J. Burnett. 2005. *Plural Policing: The Mixed Economy of Visible Patrols in England and Wales*. Bristol: Policy Press.

Culcasi, K. 2006. "Cartographically Constructing Kurdistan within Geopolitical and Orientalist Discourses." *Political Geography* 25 (6): 680–706.

Datta, A. 2016. "The Genderscapes of Hate: On Violence Against Women in India." *Dialogues in Human Geography* 6 (2): 178–81.

Datta, A., and N. Ahmed. 2020. "Intimate Infrastructures: The Rubrics of Gendered Safety and Urban Violence in Kerala, India." *Geoforum* 110: 67–76.

Davis, E. 2005. *Memories of State: Politics, History, and Collective Identity in Modern Iraq*. Berkeley: University of California Press.

Davis, E. W. 2011. "Imagined Parasites: Flows of Monies and Spirits." In *Cambodia's Economic Transformation*, edited by C Hughes and K. Un, 310–29. Copenhagen: NIAS Press.

———. 2016. *Deathpower: Buddhism's Ritual Imagination in Cambodia*. New York: Columbia University Press.

Davis, S. 2015. *The Empires' Edge: Militarization, Resistance, and Transcending Hegemony in the Pacific*. Athens: University of Georgia Press.

Debord, G.-E. (1955) 2006. "Introduction to a Critique of Urban Geography." Translated by K. Knabb. http://www.bopsecrets.org/SI/urbgeog.htm.

de Goede, M. 2012. *Speculative Security: The Politics of Pursuing Terrorist Monies.* Minneapolis: University of Minnesota Press.

de Guevara, B. B., and M. Bøås, eds. 2020. *Doing Fieldwork in Areas of International Intervention: A Guide to Research in Violent and Closed Contexts.* Bristol: Bristol University Press.

Denham, D. D. 2020. "The Logistics of Police Power: Armored Vehicles, Colonial Boomerangs, and Strategies of Circulation." *Environment and Planning D: Society and Space* 37 (6): 1045–63.

Devermont, J., and E. Columbo. 2019. *Northern Mozambique at a Crossroads: Scenarios for Violence in Resource-Rich Cabo Delgado Province.* Washington, D.C.: Center for Strategic and International Studies.

Dick, H. W. 2003. *Surabaya, City of Work: A Socioeconomic History, 1900–2000.* Singapore: NUS Press.

Dimitrov, M. K., and J. Sassoon. 2014. "State Security, Information and Repression: A Comparison of Communist Bulgaria and Ba'thist Iraq." *Journal of Cold War Studies* 18 (2): 3–31.

Dinerman, A. 2006. *Revolution, Counter-revolution and Revisionism in Postcolonial Africa: The Case of Mozambique, 1975–1994.* London: Routledge.

Dittmer, J., and N. Gray. 2010. "Popular Geopolitics 2.0: Towards New Methodologies of the Everyday." *Geography Compass* 4 (11): 1664–77.

Doyle, D., and T. Dunning. 2018. "Recognizing Fragmented Authority: Towards a Post-Westphalian Security Order in Iraq." *Small Wars and Insurgencies* 29 (3): 537–59.

Duffield, M. 2007. *Development, Security and Unending War: Governing the World of Peoples.* Cambridge: Polity.

Duggan, S. J. 1997. "The Role of International Organisations in the Financing of Higher Education in Cambodia." *Higher Education* 34 (1): 1–22.

Dumbrell, J., and D. Ryan, eds. 2007. *Vietnam in Iraq: Tactics, Lessons, Legacies and Ghosts.* London: Routledge.

Dundar, F. 2012. "'Statisquo': British Use of Statistics in the Iraqi Kurdish Question (1919–1932)." Crown Paper 7, Crown Center for Middle East Studies, Brandeis University. http://www.brandeis.edu/crown/publications/cp/CP7.pdf.

Dupont, B., P. Grabosky, and C. Shearing. 2003. "The Governance of Security in Weak and Failing States." *Criminology and Criminal Justice* 3 (4): 331–49.

Economist. 2013. "America, Vietnam and Cambodia: Realpolitik Redux." 3 August. https://www.economist.com/asia/2013/08/03/realpolitik-redux.

———. 2015. "Mozambique: A Tuna Scandal Strikes." 7 August. https://www.economist.com/middle-east-and-africa/2015/08/07/a-tuna-scandal-strikes.

Edwards, P. 2007. *Cambodge: The Cultivation of a Nation, 1860–1945.* Honolulu: University of Hawai'i Press.

Elden, S. 2010. "Land, Terrain, Territory." *Progress in Human Geography* 34 (6): 799–817.

———. 2014. *The Birth of Territory.* Chicago: University of Chicago Press.

———. 2015. "From Hinterland to the Global: New Books on Historical and Political Understandings of Territory." *Environment and Planning D* 33 (1): 185–90.

Ellis-Petersen, H. 2018. "'No Cambodia Left': How Chinese Money Is Changing Sihanoukville." *Guardian*, 31 July. https://www.theguardian.com/cities/2018/jul/31/no-cambodia-left-chinese-money-changing-sihanoukville.

Eng, N., and C. Hughes. 2017. "Coming of Age in Peace, Prosperity, and Connectivity: Cambodia's Young Electorate and Its Impact on the Ruling Party's Political Strategies." *Critical Asian Studies* 49 (3): 396–410.

Enloe, C. 2010. *Nimo's War, Emma's War: Making Feminist Sense of the Iraq War*. Berkeley: University of California Press.

Enzensberger, H. M. 2019. *Anarchy's Brief Summer: The Life and Death of Buenaventura Durruti*. Translated by M. Mitchell. Kolkata: Seagull Books.

Eski, Y. 2016. *Policing, Port Security and Crime Control: An Ethnography of the Port Securityscape*. London: Routledge.

Evans, G. 1998. *The Politics of Ritual and Remembrance: Laos since 1975*. Honolulu: University of Hawai'i Press.

Evans, G., and K. Rowley. 1984. *Red Brotherhood at War: Indochina since the Fall of Saigon*. London: Verso.

Farouk-Sluglett, M., P. Sluglett, and J. Stok. 1984. "Not Quite Armageddon: Impact of the War on Iraq." *MERIP Reports* 125/126: 22–30, 37.

Fauveaud, G. 2014. "Mutations of Real Estate Actors' Strategies and Modes of Capital Appropriation in Contemporary Phnom Penh." *Urban Studies* 51 (16): 3479–94.

Feldman, I. 2015. *Police Encounters: Security and Surveillance in Gaza under Egyptian Rule*. Stanford, Calif.: Stanford University Press.

Feldman, S., G. A. Menon, and C. Geisler. 2011. "Introduction: A New Politics of Containment." In *Accumulating Insecurity: Violence and Dispossession in the Making of Everyday Life*, edited by S. Feldman, 1–20. Athens: University of Georgia Press.

Fergie, D. 2019. "Geopolitics Turned Inwards: The Princeton Military Studies Group and the National Security Imagination." *Diplomatic History* 43 (4): 644–70.

Ferguson, J. 2005. "Seeing Like an Oil Company: Space, Security, and Global Capital in Neoliberal Africa." *American Anthropologist* 107 (3): 377–82.

———. 2007. *Global Shadows: Africa in the Neoliberal World Order*. Durham, N.C.: Duke University Press.

Filippi, J.-M. 2012. *Strolling around Phnom Penh*. Phnom Penh: Kam Éditions.

Finnegan, W. 1992. *A Complicated War: The Harrowing of Mozambique*. Berkeley: University of California Press.

Fluri, J., and R. Lehr. 2017. *The Carpetbaggers of Kabul and Other American-Afghan Entanglements*. Athens: University of Georgia Press.

Folio, F., C. Marlen, and L. C. Mutisse. 2017. "Crime, State and Civil Society Responses in Maputo (Mozambique): Between Privatisation and Civilization." *African Studies* 76 (2): 260–80.

Foreign and Commonwealth Office. 2009. "Foreign Travel Advice—Mozambique." https://webarchive.nationalarchives.gov.uk/20090430200305/http://www.fco.gov.uk

/en/travelling-and-living-overseas/travel-advice-by-country/sub-saharan-africa/mozambique.

Foucault, M. 2009. "Lecture of 1 February 1978." In *Security, Territory, Population: Lectures at the Collège de France, 1977–78*, edited by M. Senellart, translated by G. Burchell, 87–114. London: Palgrave Macmillan.

———. 2010. "Right of Death and Power over Life." In *The Foucault Reader*, edited by P. Rabinow, 258–72. New York: Vintage.

Franceschini, I. 2020. "As Far Apart as Earth and Sky: A Survey of Chinese and Cambodian Construction Workers in Sihanoukville." *Critical Asian Studies* 52: 512–29. https://doi.org/10.1080/14672715.2020.1804961.

Franzén, J. 2011. *Red Star over Iraq: Iraqi Communism before Saddam*. London: Hurst.

Freeman, J. 2010. "From the Little Tree, Half a Block toward the Lake: Popular Geography and Symbolic Discontent in Post-Sandinista Managua." *Antipode* 42 (2): 336–73.

Fregonese, S. 2012. "Beyond the 'Weak State': Hybrid Sovereignties in Beirut." *Environment and Planning D* 30 (4): 655–74.

———. 2017. "Affective Atmospheres, Urban Geopolitics and Conflict (De)escalation in Beirut." *Political Geography* 61 (November): 1–10.

Fregonese, S., and A. Ramadan. 2015. "Hotel Geopolitics: A Research Agenda." *Geopolitics* 20 (4): 793–813.

Friis, S. 2014. "Sammelrez: Security and Development: Critical Reflections on a Conceptual and Political Nexus. Reviews of Ramses Amer et al. *The Security-Development Nexus: Peace, Conflict and Development*; Joanna Spear & Paul Williams *Security and Development in Global Politics: A Critical Comparison*; and Neclâ Tschirgi et al. *Security and Development: Searching for Critical Connections*." *H-Net Online*, October. https://www.h-net.org/reviews/showpdf.php?id=42577.

Gaddis, J. L. 2005. *Strategies of Containment: A Critical Appraisal of American National Security Policy during the Cold War*. Rev. ed. Oxford: Oxford University Press.

Gainsborough, M. 2012. "Elites vs. Reform in Laos, Cambodia and Vietnam." *Journal of Democracy* 23 (2): 34–46.

Gandy, M. 2005. "Learning from Lagos." *New Left Review* 33 (May–June): 36–52.

———. 2006. "Planning, Anti-planning and the Infrastructure Crisis Facing Metropolitan Lagos." *Urban Studies* 43 (2): 371–96.

Garrett, B. L. 2014. *Explore Everything: Place Hacking and the City*. London: Verso.

Garver, J. W., and F.-L. Wang. 2010. "China's Anti-encirclement Struggle." *Asian Security* 6 (3): 238–61.

Gąsior-Niemiec, A., G. Glasze, and R. A. Pütz. 2009. "Glimpse over the Rising Walls: The Reflection of Post-Communist Transformation in the Polish Discourse of Gated Communities." *East European Politics and Societies* 23 (2): 244–65.

Ghertner, D. A. 2015. *Rule by Aesthetics: World-Class City Making in Delhi*. Oxford: Oxford University Press.

Gill, N. 2009. "Governmental Mobility: The Power Effects of the Movement of Detained Asylum Seekers around Britain's Detention Estate." *Political Geography* 28 (3): 186–96.

Giry, S. 2014. "The Genocide That Wasn't." *New York Review of Books*, 25 August. https://www.nybooks.com/daily/2014/08/25/khmer-rouge-genocide-wasnt/.

Glassman, J., and Y.-J. Choi. 2014. "The Chaebol and the US Military–Industrial Complex: Cold War Geopolitical Economy and South Korean Industrialization." *Environment and Planning A* 46 (5): 1160–80.

Glawion, T. 2020. *The Security Arena in Africa: Local Order-Making in the Central African Republic, Somaliland, and South Sudan*. Cambridge: Cambridge University Press.

Glennon, M. J. 2015. *National Security and Double Government*. Oxford: Oxford University Press.

Global Witness. 2016. *Hostile Takeover: The Corporate Empire of Cambodia's Ruling Family*. London: Global Witness.

Glück, Z. 2015. "Piracy and the Production of Security Space." *Environment and Planning D* 33 (4): 642–59.

Go, J. 2020. "The Imperial Origins of American Policing: Militarization and Imperial Feedback in the Early 20th Century." *American Journal of Sociology* 125 (5): 1193–254.

Goldsmith, A. 2002. "Policing Weak States: Citizen Safety and State Responsibility." *Policing and Society* 13 (1): 3–21.

Goldstein, D. M. 2010. "Toward a Critical Anthropology of Security. *Current Anthropology* 51 (4): 487–517.

———. 2012. *Outlawed: Between Security and Violence in a Bolivian City*. Durham, N.C.: Duke University Press.

Gottesman, E. W. 2004. *Cambodia after the Khmer Rouge: Inside the Politics of Nation-Building*. New Haven, Conn.: Yale University Press.

Gourlay, W. 2018. "Kurdayetî: Pan-Kurdish Solidarity and Cross-Border Links in Times of War and Trauma." *Middle East Critique* 27 (1): 25–42.

Graham, S. 2006. "Cities and the 'War on Terror.'" *International Journal of Urban and Regional Research* 30 (2): 255–76.

———. 2010. *Cities under Siege: The New Military Urbanism*. London: Verso.

———. 2012. "When Life Itself Is War: On the Urbanization of Military and Security Doctrine." *International Journal of Urban and Regional Research* 36 (1): 136–55.

Green, N. 2014. "Rethinking the 'Middle East' after the Oceanic Turn." *Comparative Studies of South Asia, Africa and the Middle East* 34 (3): 556–64.

Green, N., and N. Arbabzadah. 2013. "Preface and Acknowledgements." In *Afghanistan in Ink: Literature between Diaspora and Nation*, edited by N. Green and N. Arbabzadah, xv–xviii. New York: Columbia University Press.

Greenwald, G. 2014. *No Place to Hide: Edward Snowden, the NSA and the U.S. Surveillance State*. London: Hamish Hamilton.

Gregory, T. 2019. "Dangerous Feelings: Checkpoints and the Perception of Hostile Intent." *Security Dialogue* 50 (2): 131–47.

Grewal, I. 2006. "'Security Moms' in the Early Twentieth-Century United States: The Gender of Security in Neoliberalism." *Women's Studies Quarterly* 34 (1/2): 25–39.

Guillou, A. Y. 2017. "Khmer Potent Places: *Pāramī* and the Localisation of Buddhism and Monarchy in Cambodia." *Asia Pacific Journal of Anthropology* 18 (5): 421–43.

Gunter, M. 2011. *The Kurds Ascending: The Evolving Solution to the Kurdish Problem in Iraq and Turkey*. New York: Palgrave Macmillan.

———. 2014. *Out of Nowhere: The Kurds of Syria in Peace and War*. London: Hurst.

Gupta, P. 2018. *Portuguese Decolonization in the Indian Ocean World: History and Ethnography*. London: Bloomsbury.

Gupta, P., and E. Rodary. 2017. "Opening-Up Mozambique: Histories of the Present." *African Studies* 76 (2): 179–87.

Gupte, J. 2017. "'These Streets Are Ours': Mumbai's Urban Form and Security in the Vernacular." *Peacebuilding* 5 (2): 203–17.

Gurses, M. 2020. "The Evolving Kurdish Question in Turkey." *Middle East Critique* 29 (3): 307–18.

Gusterson, H. 2004. *People of the Bomb: Portraits of America's Nuclear Complex*. Minneapolis: University of Minnesota Press.

Hagberg, S. 2019. "Ethnography In/Of the Red Zone: Challenges, Frustrations, Engagements." *Mande Studies* 21: 13–31.

Haggerty, K. D., and R. V. Ericson. 2000. "The Surveillant Assemblage." *British Journal of Sociology* 51 (4): 605–22.

Hall, M., and T. Young. 1997. *Confronting Leviathan: Mozambique since Independence*. London: Hurst.

Halliday, F. 1986. *The Making of the Second Cold War*. 2nd ed. London: Verso.

Halper, J. 2015. *War against the People: Israel, the Palestinians and Global Pacification*. London: Pluto Press.

Hama, H. H. 2020. "Iraqi Kurdistan's 2017 Independence Referendum: The KDP's Public and Private Motives." *Asian Affairs* 51 (1): 109–25.

Hamdan, A. N. 2016. "Breaker of Barriers? Notes on the Geopolitics of the Islamic State in Iraq and Sham." *Geopolitics* 21 (3): 605–27.

Hamelink, W., and H. Baris. 2014. "Dengbêjs on Borderlands: Borders and the State as Seen through the Eyes of Kurdish Singer-Poets." *Kurdish Studies* 2 (1): 34–60.

Hanlon, J. 2007. "Is Poverty Decreasing in Mozambique?" Paper presented at the Inaugural Conference of the Instituto de Estudos Sociais e Económicos (IESE), Maputo, 19 September. https://www.iese.ac.mz/~ieseacmz/lib/publication/Hanlon,Joseph_Poverty.pdf.

———. 2009. "Mozambique: The Panic of the Poor." *Review of African Political Economy* 36 (119): 125–30.

———. 2010. "Mozambique: 'The War Ended 15 Years Ago, but We Are Still Poor.'" *Conflict, Security & Development* 10 (1): 77–102.

———. 2017. "Following the Donor-Designed Path to Mozambique's US$2.2 Billion Secret Debt Deal." *Third World Quarterly* 38 (3): 753–70.

Harms, E. 2011. *Saigon's Edge: On the Margins of Ho Chi Minh City*. Minneapolis: University of Minnesota Press.

———. 2012. "Beauty as Control in the New Saigon: Eviction, New Urban Zones, and Atomized Dissent in a Southeast Asian City. *American Ethnologist* 39 (4): 735–50.

Harvey, D. 1982. *The Limits to Capital*. Oxford: Basil Blackwell.

———. 1985. "The Geopolitics of Capitalism." In *Social Relations and Spatial Structures*, edited by D. Gregory and J. Urry, 128–63. Basingstoke: Macmillan.

———. 1989. *The Urban Experience.* Oxford: Basil Blackwell.

Hawkins, T. Y. 2009. "Violent Death as Essential Truth in *Dispatches*: Re-reading Michael Herr's 'Secret History' of the Vietnam War." *War, Literature & the Arts* 21 (1–2): 129–43.

Haysom, S. 2018. *Where Crime Compounds Conflict: Understanding Northern Mozambique's Vulnerabilities.* Geneva: Global Initiative Against Transnational Organized Crime.

Hazbun, W. 2018. "American Interventionism and the Geopolitical Roots of Yemen's Catastrophe." *Middle East Report* 289 (Winter): 32–37.

Heath-Kelly, C. 2020. "Designing the Pentagon Memorial: Gendered Statecraft, Heroic Victimhood and Site Authenticity in War on Terror Commemoration." *Critical Military Studies* 6 (3–4): 269–86.

Hemmersam, P., and A. Morrison. 2016. "Place Mapping—Transect Walks in Arctic Urban Landscapes." *SPOOL* 3 (1): 23–36.

Herr, M. 1977. *Dispatches.* New York: Knopf.

Higate, P., and M. Henry. 2009. *Insecure Spaces: Peacekeeping, Power and Performance in Haiti, Kosovo and Liberia.* London: Zed.

Hills, A. 2014. "Somalia Works: Police Development as State Building." *African Affairs* 113 (450): 88–107.

Hinnebusch, R. 2007. "The US Invasion of Iraq: Explanations and Implications." *Critique: Critical Middle Eastern Studies* 16 (3): 209–28.

Hinton, E. 2017. *From the War on Poverty to the War on Crime: The Making of Mass Incarceration in America.* Cambridge, Mass.: Harvard University Press.

Hörschelmann, K., and E. Reich. 2017. "Entangled (In)securities: Sketching the Scope of Geosocial Approaches for Understanding 'Webs of (In)security.'" *Geopolitics* 22 (1): 73–90.

Houssay-Holzschuch, M., and A. Teppo. 2009. "A Mall for All? Race and Public Space in Post-apartheid Cape Town." *Cultural Geographies* 16 (3): 351–79.

Huang, T. M. 2004. *Walking between Slums and Skyscrapers: Illusions of Open Space in Hong Kong, Tokyo and Shanghai.* Hong Kong: Hong Kong University Press.

Hughes, C. 2003. *The Political Economy of Cambodia's Transition, 1991–2001.* London: Routledge.

Hughes, C., and K. Un. 2011. "Cambodia's Economic Transformation: Historical and Theoretical Frameworks." In *Cambodia's Economic Transformation,* edited by C. Hughes and K. Un, 1–26. Copenhagen: NIAS Press.

Hughes, R. 2008. "Dutiful Tourism: Encountering the Cambodian Genocide." *Asia Pacific Viewpoint* 49 (3): 318–30.

Human Rights Watch. 2019. "'Everyone Must Confess': Abuses Against Children Suspected of ISIS Affiliation in Iraq." March. https://www.hrw.org/sites/default/files/report_pdf/iraq0319_web_1.pdf.

———. 2020a. "Cambodia: Covid-19 Spurs Bogus 'Fake News' Arrests." 29 April. https://www.hrw.org/news/2020/04/29/cambodia-covid-19-spurs-bogus-fake-news-arrests.

———. 2020b. "Cambodia: Hun Sen and His Abusive Generals. Video Shows Unexplained Wealth of 'Dirty Dozen' as Number of Political Prisoners Mounts." 22 October. https://www.hrw.org/news/2020/10/22/cambodia-hun-sen-and-his-abusive-generals.

Hunt, L. 2015. "Cambodia's Well-Heeled Military Patrons." *Diplomat,* 10 August. https://thediplomat.com/2015/08/cambodias-well-heeled-military-patrons/.

Hutta, J. S. 2009. "Geographies of *Geborgenheit*: Beyond Feelings of Safety and the Fear of Crime." *Environment and Planning D* 27 (2): 251–27.

Igreja, V. 2008. "Memories as Weapons: The Politics of Peace and Silence in Post–Civil War Mozambique." *Journal of Southern African Studies* 34 (3): 539–56.

Inhorn, M. C. 2015. *Cosmopolitan Conceptions: IVF Sojourns in Global Dubai*. Durham, N.C.: Duke University Press.

Jabar, F. A., and H. Dawod, eds. 2006. *The Kurds: Nationalism and Politics*. London: Saqi.

Jaffe, R., ed. 2017. "The City at War: Reflections on Paris, Beirut, Brussels, and Beyond." *International Journal of Urban and Regional Research.* https://www.ijurr.org/spotlight-on/the-city-at-war-reflections-on-beirut-brussels-and-beyond/the-city-at-war/.

Jaffe, R., and T. Diphoorn. 2019. "Old Boys and Badmen: Private Security in (Post)colonial Jamaica." *Interventions* 21 (7): 909–27.

Jarvis, L., and J. Holland. 2015. *Security: A Critical Introduction*. New York: Palgrave Macmillan.

Jeganathan, P. 2004. "Checkpoint: Anthropology, Identity and the State." In *Anthropology in the Margins of the State*, edited by V. Das and D. Poole, 67–80. Santa Fe, N.Mex.: School of American Research Press.

Jentzsch, C. 2017. "Auxiliary Armed Forces and Innovations in Security Governance in Mozambique's Civil War." *Civil Wars* 19 (3): 325–47.

Jeursen, T., and C. van der Borgh. 2014. "Security Provision after Regime Change: Local Militias and Political Entities in Post-Qaddafi Tripoli." *Journal of Intervention and Statebuilding* 8 (2–3): 173–91.

Johnson, L. B. 1971. *The Vantage Point: Perspectives of the Presidency 1963–1969*. New York: Holt, Reinhart and Winston.

Johnston, L. 1992. *The Rebirth of Private Policing*. London: Routledge.

Jokela-Pansini, M. 2020. "Complicating Notions of Violence: An Embodied View of Violence against Women in Honduras." *Environment and Planning C* 38 (5): 848–65.

Jones, R., and P. Merriman. 2012. "Network Nation." *Environment and Planning A* 44 (4): 937–53.

Jones, T., and T. Newburn. 1998. *Private Security and Public Policing*. Oxford: Oxford University Press.

———, eds. 2006. *Plural Policing: A Comparative Perspective*. Abingdon: Routledge.

Jongerden, J. 2019. "Governing Kurdistan: Self-Administration in the Kurdistan Regional

Government in Iraq and the Democratic Federation of Northern Syria." *Ethnopolitics* 18 (1): 61–75.

Jorge, S. 2020. "The Financialization of the Margins of Maputo, Mozambique." *Housing Policy Debate* 30 (4): 606–22.

Kaarsholm, P. 2014. "Zanzibaris or Amakhuwa? Sufi Networks in South Africa, Mozambique, and the Indian Ocean." *Journal of African History* 55 (2): 191–210.

Kadhim, A. 2012. *Reclaiming Iraq: The 1920 Revolution and the Founding of the Modern State.* Austin: University of Texas Press.

Kaiser, D. 2017. "'Makers of Bonds and Ties': Transnational Socialisation and National Liberation in Mozambique." *Journal of Southern African Studies* 43 (1): 29–48.

Kaldor, M. 2018. *Global Security Cultures.* Cambridge: Polity.

Kaldor, M., and S. Sassen, eds. 2020. *Cities at War: Global Insecurity and Urban Resistance.* New York: Columbia University Press.

Kammen, D. 2017. "World Turned Upside Down: Benedict Anderson, Ruth Mcvey, and the 'Cornell Paper.'" *Indonesia* 104: 1–26.

Kapuscinski, R. 1988. *Another Day of Life.* London: Picador.

Kasperson, R. E., and J. V., Minghi, eds. 1970. *The Structure of Political Geography.* London: University of London Press.

Kausikan, B. 2020. "Asean May Have to Cut Members if They Continue to Be Led by an External Power." Excerpt of remarks on "Asean's Agency in the Midst of Great Power Competition" at the 35th Asean Roundtable on the COVID-19 Crisis: Impact on Asean and the Way Forward, Session III: Dealing with a Volatile World, 23 October, hosted by the Asean Studies Centre, ISEAS-Yusof Ishak Institute, Singapore. https://mothership.sg/2020/10/bilahari-asean-china/.

Kempa, M., P. Stenning, and J. Wood. 2004. "Policing Communal Spaces: A Reconfiguration of the 'Mass Private Property' Hypothesis." *British Journal of Criminology* 44 (4): 562–81.

Kent, A. 2006. "Reconfiguring Security: Buddhism and Moral Legitimacy in Cambodia." *Security Dialogue* 37 (3): 343–61.

———. 2007. "Purchasing Power and Pagodas: The Sīma Monastic Boundary and Consumer Politics in Cambodia." *Journal of Southeast Asian Studies* 38 (2): 335–54.

Khan, S. 2012. "Disasters: Contributions of Hazardscape and Gaps in Response Practices." *Natural Hazards and Earth System Sciences* 12 (12): 3775–87.

Khan, S. P., M. P. Meneses, and B. E. Bertelsen, eds. 2019. *Mozambique on the Move: Challenges and Reflections.* Leiden: Brill.

Kidron, C. A. 2020. "The 'Perfect Failure' of Communal Genocide Commemoration in Cambodia: Productive Friction or Bone Business?" *Current Anthropology* 61 (3): 304–34.

Kinder, K. 2014. "Guerrilla-Style Defensive Architecture in Detroit: A Self-Provisioned Security Strategy in a Neoliberal Space of Disinvestment." *International Journal of Urban and Regional Research* 38 (5): 1767–84.

King, D. E. 2008. "The Personal Is Patrilineal: *Namus* as Sovereignty." *Identities* 15 (3): 317–42.

———. 2014. *Kurdistan on the Global Stage: Kinship, Land, and Community in Iraq.* New Brunswick, N.J.: Rutgers University Press.

Kirmanj, S. 2014. "Kurdish History Textbooks: Building a Nation-State within a Nation-State." *Middle East Journal* 68 (3): 367–84.

Klauser, F. R. 2010. "Splintering Spheres of Security: Peter Sloterdijk and the Contemporary Fortress City." *Environment and Planning D* 28 (2): 326–40.

Klem, B., and S. Maunaguru. 2017. "Insurgent Rule as Sovereign Mimicry and Mutation: Governance, Kingship, and Violence in Civil Wars." *Comparative Studies in Society and History* 59 (3): 629–56.

Koch, N. 2018. "The Geopolitics of Sport beyond Soft Power: Event Ethnography and the 2016 Cycling World Championships in Qatar." *Sport in Society* 21 (12): 2010–31.

Kongkea, B. R. 2012. "'Police Law' in Effect for Busted Duo." *Phnom Penh Post*, 26 March. https://www.phnompenhpost.com/national/%E2%80%98police-law%E2%80%99 -effect-busted-duo.

Koopman, S. 2011. "Alter-geopolitics: Other Securities Are Happening." *Geoforum* 42 (3): 274–84.

Kösebalaban, H. 2020. "Transformation of Turkish Foreign Policy toward Syria: The Return of Securitization." *Middle East Critique* 29 (3): 335–44.

Kowalewski, M., and R. Bartłomiejski. 2020. "Is It Research or Just Walking? Framing Walking Research Methods as 'Non-scientific.'" *Geoforum* 114 (August): 59–65.

Krasmann, S., and C. Hentschel. 2019. "'Situational Awareness': Rethinking Security in Times of Urban Terrorism." *Security Dialogue* 50 (2): 181–97.

Kuddus, R. 2017. "The Ghosts of 1965: Politics and Memory in Indonesia." *New Left Review* 104 (March–April): 45–92.

———. 2020. "Lemongrass and Prayer." *New Left Review* 122 (March–April): 35–41.

Kuus, M. 2008. "Professionals of Geopolitics: Agency in International Politics." *Geography Compass* 2 (6): 2062–79.

Kwon, H. 2006. *After the Massacre: Commemoration and Consolation in Ha My and My Lai.* Berkeley: University of California Press.

Kyed, H. M. 2007a. "The Politics of Policing: Re-capturing 'Zones of Confusion' in Rural Postwar Mozambique." In *The Security Development Nexus: Expressions of Sovereignty and Securitization in Southern Africa*, edited by L. Buur, S. Jensen, and F. Stepputat, 132–51. Uppsala: HSRC Press.

———. 2007b. "State Vigilantes and Political Community on the Margins in Post-war Mozambique." In *Global Vigilantes*, edited by D. Pratten and A. Sen, 393–418. London: Hurst.

———. 2009. "Community Policing in Post-war Mozambique." *Policing and Society* 19 (4): 354–71.

———. 2017. "Predicament: Interpreting Police Violence (Mozambique)." In *Writing the World of Policing: The Difference Ethnography Makes*, edited by D. Fassin, 113–38. Chicago: University of Chicago Press.

———. 2020. "Provisional Police Authority in Maputo's Inner-City Periphery." *Environment and Planning D* 38 (3): 528–45.

Langley, P. 2017. "Finance/Security/Life." *Finance and Society* 3 (2): 173–79.

Larrabee, S. F. 2013. "Turkey's New Kurdish Opening." *Survival* 55 (5): 133–46.

Lawreniuk, S. 2020. "Intensifying Political Geographies of Authoritarianism: Toward an Anti-geopolitics of Garment Worker Struggles in Neoliberal Cambodia." *Annals of the American Association of Geographers* 110: 1174–91. https://doi.org/10.1080/24694452.2019.1670040.

Leander, A. 2005. "The Power to Construct International Security: On the Significance of Private Military Companies." *Millennium: Journal of International Studies* 33 (3): 803–25.

Leão, A. 2004. *Weapons in Mozambique: Reducing Availability and Demand*. ISS monograph 94. Pretoria: Institute for Security Studies.

Le Billon, P. 2002. "Logging in Muddy Waters: The Politics of Forest Exploitation in Cambodia." *Critical Asian Studies* 34 (4): 563–86.

Leezenberg, M. 2006. "Urbanization, Privatization and Patronage: The Political Economy of Iraqi Kurdistan." In *The Kurds: Nationalism and Politics*, edited by F. A. Jabar and H. Dawod, 151–79. London: Saqi. http://home.hum.uva.nl/oz/leezenberg/Urbanization.pdf.

———. 2016. "The Ambiguities of Democratic Autonomy: The Kurdish Movement in Turkey and Rojava." *Southeast European and Black Sea Studies* 16 (4): 671–90.

———. 2019. "The Rise of the White Kurds: An Essay in Regional Political Economy." In *The Kurds in a Changing Middle East: History, Politics and Representation*, edited by F. A. Jabar and R. Mansour, 86–117. London: I. B. Tauris.

Lefort, B. 2020. "Cartographies of Encounters: Understanding Youth Conflict Transformation through a Collaborative Exploration of Youth Spaces in Beirut." *Political Geography* 76 (January): 1–12.

Leisch, H. 2002. "Gated Communities in Indonesia." *Cities* 19 (5): 341–50.

Lemke, T. 2011. *Biopolitics: An Advanced Introduction*. Translated by E. F. Trump. New York: New York University Press.

Lennon, J., and M. Foley. 2000. *Dark Tourism: The Attraction of Death and Disaster*. London: Continuum.

Lentz, C. C. 2014. "The King Yields to the Village? A Micropolitics of Statemaking in Northwest Vietnam." *Political Geography* 39 (March): 1–10.

Levy, A., and C. Scott-Clark. 2008. "Country for Sale." *Guardian Weekend Magazine*, 26 April, 30–41. http://www.guardian.co.uk/world/2008/apr/26/Cambodia.

Lewis, S. 2012. "Hun Sen Denies China Influencing Cambodia." *Cambodia Daily*, 5 April. https://www.cambodiadaily.com/news/hun-sen-denies-china-influencing-cambodia-599/.

———. 2013. "NagaWorld Boss Acquires Billionaire Status." *Cambodia Daily*, 4 March. https://www.cambodiadaily.com/news/nagaworld-boss-acquires-billionaire-status-64112/.

Light, J. S. 2002. "Urban Security from Warfare to Welfare." *International Journal of Urban and Regional Research* 26 (3): 607–13.

Lindell, I. 2008. "The Multiple Sites of Urban Governance: Insights from an African City." *Urban Studies* 45 (9): 1879–1901.

Linehan, D. 2007. "Re-ordering the Urban Archipelago: Kenya Vision 2030, Street Trade and the Battle for Nairobi City Centre." *Aurora Geography Journal* 1: 21–42.

Lipman, A., and H. Harris. 1999. "Fortress Johannesburg." *Environment and Planning B: Planning and Design* 26 (5): 727–40.

Lippert, R., and D. O'Conner. 2003. "Security Assemblages: Airport Security, Flexible Work and Liberal Governance." *Alternatives* 28 (3): 331–58.

Lisle, D. 2016. *Holidays in the Danger Zone: Entanglements of War and Tourism.* Minneapolis: University of Minnesota Press.

Little, D. 2010. "The United States and the Kurds: A Cold War Story." *Journal of Cold War Studies* 12 (4): 63–98.

Loader, I. 1999. "Consumer Culture and the Commodification of Policing and Security." *Sociology* 33 (2): 373–92.

———. 2000. "Plural Policing and Democratic Governance." *Social and Legal Studies* 9 (3): 323–45.

Lohnert, M. 2019. "Security Is a Mental Game: The Psychology of Bordering Checkposts in Pakistan." *Geopolitics* 24 (2): 366–90.

Lombard, L., and T. Carayannis. 2015. "Making Sense of CAR: An Introduction." In *Making Sense of the Central African Republic*, edited by T. Carayannis and L. Lombard, 1–16. London: Zed.

Loong, S. 2018. "'This Country, Law Very Strong': Securitization beyond the Border in the Everyday Lives of Bangladeshi Migrant Workers in Singapore." *Geoforum* 90: 11–19.

Lorey, I. 2015. *State of Insecurity: Government of the Precarious.* Translated by A. Derieg. London: Verso.

Low, S. 2003. *Behind the Gates: Life, Security and the Pursuit of Happiness in Fortress America.* London: Routledge.

Low, S., and M. Maguire, eds. 2019. *Spaces of Security: Ethnographies of Securityscapes, Surveillance, And control.* New York: New York University Press.

Lund, C. 2016. "Rule and Rupture: State Formation through the Production of Property and Citizenship." *Development and Change* 47: 1199–228.

Machaqueiro, M. 2012. "The Islamic Policy of Portuguese Colonial Mozambique, 1960–1973." *Historical Journal* 55 (4): 1097–116.

Machava, B. L. 2011. "State Discourse on Internal Security and the Politics of Punishment in Post-independence Mozambique (1975–1983)." *Journal of Southern African Studies* 37 (3): 593–609.

Macklin, A. 2004. "Like Oil or Water, with a Match: Militarized Commerce, Armed Conflict and Human Security in Sudan." In *Sites of Violence: Gender and Conflict Zones*, edited by W. Giles and J. Hyndman, 75–107. Berkeley: University of California Press.

Macuane, J. J., L. Buur, and C. M. Monjane. 2018. "Power, Conflict and Natural Resources: The Mozambican Crisis Revisited." *African Affairs* 117 (468): 415–38.

Maddrell, A., and J. D. Sidaway, eds. 2010. *Deathscapes: Spaces for Death, Dying, Mourning and Remembrance.* Farnham: Ashgate.

Maguire, M., C. Frois, and N. Zurawski, eds. 2014. *The Anthropology of Security: Perspectives from the Frontline of Policing, Counter-terrorism and Border Control.* London: Pluto.

Maguire, M., and S. Low. 2019. "Introduction: Exploring Spaces of Security." In *Spaces of Security: Ethnographies of Securityscapes, Surveillance, and Control*, edited by S. Low and M. Maguire, 1–30. New York: New York University Press.

Makiya, K. 1998. *Republic of Fear. The Politics of Modern Iraq*. Updated ed. Berkeley: University of California Press.

Manning, C. L. 2002. *The Politics of Peace in Mozambique: Post-conflict Democratization*. Westport, Conn.: Praeger.

Marcus, A. 2007. *Blood and Belief: The PKK and the Kurdish Fight for Independence*. New York: New York University Press.

Marcuse, P. 2006. "Security or Safety in Cities? The Threat of Terrorism after 9/11." *International Journal of Urban and Regional Research* 30 (4): 919–29.

Martin, M. 2014. *An Intimate War: An Oral History of the Helmand Conflict*. London: Hurst.

Masco, J. 2014. *The Theater of Operations: National Security Affect from the Cold War to the War on Terror*. Durham, N.C.: Duke University Press.

Mater, A. 2016. *Desert of Pharan: Unofficial Histories behind the Mass Expansion of Mecca*. Edited by C. David. Zurich: Lars Müller.

McCoy, A. W. 2009. *Policing America's Empire: The United States, the Philippines, and the Rise of the Surveillance State*. Madison: University of Wisconsin Press.

McDonald, M. 2018. "Climate Change and Security: Towards Ecological Security?" *International Theory* 10 (2): 153–80.

McDowall, D. 2004. *A Modern History of the Kurds*. London: I. B. Tauris.

McGregor, A. 2019. "Why Mozambique Is Outsourcing Counter-insurgency to Russia: Hidden Loans and Naval Bases." *Eurasia Daily Monitor* 16 (153), 4 November. https://jamestown.org/program/why-mozambique-is-outsourcing-counter-insurgency-to-russia-hidden-loans-and-naval-bases/.

McKinnon, M. 2011. *Asian Cities: Globalization, Urbanization and Nation-Building*. Copenhagen: NIAS Press.

Megoran, N. 2006. "For Ethnography in Political Geography: Experiencing and Reimagining Ferghana Valley Boundary Closures." *Political Geography* 25 (6): 622–40.

Menkhaus, K. 2007. "Governance without Government in Somalia: Spoilers, State Building, and the Politics of Coping." *International Security* 31 (3): 74–106.

Mertha, A. 2014. *Brothers in Arms: Chinese Aid to the Khmer Rouge, 1975–1979*. Ithaca, N.Y.: Cornell University Press.

Miller, T. 2019. *Empire of Borders. The Expansion of the US Border around the World*. London: Verso.

Milne, S. 2015. "Cambodia's Unofficial Regime of Extraction: Illicit Logging in the Shadow of Transnational Governance and Investment." *Critical Asian Studies* 47 (2): 200–228.

Milne, S., and W. M. Adams. 2012. "Market Masquerades: Uncovering the Politics of Community-Level Payments for Environmental Services in Cambodia." *Development and Change* 43 (1): 133–58.

Minnaar, A., and D. Mistry. 2004. "Outsourcing and the South African Police Service." In *Private Muscle: Outsourcing the Provision of Criminal Justice Services*, edited by

M. Schönteich, A. Minnaar, D. Mistry, and K. C. Goyer, 38–54. ISS monograph 93, Institute for Security Studies, Cape Town. https://www.africaportal.org/publications /private-muscle-outsourcing-the-provision-of-criminal-justice-services/.

Minnaar, A., and P. Ngoveni. 2004. "The Relationship between the South African Police Service and the Private Security Industry: Any Role for Outsourcing in the Prevention of Crime?" *Acta Criminologica* 17 (1): 42–65.

Mitchell, D. 2005. "The S.U.V. Model of Citizenship: Floating Bubbles, Buffer Zones, and the Rise of the 'Purely Atomic' Individual." *Political Geography* 24 (1): 77–100.

Mitchell, T. 1991. "The Limits of the State: Beyond Statist Approaches and Their Critics." *American Political Science Review* 85 (1): 77–96.

Mohammad, R., and J. D. Sidaway. 2011. "Intervention: Stalingrad in the Hindu Kush? AFPAK, Crucibles and Chains of Terror." *Antipode* 43 (2): 199–204.

Mojab, S. 2004. "No 'Safe Haven': Violence against Women in Iraqi Kurdistan." In *Sites of Violence: Gender and Conflict Zones*, edited by W. Giles and J. Hyndman, 108–33. Berkeley: University of California Press.

Molotch, H. 2003. "Introduction. Symposium on Urban Terror." *International Journal of Urban and Regional Research* 27 (3): 649–50.

Moran, D., L. Piacentini, and J. Pallot. 2012. "Disciplined Mobility and Carceral Geography: Prisoner Transport in Russia." *Transactions of the Institute of British Geographers* 37 (3): 446–60.

Morgenbesser, L. 2018. "Misclassification on the Mekong: The Origins of Hun Sen's Personalist Dictatorship." *Democratization* 25 (2): 191–208.

Morier-Genoud, E. 2020. "The Jihadi Insurgency in Mozambique: Origins, Nature and Beginning." *Journal of Eastern African Studies* 14 (3): 396–412.

Morier-Genoud, E., M. Cahen, and D. M. do Rosário, eds. 2018. *The War Within: New Perspectives on the Civil War in Mozambique 1976–1992*. Woodbridge: James Currey.

Morris, S. J. 1999. *Why Vietnam Invaded Cambodia: Political Culture and the Causes of War*. Stanford, Calif.: Stanford University Press.

Morrissey, J. 2017. *The Long War: CENTCOM, Grand Strategy, and Global Security*. Athens: University of Georgia Press.

Morton, D. 2018. "The Shape of Aspiration: Clandestine Masonry House Construction in Lourenço Marques, Mozambique (1960–75)." *Journal of African History* 59 (2): 283–304.

———. 2019. *Age of Concrete: Housing and the Shape of Aspiration in the Capital of Mozambique*. Athens: Ohio University Press.

Morton, E. 2014. "Naga Aircraft Set to Take Flight." *Phnom Penh Post*, 11 August. https:// www.phnompenhpost.com/business/naga-aircraft-set-take-flight.

Mott, C., and S. Roberts. 2014. "Not Everyone Has the Balls: Urban Exploration and the Persistence of Masculinist Geography." *Antipode* 46: 229–45.

MPA-International. 2012a. "Secured Logistics." http://www.mpacambodia.com/secured logistics.html.

———. 2012b. "Other Services." http://www.mpacambodia.com/otherservices.html.

Mufti, M. 1996. *Sovereign Creations: Pan-Arabism and Political Order in Syria and Iraq*. Ithaca, N.Y.: Cornell University Press.

Müller, M. 2008. "Reconsidering the Concept of Discourse for the Field of Critical Geopolitics: Towards Discourse as Language and Practice." *Political Geography* 27 (3): 322–38.

Murphy, A. B. 2012. "Territory's Continuing Allure." *Annals of the Association of American Geographers* 103 (5): 1212–26.

Murray, M. J. 2020. *Panic City: Crime and the Fear Industries in Johannesburg.* Stanford, Calif.: Stanford University Press.

Nachemson, A. 2018. "Hun Sen's Monument to Himself." *Diplomat,* 31 December. https://thediplomat.com/2018/12/hun-sens-monument-to-himself/.

NagaCorp. 2012a. "Directors and Senior Management." http://www.nagacorp.com/eng/overview/management.php.

———. 2012b. "Optimistic on 2012." http://www.nagacorp.com/assets/files/eng/analyst/research/research_120223.pdf.

Nam, S. 2017. "Urban Speculation, Economic Openness, and Market Experiments in Phnom Penh." *positions* 25 (4): 645–67.

Natali, D. 2008. "The Kirkuk Conundrum." *Ethnopolitics* 7 (4): 433–43.

———. 2010. *The Kurdish Quasi-State.* Syracuse, N.Y.: Syracuse University Press.

Natarajan, U. 2011. "Creating and Recreating Iraq: Legacies of the Mandate System in Contemporary Understandings of Third World Sovereignty." *Leiden Journal of International Law* 24 (4): 799–822.

National Assembly of the Kingdom of Cambodia. 2005. "Law on the Management of Weapons, Explosives and Ammunition, Adopted 26 April." https://www.icj.org/wp-content/uploads/2013/04/Cambodia-Law-on-the-Management-of-Weapons-Explosives-and-Ammunition-2005-eng.pdf.

Neisser, F., and S. Runkel. 2017. "The Future Is Now! Extrapolated Riskscapes, Anticipatory Action and the Management of Potential Emergencies." *Geoforum* 82: 170–79.

Németh, J. 2010. "Security in Public Space: An Empirical Assessment of Three US Cities." *Environment and Planning A* 42 (10): 2487–507.

Neocleous, M. 2011. "Security as Pacification." In *Anti-security,* edited by M. Neocleous and G. S. Rigakos, 23–56. Ottawa: Red Quill Books.

Neocleous, M., and G. S. Rigakos. 2011. "Anti-security: A Declaration." In *Anti-security,* edited by M. Neocleous and G. S. Rigakos, 15–21. Ottawa: Red Quill Books.

Nevins, J. 2005. *A Not-So-Distant Horror: Mass Violence in East Timor.* Ithaca, N.Y.: Cornell University Press.

Nguyen, M. 2018. *America's Vietnam: The Longue Durée of U.S. Literature and Empire.* Philadelphia: Temple University Press.

Nguyen, N. 2015. "Chokepoint: Regulating US Student Mobility through Biometrics." *Political Geography* 46 (May): 1–10.

———. 2019. *Suspect Communities: Anti-Muslim Racism and the Domestic War on Terror.* Minneapolis: University of Minnesota Press.

Nguyen, V. T. 2016. *Nothing Ever Dies. Vietnam and the Memory of War.* Cambridge, Mass.: Harvard University Press.

Nielsen, M., J. Sumich, and B. E. Bertelsen. 2021. "Enclaving: Spatial Detachment as an

Aesthetics of Imagination in an Urban Sub-Saharan Context." *Urban Studies* 58 (5): 881–902.

Nimol, T., and S. Worrell. 2012. "Banners versus Batons." *Phnom Penh Post*, 28 March. https://www.phnompenhpost.com/national/banners-versus-batons.

Nixon, R. 1970. "Address to the Nation on the Situation in Southeast Asia, April 30." American Presidency Project. https://www.presidency.ucsb.edu/documents/address -the-nation-the-situation-southeast-asia-1.

Nordholt, H. S. 2011. "Indonesia in the 1950s: Nation, Modernity, and the Post-colonial State." *Bijdragen tot de Taal-, Land-en Volkenkunde* 167 (4): 386–404.

Nordstrom, C., and A. C. G. M. Robben, eds. 1996. *Fieldwork under Fire: Contemporary Studies of Violence and Culture*. Berkeley: University of California Press.

Norén-Nilsson, A. 2013. "Performance as (Re)incarnation: The Sdech Kân Narrative." *Journal of Southeast Asian Studies* 44 (1): 4–23.

Noxolo, P. 2014. "Towards an Embodied Securityscape: Brian Chikwava's Harare North and the Asylum Seeking Body as Site of Articulation." *Social & Cultural Geography* 15 (3): 291–312.

Öcalan, A. 2011. *Democratic Confederalism*. London: Transmedia.

O'Connor, D., R. Lippert, D. Spencer, and L. Smylie. 2008. "Seeing Private Security Like a State." *Criminology and Criminal Justice* 8 (2): 203–26.

OED Online. 2020. "Security, n." Oxford University Press.

Oestmann, K., and A. M. Korschinek. 2020. "How to Live with a Female Body: Securityscapes against Sexual Violence and Related Interpretation Patterns of Kyrgyz Women." In *Surviving Everyday Life: The Securityscapes of Threatened People in Kyrgyzstan*, edited by M. von Boemcken, N. Bagdasarova, A. Ismailbekova, and C. Schetter, 131–54. Bristol: Bristol University Press.

Office of the Council of Ministers. 2019. "Remark Samdech Techo Hun Sen, at the 20th Anniversary of the Establishment of the Royal Cambodian Army Command Headquarters" [Unofficial translation]. 24 January. https://pressocm.gov.kh/en/archives/46870.

Offner, A. C. 2019. *Sorting Out the Mixed Economy: The Rise and Fall of Welfare and Developmental States in Americas*. Princeton, N.J.: Princeton University Press.

Öjendal, J., and K. Sedra. 2006. "*Korob, kaud, klach*: In Search of Agency in Rural Cambodia." *Journal of Southeast Asian Studies* 37 (3): 507–26.

Olds, K., J. D. Sidaway, and M. Sparke. 2005. "White Death." *Environment and Planning D* 23 (4): 475–79.

O'Leary, B. 2012. "The Federalization of Iraq and the Break-up of Sudan." *Government and Opposition* 47 (4): 481–516.

Opello, W. C., Jr. 1975. "Pluralism and Elite Conflict in an Independence Movement: FRELIMO in the 1960s." *Journal of Southern African Studies* 2 (1) 66–82.

Osborne, M. 1973. *Politics and Power in Cambodia: The Sihanouk Years*. Melbourne: Longmans.

Ó Tuathail, G. 1996. "An Anti-geopolitical Eye: Maggie O'Kane in Bosnia, 1992–93." *Gender, Place & Culture* 3 (2): 171–86.

Owen, R. 2014. *The Rise and Fall of the Arab Presidents for Life*. Cambridge, Mass.: Harvard University Press.

Özcan, A. K. 2005. *Turkey's Kurds: A Theoretical Analysis of the PKK and Abdullah Öcalan*. London: Routledge.

Paasche, T. F. 2012. "Creating Parallel Public Spaces through Private Governments: A South African Case Study." *South African Geographical Journal* 94 (1): 46–59.

——. 2015. "Syrian and Iraqi Kurds: Conflict and Cooperation." *Middle East Policy* 22 (1): 77–88.

——. 2016. "Co-producing Fieldwork under Fire—Collaborating with Journalists in Syria and Iraq." *Geographical Journal* 182 (3): 289–93.

Paasche, T. F., and H. Mansurbeg. 2014. "Kurdistan Regional Government–Turkish Energy Relations: A Complex Partnership." *Eurasian Geography and Economics* 55 (2): 111–32.

Paasche, T. F., and J. D. Sidaway. 2010. "Transecting Security and Space in Maputo." *Environment and Planning A* 42 (7): 1555–76.

——. 2015. "Transecting Security and Space in Kurdistan, Iraq." *Environment and Planning A* 47 (10): 2113–33.

Paasche, T. F., R. Yarwood, and J. D. Sidaway. 2014. "Territorial Tactics: The Socio-spatial Significance of Private Policing Tactics in Cape Town." *Urban Studies* 51 (8): 1559–75.

Paglen, T. 2009. *Blank Spots on the Map: The Dark Geography of the Pentagon's Secret World*. New York: Dutton.

Painter, J. 2010. Rethinking Territory. *Antipode* 42 (5): 1090–118.

Paling, W. 2012. "Planning a Future for Phnom Penh: Mega Projects, Aid Dependence and Disjointed Governance." *Urban Studies* 49 (13): 2889–912.

Panzer, M. G. 2013. "Building a Revolutionary Constituency: Mozambican Refugees and the Development of the FRELIMO Proto-state, 1964–1968." *Social Dynamics* 39 (1): 5–23.

Pearce, J. 2020. "History, Legitimacy and Renamo's Return to Arms in Central Mozambique." *Africa* 90 (4): 774–95.

Pedelty, M. 1995. *War Stories: The Culture of Foreign Correspondents*. London: Routledge.

Peou, S. 2005. "Collaborative Human Security? The UN and Other Actors in Cambodia." *International Peacekeeping* 12 (1): 105–24.

Percival, T., and P. Waley. 2012. "Articulating Intra-Asian Urbanism: The Production of Satellite Cities in Phnom Penh." *Urban Studies* 49 (13): 2873–88.

Persson, A., B. Rothstein, and J. Teorell. 2010. "The Failure of Anti-corruption Policies. A Theoretical Mischaracterization of the Problem." QoG Working Paper Series No. 19, Quality of Government Institute, University of Gothenburg. https://www.qog.pol.gu.se/digitalAssets/1350/1350163_2010_19_persson_rothstein_teorell.pdf.

Peters, R. 2013. *Surabaya, 1945–2010: Neighbourhood, State and Economy in Indonesia's City of Struggle*. Singapore: NUS Press.

Peycam, M. F. 2010. "Sketching an Institutional History of Academic Knowledge Production in Cambodia (1863–2009)—Part 1." *Sojourn* 25 (2): 153–77.

Philo, C. 2014. "Guest Editorial: State Security and the 'Hostile Acres.'" *Environment and Planning D* 32 (5): 753–61.

Pitcher, M. A. 2002. *Transforming Mozambique: The Politics of Privatization, 1975–2000.* Cambridge: Cambridge University Press.

———. 2006. "Forgetting from Above and Memory from Below: Strategies of Legitimation and Struggle in Postsocialist Mozambique." *Africa* 76 (1): 88–112.

———. 2020. "Mozambique Elections 2019: Pernicious Polarization, Democratic Decline, and Rising Authoritarianism." *African Affairs* 119: 468–86.

Pitcher, M. A., and K. M. Askew. 2006. "African Socialisms and Postsocialisms." *Africa* 76 (1): 1–14.

Pitcher, M. A., and G. Graham. 2007. "Cars Are Killing Luanda: Cronyism, Consumerism, and Other Assaults on Angola's Post-war Capital City. In *Cities in Contemporary Africa*, edited by M. J. Murray and G. A. Myers, 173–94. New York: Palgrave Macmillan.

Post, K., and P. Wright. 1989. *Socialism and Underdevelopment.* London: Routledge.

Pow, C. P. 2014. "Urban Dystopia and Epistemologies of Hope." *Progress in Human Geography* 39 (4): 1–22.

Power, M. 2020. "(Luso)tropicality and the Materiality of Decolonization." *Singapore Journal of Tropical Geography* 41 (1): 154–58.

Preston, A. 2014. "Monsters Everywhere: A Genealogy of National Security." *Diplomatic History* 38 (3): 477–500.

Qabaha, A. 2019. "Decolonizing History and Depoliticizing Territory: Raja Shehadeh's *Palestinian Walks: Notes on a Vanishing Landscape.*" *Interventions* 21 (7): 1030–44.

Raco, M. 2003. "Remaking Place and Securitising Space: Urban Regeneration and the Strategies, Tactics and Practices of Policing in the UK." *Urban Studies* 40 (9): 1869–87.

Rajaram, P. K., and C. Grundy-Warr, eds. 2007. *Borderscapes: Hidden Geographies and Politics at Territory's Edge.* Minneapolis: University of Minnesota Press.

Rankin, W. 2018. *After the Map: Cartography, Navigation and the Transformation of Territory in the Twentieth Century.* Chicago: University of Chicago Press.

Reid-Henry, S. 2011. "Spaces of Security and Development." *Security Dialogue* 42 (1): 97–104.

Reporters Without Borders. 2020. "Iraqi Kurdistan: Wave of Arrests of Journalists since Covid-19's Arrival." 17 April. https://rsf.org/en/news/iraqi-kurdistan-wave-arrests-journalists-covid-19s-arrival.

Reuters. 2012. "Cambodians Held over Eviction Protest before Obama Visit, 15 November." http://www.reuters.com/article/2012/11/15/us-cambodia-obama-idUSBRE8AE0FE20121115.

Reyntjens, F. 2005. "The Privatisation and Criminalisation of Public Space in the Geopolitics of the Great Lakes Region." *Journal of Modern African Studies* 43 (4): 587–607.

Richardson, T., ed. 2015. *Walking Inside Out: Contemporary British Psychogeography.* London: Rowman & Littlefield.

Rigakos, G. S. 2002. *The New Parapolice: Risk Markets and Commodified Social Control.* Toronto: University of Toronto Press.

———. 2011. "'To Extend the Scope of Productive Labour': Pacification as a Police Project." In *Anti-Security*, edited by M. Neocleous and G. S. Rigakos, 57–83. Ottawa: Red Quill Books.

Rijke, A. 2019. "The Land of the Checkpoints: A Study of the Daily Geographies of Checkpoints in the Occupied Palestinian Territories." PhD thesis, Wageningen University, Wageningen, Netherlands. https://doi.org/10.18174/501665.

Rivas, A.-M., and B. C. Browne, eds. 2019. *Experiences in Researching Conflict and Violence: Fieldwork Interrupted*. Bristol: Bristol University Press.

Rivera-Amarillo, C., and A. Camargo. 2020. "Zika Assemblages: Women, Populationism, and the Geographies of Epidemiological Surveillance." *Gender, Place & Culture* 27 (3): 412–28.

Roberts, G. 2017. "The Assassination of Eduardo Mondlane: FRELIMO, Tanzania, and the Politics of Exile in Dar es Salaam." *Cold War History* 17 (1): 1–19.

Roberts, R. 2008. "Cambodia: Surplus Destruction after War and Genocide." *Contemporary Security Policy* 29 (1): 103–28.

Robic, M.-C. 2004. "Section, Transect." *Hypergeo*. http://www.hypergeo.eu/spip.php?article345#.

Robinson, G. 2018. *The Killing Season: A History of the Indonesian Massacres, 1965–66*. Princeton, N.J.: Princeton University Press.

Robinson, J. 2002. "Global and World Cities: A View from Off the Map." *International Journal of Urban and Regional Research* 26 (3): 531–54.

Rodgers, D. 2004. "'Disembedding' the City: Crime, Insecurity, and Spatial Organisation in Managua, Nicaragua." *Environment and Urbanization* 16 (2): 113–24.

Rodgers, G. 2008. "Everyday Life and the Political Economy of Displacement on the Mozambique–South Africa Borderland." *Journal of Contemporary African Studies* 26 (4): 385–99.

Rojava Information Center. 2019. "Beyond the Frontlines: The Building of the Democratic System in North and East Syria." RIC Report, 19 December. Qamishli, Syria: RIC. https://rojavainformationcenter.com/storage/2019/12/Beyond-the-frontlines-The-building-of-the-democratic-system-in-North-and-East-Syria-Report-Rojava-Information-Center-December-2019-V4.pdf.

Rokem, J., S., Fregonese, A. Ramadan, E. Pascucci, G. Rosen, I. Charney, T. F. Paasche, and J. D. Sidaway. 2017. "Interventions in Urban Geopolitics." *Political Geography* 61: 253–62.

Romano, D. 2007. "The Future of Kirkuk." *Ethnopolitics* 6 (2): 265–83.

Roque, S., M. Mucavele, and N. Noronha. 2016. "Subúrbios and *Cityness*: Exploring Imbrications and Urbanity in Maputo, Mozambique." *Journal of Southern African Studies* 42 (4): 643–58.

Rose, N., and P. Miller. 1992. "Political Power beyond the State: Problematics of Government." *British Journal of Sociology* 43 (2): 173–205.

Ross, N., and A. Mohammadpour. 2018. "Imagined or Real: The Intersection of Tribalism and Nationalism in the Kurdish Regional Government (KRG)." *British Journal of Middle Eastern Studies* 45 (2): 194–211.

Roy, A. 2009. "The 21st-Century Metropolis: New Geographies of Theory." *Regional Studies* 43: 819–30.

Roy, A., and A. Ong, eds. 2011. *Worlding Cities: Asian Experiments and the Art of Being Global*. Malden, Mass.: Wiley-Blackwell.

Ruggie, J. G. 1993. "Territoriality and Beyond: Problematizing Modernity in International Relations." *International Organization* 47 (1): 139–74.

Rusty Compass. 2011. "Cambodiana Hotel, Phnom Penh—Review by Mark Bowyer." 7 February. https://www.rustycompass.com/cambodia-travel-guide-37/phnom-penh-7/hotels-15/cambodiana-hotel-phnom-penh-149#.XKzH0Gd7kkI.

Salter, M. B., and C. E. Mutlu, eds. 2013. *Research Methods in Critical Security Studies: An Introduction*. Abingdon: Routledge.

Sarma, J., and J. D. Sidaway. 2020. "Securing Urban Frontiers: A View from Yangon, Myanmar." *International Journal of Urban and Regional Research* 44 (3): 447–68.

Sarmento, J., and D. Linehan. 2019. "The Colonial Hotel: Spacing Violence at the Grande Hotel, Beira, Mozambique." *Environment and Planning D: Society and Space* 37 (2): 276–93.

Sassen, S. 2001. *The Global City: New York, London, Tokyo*. Rev. ed. Princeton, N.J.: Princeton University Press.

———. 2013. "When Territory Deborders Territoriality." *Territory, Politics, Governance* 1 (1): 21–45.

Saul, J. S. 2020a. "The African Hero in Mozambican History: On Assassinations and Executions—Part I." *Review of African Political Economy* 47 (163): 153–65.

———. 2020b. "The African Hero in Mozambican History: On Assassinations and Executions—Part II." *Review of African Political Economy* 47 (164): 335–45.

Savage, P. 2019. "Avenida Mao Tse Tung (or How Artists Navigated the Mozambican Revolution)." In *Art, Global Maoism and the Chinese Cultural Revolution*, ed. J. Galimberti and V. H. F. Scott, 249–67. Manchester: Manchester University Press.

Schmidinger, T. 2018. *Rojava: Revolution, War and the Future of Syria's Kurds*. Translated by M. Schiffmann. 4th ed. London: Pluto.

Schoenberger, L., and A. Beban. 2018. "'They Turn Us into Criminals': Embodiments of Fear in Cambodian Land Grabbing." *Annals of the American Association of Geographers* 108 (5): 1338–53.

Schomerus, M., and L. de Vries. 2014. "Improvising Border Security: 'A Situation of Security Pluralism' along South Sudan's Borders with the Democratic Republic of the Congo." *Security Dialogue* 45 (3): 279–94.

Schrader, S. 2019. *Badges without Borders: How Global Counterinsurgency Transformed American Policing*. Berkeley: University of California Press.

Scott, J. 1998. *Seeing Like a State: How Certain Schemes to Improve the Human Condition Have Failed*. New Haven, Conn.: Yale University Press.

Sefalafala, T., and E. Webster. 2013. "Working as a Security Guard: The Limits of Professionalisation in a Low Status Occupation." *South African Review of Sociology* 44 (2): 76–97.

Seigel, M. 2018. *Violence Work: State Power and the Limits of Police*. Durham, N.C.: Duke University Press.

Shatkin, G. 1998. "'Fourth World' Cities in the Global Economy: The Case of Phnom Penh, Cambodia." *International Journal of Urban and Regional Research* 22 (3): 378–93.

Shaw, I. G. R. 2016. *Predator Empire: Drone Warfare and Full Spectrum Dominance*. Minneapolis: University of Minnesota Press.

Shawcross, W. 1979. *Sideshow: Kissinger, Nixon and the Destruction of Cambodia.* New York: Simon & Schuster.

Shearing, C. D., and M. Kempa. 2000. "The Role of 'Private Security' in Transitional Democracies." In *Crime and Policing in Transitional Societies*, 205–14. https://www.kas .de/c/document_library/get_file?uuid=092f7296-f4ec-371b-b5ce-c7bc0a678e1b& groupId=252038.

Shearing, C. D., and P. C. Stenning. 1983. "Private Security: Implications for Social Control." *Social Problems* 30 (5): 493–506.

——— . 1985. "From the Panopticon to Disney World: The Development of Discipline." In *Perspectives in Criminal Law: Essays in Honour of John Ll. J. Edwards*, edited by A. N. Doob and E. L. Greenspan, 335–49. Toronto: Canada Law Book.

Shearing, C. D., and J. Wood. 2003. "Nodal Governance, Democracy, and the New 'Denizens.'" *Journal of Law and Society* 30 (3): 400–419.

Shehadeh, R. 2007. *Palestinian Walks: Notes on a Vanishing Landscape.* London: Profile Books.

Shipley, T., and M. Jenkins. 2019. *Grand Corruption and the SDG's: The Visible Costs of Mozambique's Hidden Debt's Scandal.* Berlin: Transparency International. https:// www.transparency.org/en/publications/grand-corruption-and-the-sdgs-the-visible -costs-of-mozambiques-hidden-debts.

Short, P. 2004. *Pol Pot: The Anatomy of a Nightmare.* London: John Murray.

Shukaitis, S. 2014. "'Theories Are Made Only to Die in the War of Time': Guy Debord and the Situationist International as strategic thinkers." *Culture and Organization* 20 (4): 251–68.

Sidaway, J. D. 1992. "Mozambique: Destabilization, State, Society and Space." *Political Geography* 11 (3): 239–58.

——— . 1993. "Urban and Regional Planning in Post-independence Mozambique." *International Journal of Urban and Regional Research* 17 (2): 241–59.

——— . 2002. "Signifying Boundaries: Detours around the Portuguese-Spanish (Algarve/Alentejo-Andalucía) Borderlands." *Geopolitics* 7 (1): 139–64.

——— . 2003. "Sovereign Excesses? Portraying Postcolonial Sovereigntyscapes." *Political Geography* 22 (2): 157–78.

——— . 2005. "The Poetry of Boundaries: Reflections from the Portuguese-Spanish Borderlands." In *B/ordering space*, edited by H. Van Houtum, O. Kramsch, and W. Zierhofer, 189–206. Farnham: Ashgate.

——— . 2007a. "Enclave Space: A New Metageography of Development?" *Area* 39 (3): 331–39.

——— . 2007b. "Bordermarks: The Poetry of Boundaries." In *Borderscapes: Hidden Geographies and Politics at Territory's Edge*, edited by P. K. Rajaram and C. Grundy-Warr, 161–81. Minneapolis: University of Minnesota Press.

——— . 2009. "Shadows on the Path: Negotiating Geopolitics on an Urban Section of Britain's South West Coast Path." *Environment and Planning D* 27 (6): 1091–1116.

——— . 2012. "Subaltern Geopolitics: Libya in the Mirror of Europe." *Geographical Journal* 178 (4): 296–301.

——— . 2017. "Afterword: Lineages of Urban Geopolitics." In *Rethinking Planning and*

Urban Geopolitics in Contested Cities, edited by J. Rokem and C. Boano, 234–36. Abingdon: Routledge.

Sidaway, J. D., and P. Mayell. 2007. "Cultural Geographies in Practice. Monumental Geographies: Re-situating the State." *Cultural Geographies* 14 (1): 147–54.

Sidaway, J. D., T. F. Paasche, C. Y. Woon, and P. Keo. 2014. "Transecting Security and Space in Phnom Penh." *Environment and Planning A* 46 (5): 1181–202.

Sidaway, J. D., and M. Power. 1995. "Sociospatial Transformations in the 'Postsocialist' Periphery: The Case of Maputo, Mozambique." *Environment and Planning A* 27 (9): 1463–91.

Simon, D. 1992. *Cities, Capital and Development: African Cities in the World Economy.* London: Belhaven Press.

Simone, A. M. 2006. "Pirate Towns: Reworking Social and Symbolic Infrastructures in Johannesburg and Douala." *Urban Studies* 43 (2): 357–70.

——— . 2019. *Improvised Lives: Rhythms of Endurance in the Urban South.* Cambridge, Mass.: Polity.

Singer, P. W. 2005. "Outsourcing War." *Foreign Affairs* 84 (2): 119–32.

Singh, N. P. 2019. *Race and America's Long War.* Oakland: University of California Press.

Sion, B. 2011. "Conflicting Sites of Memory in Post-genocide Cambodia." *Humanity* 2 (1): 1–21.

Sklair, L. 2005. "The Transnational Capitalist Class and Contemporary Architecture in Globalizing Cities." *International Journal of Urban and Regional Research* 29 (3): 485–500.

Smith, P. 2010. "The Contemporary Dérive: A Partial Review of Issues Concerning the Contemporary Practice of Psychogeography." *Cultural Geographies* 17 (1): 103–22.

Soenthrith, S. 2012a. "Police Official Kills Villager after Dispute, Now on the Run." *Cambodia Daily*, 2 April.

——— . 2012b. "Police Officials Arrested for Firing Guns at Random while Drunk." *Cambodia Daily*, 3 April.

Sokhean, B. 2019. "Soldiers Banned from Providing Private Security Services." *Khmer Times*, 9 September. https://www.khmertimeskh.com/641322/soldiers-banned-from-providing-private-security-services-2/.

Soleimani, K., and A. Mohammadpour. 2020a. "The Securitisation of Life: Eastern Kurdistan under the Rule of a Perso-Shi'i State." *Third World Quarterly* 41 (4): 663–82.

——— . 2020b. "Life and Labor on the Internal Colonial Edge: Political Economy of Kolberi in Rojhelat." *British Journal of Sociology* 71 (4): 741–60.

Sosnowski, M. 2020. "Negotiating Statehood through Ceasefires: Syria's De-escalation Zones." *Small Wars and Insurgencies* 31 (7–8): 1395–1414.

Sotharith, C. 2010. "Trade, FDI, and ODA between Cambodia and China/Japan/Korea." In *Economic Relations of China, Japan and Korea with the Mekong River Basin Countries*, edited by M. Kagami, 10–44. BRC Research Report 3, Bangkok Research Centre, IDE-JETRO. http://www.ide.go.jp/library/English/Publish/Download/Brc/pdf/03_chapter1.pdf.

Sovacool, B., and S. Halfon. 2007. "Reconstructing Iraq: Merging Discourses of Security and Development." *Review of International Studies* 33 (2): 223–43.

Sovuthy, K. 2012. "Three Police Officers Sentenced to Life for Viral Video Murder." *Cambodia Daily*, 4 April.

Sparke, M. 2005. *In the Space of Theory: Postfoundational Geographies of the Nation-State*. Minneapolis: University of Minnesota Press.

Spencer, J., J. Goodhand, S. Hasbullah, B. Klem, B. Korf, and K. T. Silva. 2015. *Checkpoint, Temple, Church and Mosque: A Collaborative Ethnography of War and Peace*. London: Pluto Press.

Spivak, G. C. 1993. *Outside in the Teaching Machine*. New York: Routledge.

Springer, S. 2009. "Culture of Violence or Violent Orientalism? Neoliberalisation and Imagining the 'Savage Other' in Post-transitional Cambodia." *Transactions of the Institute of British Geographers* NS 34 (3): 305–19.

———. 2010. *Cambodia's Neoliberal Order: Violence, Authoritarianism and the Contestation of Public Space*. London: Routledge.

———. 2011. "Articulated Neoliberalism: The Specificity of Patronage, Kleptocracy, and Violence in Cambodia's Neoliberalization." *Environment and Planning A* 43 (11): 2554–70.

Sriram, C. L., J. C. King, J. A. Mertus, O. Martin-Ortega, and J. Herman, eds. 2009. *Surviving Field Research: Working in Violent and Difficult Situations*. London: Routledge.

Stanek, Ł. 2020. "Socialist Worldmaking: Architecture and Global Urbanization in the Cold War." In *Alternative Globalizations: Eastern Europe and the Postcolonial World*, edited by J. Mark, A. M. Kalinovsky, and S. Marung, 166–86. Bloomington: Indiana University Press.

Stansfield, G. 2013. "The Unravelling of the Post–First World War State System? The Kurdistan Region of Iraq and the Transformation of the Middle East." *International Affairs* 89 (2): 259–82.

Steele, J. 2011. *Ghosts of Afghanistan: The Haunted Battlefield*. Berkeley, Calif.: Counterpoint.

Stenning, P. 2009. "Governance and Accountability in a Plural Policing Environment—The Story So Far." *Policing* 3 (1): 22–33.

Stern, M., and J. Öjendal. 2010. "Mapping the Security-Development Nexus: Conflict, Complexity, Cacophony, Convergence?" *Security Dialogue* 41 (1): 5–29.

Stone, O., and P. Kuznick. 2013. *The Untold History of the United States*. London: Ebury Press.

Story, B. 2019. *Prison Land: Mapping Carceral Power across Neoliberal America*. Minneapolis: University of Minnesota Press.

Strangio, S. 2014. *Hun Sen's Cambodia*. New Haven, Conn.: Yale University Press.

———. 2020. "Could ASEAN Really Cut Laos and Cambodia Loose?" *Diplomat*, 29 October. https://thediplomat.com/2020/10/could-asean-really-cut-laos-and-cambodia-loose/.

Sullivan, M. 2011. "China's Aid to Cambodia." In *Cambodia's Economic Transformation*, edited by C. Hughes and K. Un, 50–69. Copenhagen: NIAS Press.

Sumich, J. 2008a. "Construir uma nacão: ideologia de modernidade da elite moçambicana" [Building a Nation: Elite Ideologies of Modernity in Mozambique]. *Análise So-*

cial 43 (2): 319–45. http://analisesocial.ics.ul.pt/documentos/1218639505B4yEE8zd4
Lm89HK9.pdf.

———. 2008b. "Politics after the Time of Hunger in Mozambique: A Critique of the Neopatrimonial Interpretation of Elites." *Journal of Southern African Studies* 34 (1): 111–25.

———. 2018. *The Middle Class in Mozambique: The State and Politics of Transformation in Southern Africa.* Cambridge: Cambridge University Press.

———. 2021. "'Just Another African Country': Socialism, Capitalism and Temporality in Mozambique." *Third World Quarterly* 42 (3): 582–98.

Sumich, J., and M. Nielsen. 2020. "The Political Aesthetics of Middle Class Housing in (Not So) Neoliberal Mozambique." *Antipode* 52 (4): 1216–34.

Tang, S. 2009. "The Security Dilemma: A Conceptual Analysis." *Security Studies* 18 (3): 587–623.

Telepneva, N. 2017. "Mediators of Liberation: Eastern-Bloc Officials, Mozambican Diplomacy and the Origins of Soviet Support for Frelimo, 1958–1965." *Journal of Southern African Studies* 43 (1): 67–81.

Tidwell, A. S. D., and J. M. Smith. 2015. "Morals, Materials, and Technoscience: The Energy Security Imaginary in the United States." *Science, Technology and Human Values* 40 (5): 687–711.

Toal, G., and C. T. Dahlman. 2011. *Bosnia Remade: Ethnic Cleansing and Its Reversal.* New York: Oxford University Press.

Topak, Ö. E. 2019. "The Authoritarian Surveillant Assemblage: Authoritarian State Surveillance in Turkey." *Security Dialogue* 50 (5): 454–72.

Törne, A. 2015. "'On the Grounds Where They Will Walk in a Hundred Years' Time'— Struggling with the Heritage of Violent Past in Post-genocidal Tunceli." *European Journal of Turkish Studies* 20. https://doi.org/10.4000/ejts.5099.

Tripp, C. 2013. *The Power and the People: Paths of Resistance in the Middle East.* Cambridge: Cambridge University Press.

Tyner, J. A., G. B. Alvarez, and A. R. Colucci. 2012. "Memory and the Everyday Landscape of Violence in Post-genocide Cambodia." *Social and Cultural Geography* 13 (8): 853–71.

Tyner, J. A., S. Henkin, S. Sirik, and S. Kimsroy. 2014. "Phnom Penh during the Cambodian Genocide: A Case of Selective Urbicide." *Environment and Planning A* 46 (8): 1873–91.

United Nations High Commissioner for Refugees (UNHCR). 2020. "Civilians Bear the Brunt of Violence in Mozambique's Cabo Delgado." News release, 13 November. https://www.unhcr.org/news/briefing/2020/11/5fae44df4/civilians-bear-brunt-violence-mozambiques-cabo-delgado.html.

U.S. Department of State. 2006. "Corruption in the Kurdish North." Confidential cable from Regional Embassy Office Kirkuk, Iraq to Baghdad offices of DoS, Iraq Reconstruction Management Office, National Coordination Team and USAID, 16 February. https://wikileaks.org/plusd/cables/06KIRKUK37_a.html.

———. 2009. "Mozambique: Country Specific Information." http://travel.state.gov/travel/cispatw/cis/cis976.html#safety.

Vail, L. 1976. "Mozambique's Chartered Companies: The Rule of the Feeble." *Journal of African History* 17 (3): 389–416.

van de Kamp, L. 2016. *Violent Conversion: Brazilian Pentecostalism and Urban Women in Mozambique.* Woodbridge: James Currey.

Verdery, K. 2019. "Comparative Surveillance Regimes: A Preliminary Essay." In *Spaces of Security: Ethnographies of Securityscapes, Surveillance, and Control*, edited by S. Low and M. Maguire, 57–77. New York: New York University Press.

Verver, M., and H. Dahles. 2015. "The Institutionalisation of *Oknha*: Cambodian Entrepreneurship at the Interface of Business and Politics." *Journal of Contemporary Asia* 45 (1): 48–70.

Violi, P. 2012. "Trauma Site Museums and Politics of Memory: Tuol Sleng, Villa Grimaldi and Bologna Ustica Museum." *Theory, Culture, Society* 29 (1): 36–75.

Visser, R. 2012. "The Sectarian Master Narrative in Iraqi Historiography." In *Writing the Modern History of Iraq: Historiographical and Political Challenges*, edited by J. Tejel, P. Sluglett, R. Bocco, and H. Bozarslan, 47–60. Singapore: World Scientific.

Vollmer, B. A. 2019. "The Paradox of Border Security—An Example from the UK." *Political Geography* 71 (May): 1–9.

von Boemcken, M. 2019. "Smooth Security: Creative Adaption, Mimicry and Deception in Everyday Securityscapes." *Critical Studies on Security* 7 (2): 91–106.

von Boemcken, M., H. Boboyorov, and N. Bagdasarova. 2018. "Living Dangerously: Securityscapes of Lyuli and LGBT People in Urban Spaces of Kyrgyzstan." *Central Asian Survey* 37 (1): 68–84.

von Hirsch, A., and C. Shearing. 2000. "Exclusion from Public Space." In *Ethical and Social Perspectives on Situational Crime Prevention*, edited by A. Von Hirsch, G. Garland, and A. Wakefield, 77–96. Oxford: Hart.

Vulliamy, E. 2000. "It Ain't Over Till It's Over." *Observer*, 16 July. https://www.theguardian.com/books/2000/jul/16/film#maincontent.

Wacquant, L. 2002. "From Slavery to Mass Incarceration: Rethinking the 'Race Question' in the US." *New Left Review* 13: 41–60.

Wakefield, A. 2003. *Selling Security: The Private Policing of Public Space.* Cullompton: Willan.

Wall, T., and T. Monahan. 2011. "Surveillance and Violence from Afar: The Politics of Drones and Liminal Security-Scapes." *Theoretical Criminology* 15 (3): 239–54.

Wang, C., and A. Moody. 2014. "Willingness to Diversity [*sic*] Pays Dividends." *China Daily Africa*, 20 June. http://www.chinadaily.com.cn/a/201406/20/WS5a2a45daa3101a51ddf900e3.html.

Watts, N. F. 2012. "The Role of Symbolic Capital in Protest: State-Society Relations and the Destruction of the Halabja Martyrs Monument in the Kurdistan Region of Iraq." *Comparative Studies of South Asia, Africa and the Middle East* 32 (1): 70–85.

Wehner, P. 2019. "Trump Betrayed the Kurds. He Couldn't Help Himself." *Atlantic*, 15 October. https://www.theatlantic.com/ideas/archive/2019/10/trump-betrayed-kurds-whos-next/600004/.

Weiss, L. 2014. *America Inc? Innovation and Enterprise in the National Security State.* Ithaca, N.Y.: Cornell University Press.

West, H. G. 1997. "Creative Destruction and Sorcery of Construction: Power, Hope and Suspicion in Post-war Mozambique." *Cahiers d'Etudes Africaines* 147 (3): 675–98.

——. 2001. "Sorcery of Construction and Socialist Modernization: Ways of Understanding Power in Postcolonial Mozambique." *American Ethnologist* 28 (1): 119–50.

——. 2005. *Kupilikula: Governance and the Invisible Realm in Mozambique.* Chicago: University of Chicago Press.

White House. 2020. "Remarks by President Trump on Operation LeGend: Combatting Violent Crime in American Cities." 22 July. https://www.whitehouse.gov/briefings -statements/remarks-president-trump-operation-legend-combatting-violent-crime -american-cities/.

Williams, P. 2004. "Witnessing Genocide: Vigilance and Remembrance at Tuol Sleng and Choeung Ek." *Holocaust and Genocide Studies* 18 (2): 234–54.

Willis, J. M. 2012. *Unmaking North and South: Cartographies of the Yemeni Past.* London: Hurst.

Wilson, K. B. 1992. "Cults of Violence and Counter-violence in Mozambique." *Journal of Southern African Studies* 18 (3): 527–82.

Winch, B. 2017. "'*La iha fiar, la iha seguransa*': The Spiritual Landscape and Feeling Secure in Timor-Leste." *Third World Thematics* 2 (2–3): 197–210.

Wolff, S. 2010. "Governing (in) Kirkuk: Resolving the Status of a Disputed Territory in Post-American Iraq." *International Affairs* 86 (6): 1361–79.

Woon, C. Y. 2013. "For 'Emotional Fieldwork' in Critical Geopolitical Research on Violence and Terrorism." *Political Geography* 33: 31–41.

Work, C. 2014. "Sacred Bribes and Violence Deferred: Buddhist Ritual in Rural Cambodia." *Journal of Southeast Asian Studies* 45 (1): 4–24.

Wuyts, M. E. 1989. *Money and Planning for Socialist Transition: The Mozambican Experience.* Aldershot: Gower.

Yamada, T. S. 2017. "Phnom Penh's NagaWorld Resort and Casino." *Pacific Affairs* 90 (4): 743–65.

Yarwood, R. 2007. "The Geographies of Policing." *Progress in Human Geography* 31 (4): 447–65.

Yusuf Ali, A. (1934) 2009. *The Meaning of the Holy Qur'ān: Text, Translation and Commentary.* Petaling Jaya, Selangor: Islamic Book Trust.

Zedner, L. 2009. *Security.* Abingdon: Routledge.

Zuboff, S. 2019. *The Age of Surveillance Capitalism: The Fight for a Human Future at the New Frontier of Power.* New York: PublicAffairs.

Zucker, E. M. 2013. *Forest of Struggle: Moralities of Remembrance in Upland Cambodia.* Honolulu: University of Hawai'i Press.

INDEX

GEOGRAPHIES OF JUSTICE AND SOCIAL TRANSFORMATION